Fine Arts

FINE ARTS

A Bibliographic Guide to Basic Reference Works, Histories, and Handbooks

DONALD L. EHRESMANN

Appendix by Julia M. Ehresmann

1975

Libraries Unlimited, Inc., Littleton, Colo.

LIBRARIES UNLIMITED, INC.
P.O. Box 263
Littleton, Colorado 80120

Library of Congress Cataloging in Publication Data

Ehresmann, Donald L   1937–
    Fine arts.

    Includes index.
    1. Art--Bibliography.   I. Title.
Z5931.E47   016.7   74-32452

ISBN 0-87287-070-7

For Sibylle

TABLE OF CONTENTS

PART II–HISTORIES AND HANDBOOKS
OF WORLD ART HISTORY

PREFACE

It has been thirteen years since the last systematic bibliography of reference books in the fine arts was published. Since then fine arts publishing, both in this country and abroad, has expanded at an extraordinary pace. In the United States alone over one thousand new titles have appeared annually. European publishers have been even more prolific. In 1962, for example, there were over five thousand fine arts in-print titles in France alone. This increase has been manifest at practically all levels of the subject, from scholarly encyclopedias and handbooks to popular works directed to an ever-increasing, avid, and educated general readership.

It is perhaps in the last category of popular fine arts books that the dramatic increase in fine arts publishing is most apparent. Until a few years ago there seemed to be an endless array of sumptuously illustrated books whose detractors designated them as picture books or cocktail table books. Spiraling costs seem to have diminished their increase recently, but they remain a characteristic phenomenon of mid-century art publishing. Except for some of the obviously ephemeral luxury items, they constitute a most valuable addition to the literature of the fine arts. They have stimulated the production of moderately priced histories and handbooks with a high quantity and quality of illustrations—books that were decidedly rare before 1958.

This great increase in fine arts publishing is the reason for the present bibliography, whose aim is to guide the general reader, the beginning student, and the advanced student to the basic books in the field of art history. To accomplish this aim it has been necessary to set tight limits of scope and to avoid unnecessary duplication. Keeping the overall number to fewer than 1,200 entries while at the same time seeking to serve both the advanced university student of art history and the general reader would have been an impossibility without the help of Chamberlin's standard bibliography of art reference books. Because her excellent work is readily available, it has been possible for the present bibliography to ignore all books published before 1900; of works published between 1900 and 1958 (the completion date of Chamberlin's bibliography) only classic or standard works are included here. The cut-off date for inclusion was December 31, 1973, though a few very important works published after that date are also to be found here. The limitations of scope have allowed adequate treatment of basic reference works, with a generous number of earlier works included along with the more recent. In order to achieve an advantageous selection of the remaining 800 or so entries, however, it was necessary to restrict basic histories and handbooks to books that are written in Western European languages that deal with at least two of the major art forms of architecture, sculpture, and painting, and that treat these art forms within a classification system reflecting the varying depths of our knowledge of research in the history of the world's art.

This bibliography is divided into two parts. Part I is a fairly exhaustive list of basic reference tools. Part II is a selected list of basic histories and handbooks of world art history. Collecting, museology, and the history of the minor arts will be served by a subsequent bibliography. Within its prescribed scope, the bibliography intends to serve three levels of readers: the general reader who may not have a university background in the history of art but who is interested in serious study, the beginning student involved in survey and intermediate-level university or college courses of art history, and the advanced undergraduate and graduate student studying the history of art in advanced and specialized courses and conducting independent study and research. Throughout the bibliography—but especially in Part II, where greater selectivity was necessary—these levels of readership are served directly by the critical and descriptive annotations; every effort has been made to evaluate the depth of the work and to describe the features that will be of most interest to the student and general reader. Those books in Part II with especially extensive bibliographies are marked with an asterisk (*) at the beginning of the entry. It is hoped that the specific usefulness of the books listed there is readily apparent.

The classification system employed in this bibliography follows essentially a geographical pattern by dividing the world's art into four broad areas: Europe, Orient, New World, and Africa and Oceania. Each area is further subdivided into nations and regions. Reflecting the state of our knowledge, Europe is further divided into major periods and styles. Each major category in the bibliography is provided with a short introduction that discusses the state of research. The complete classification is given in the table of contents. The index provides author, title, and subject access. The appendix gives a selected list of titles for a fine arts collection in a public library of moderate size.

Many people have helped to make this work possible. I wish especially to thank Ruth E. Schoneman, Director, and Cecilia Chin, Head of the Reference Department, of the Library of the Art Institute of Chicago and my colleagues in the Department of the History of Architecture and Art at the University of Illinois at Chicago Circle, whose assistance and advice have been valuable.

D.L.E.

Part I

REFERENCE WORKS

CHAPTER ONE

BIBLIOGRAPHIES

I. INTRODUCTION

The history of fine arts bibliography reaches back beyond the eighteenth century.[1] Although some of those early bibliographies are valuable sources for specialized studies in the historiography of the fine arts, nearly all are bibliophilic efforts, and for that reason they are chiefly of antiquarian interest today. Scientific bibliography in the fine arts does not begin until the early years of the present century. At that time two trends in fine arts bibliography appeared that, in differing proportions, continue to characterize the field of fine arts bibliography to the present. One trend was toward the production of international serial bibliographies that cataloged, if not annotated, the major literature in books and periodical articles on a regular (usually annual) basis. This was a direct response to the tremendous increase in far-reaching art historical research that characterized the first quarter of the twentieth century. In international bibliography the first such serial was produced in Germany (20); it continues, in a somewhat changed form, in the annual bibliography published in the German art historical periodical, *Zeitschrift für Kunstgeschichte* (25). It was followed soon after by the *Répertoire d'Art et d'Archéologie* (22) produced by the University of Paris. The *Répertoire* remains today the chief representative of the international serial bibliography.

The second trend—that of specifically delimited national and regional retrospective and serial fine arts bibliographies—began very modestly in the form of Hermann Sepp's bibliography of Bavarian art (78). It grew rapidly, however, in the years between the two wars. Today it is the dominant trend in fine arts bibliography; although it is still far from being represented in the majority of the countries that produce the major scholarship, it has been of sufficient magnitude to threaten the trend towards international serial bibliographies. In 1969, the Centre National de la Recherche Scientifique: Sciences Humaines in Paris sponsored a colloquium on fine arts bibliography; one of the purposes of the colloquium was to explore the possibility of coordinating the increasing activity in national fine arts bibliography with the production of the chief international bibliography, the *Répertoire.*[2] Although until recently little that was concrete had been advanced in that direction, the Paris colloquium did point out the need for both types of fine arts bibliography. The interest in national, regional, and ethnic art has increased tremendously in the past quarter century, and the literature directed to that interest has increased correspondingly. The nature of such literature, often locally produced and distributed, makes it quite clear that only regional bibliographies can handle this aspect of the study of the fine arts. But at the same time, increasing internationality in travel, culture, and study has developed a heightened appetite for information on the art of other nations and cultures. The mass of detailed and locally significant literature covered by the national and regional bibliographies frustrates this appetite. There is a continuing need for a critically selective international serial bibliography that provides access to this information. In the past year the College Art Association of America has recognized this need and has proposed the establishment of a new international bibliography of the fine arts modeled after the new, computerized bibliography of musicology, *Répertoire international de littérature musicale*, produced by the American Council of Learned Societies. If it should receive adequate support, the new fine arts bibliography should begin publication soon under the title *Répertoire international de la littérature de l'art* (RILA). Although the precise nature of the new bibliography's scope and depth have yet to be worked out, one hopes that it will aim to select major works, perhaps with the assistance of the various existing national bibliographies, and annotate or abstract them so that their value is readily apparent to the generalist and specialist alike. A major obstacle to the attainment of this possibly utopian goal is the conspicuous lack of national bibliographies for most countries of the world. This is true even if one restricts the task to Western art. This imperfect state of bibliographic coverage is most likely to be with us through the remaining years of this century. Therefore, it is essential that the serious student and conscientious librarian be aware of the strengths and weaknesses of the current situation in fine arts bibliography.

The only truly international fine arts bibliographies are the now obsolete retrospective bibliographies compiled by Lucas (7) and Chamberlin (2). The two serial bibliographies mentioned above (22 and 25) were of broader scope when they began than they are now. Both restrict themselves to Western art from the end of the ancient world to the twentieth century. Access to literature on non-Western art is seriously hampered by this, for to date only a few special bibliographies have appeared to fill the gap. Those that have appeared give excellent access to Islamic art, African art, and the art of ancient Greece and Rome. Far Eastern art and the art of pre-Columbian America have only weak and spotty bibliographic coverage, which has been an impediment to serious scholarship.

If Western art is tolerably served by the serial bibliographies, serious study in many areas of Western art history is frustrated by the uneven coverage at the national level. Only the German-speaking countries (Germany, Austria, Switzerland), Denmark, and Sweden are thoroughly covered by retrospective bibliographies; the entire Pan-German sphere is covered by the most exhaustive, classified, and annotated serial bibliography in the field of the fine arts (69). Denmark and Sweden both have excellent retrospective bibliographies and have recently instituted serial bibliographies on the German model. The rest of Europe has approached the task of fine arts bibliography less systematically. Italy has a fine retrospective bibliography (84) but has had uneven success in serial bibliography.

Considering the great importance of Italian art in the history of Western art, this situation is lamentable. Spain has a good retrospective bibliography and has gradually increased the thoroughness of the serial bibliography published in the *Archivo español* (94). The Netherlands has concentrated on painting and the graphic arts but has recently begun a serial bibliography of more universal scope in its periodical *Simiolus* (88). The weakest links in the chain of Western European countries are France and Britain. France has no national bibliography, although much of the literature is covered by the international serial *Répertoire* (22). England began a serial fine arts bibliography in the 1930s but discontinued it in 1957. Retrospective and serial bibliographies for these important countries are much needed. Only a few of the East European countries have attempted fine arts bibliographies. Most surprising of all, however, considering American accomplishments in international fine arts bibliography, there are no American national serial or retrospective fine arts bibliographies comparable to the European productions.

A third approach to fine arts bibliography that promises to be a fertile area for bibliographic contribution has been concerned with preparing bibliographies devoted to periods of Western art. Most of these have been concentrated at the two ends of the time spectrum (ancient art and art of the nineteenth and twentieth centuries), which is explained by the fact that most international and many national bibliographies omit these periods. In the case of the bibliography on nineteenth century art by Hilda Leitzmann (63), these period bibliographies have provided a great impetus to scholarship. The bibliography of the German archaeological institute (34) provides specialists in ancient art with an incomparable bibliographic tool. It is conceivable that this type of fine arts bibliography will increase in the future as will compilations from national bibliographies.

Lastly should be mentioned several contributions in the field of special subject bibliography within the fine arts. Iconography, the study of subject matter in the visual arts, cuts across all periods and nations and has been a growing subsidiary of art history. Until recently, however, there has been little access to literature on this subject. The situation has been dramatically changed by the appearance of a number of excellent dictionaries of iconography, with separate bibliographies (335), and the serial bibliography of symbolism edited by Manfred Lurker. Lurker's bibliography is to be praised not only for its scope but for the thoroughness of its annotations, which were written by specialists in the field of symbolism. Because of the great importance of bibliographies to any serious study in the fine arts, I have endeavored in this section to be as complete as has been practicable. International, national, and regional fine arts bibliographies are included; so are bibliographies dealing with specific periods, civilizations, and subjects. In addition to the fairly well-known serial and retrospective bibliographies published as books, I have included another class of bibliographies that is seldom included in retrospective bibliographies. These are the important short bibliographies that usually deal with a small area in the fine arts and often with critical commentary appearing from time to time in various fine arts periodicals. Some of these bibliographies are the sole bibliographic resource for a special area of study; others, as previously mentioned, amount to extremely comprehensive national serial bibliographies. Their inclusion here should provide the student and librarian with access to a full panorama of bibliographic aids. The fullness will be even greater if the user bears in mind that excellent bibliographies, often classified and occasionally annotated as well, can be found in basic histories and handbooks. These are listed in Part II; those that provide bibliographies are noted in the annotations.

---

1. K. Steinitz, "Early Art Bibliographies. Who Compiled the First Art Bibliography?" *Burlington Magazine* 114, 1972, pp. 829-37.
2. *Bibliographie d'Histoire de l'Art.* Paris, Ed. du Centre, 1969.

II. GENERAL SYSTEMATIC BIBLIOGRAPHIES

1   Besterman, Theodore. **Art and Architecture: A Bibliography of Bibliographies.** Totowa, N.J., Rowman and Littlefield, 1971. 216p. LC 74-29568.

Reissue of the sections on art and architecture in the author's *World Bibliography of Bibliographies*, 4th ed. (1965-1966). Classified bibliography of bibliographies.

2   Chamberlin, Mary W. **Guide to Art Reference Books.** Chicago, American Library Association, 1959. 418p. index. LC 59-10457.

Classified and annotated bibliography of 2,489 books on the fine arts. Covers reference tools, basic histories and handbooks, periodicals, documents and sources, and series publications. Includes only books written in Western languages. General index. Although no longer up to date, it is still an indispensable reference tool for students and librarians. A useful feature is the appendix, with a descriptive list of art reference libraries in the United States and Europe.

3   Crouslé, Maurice, comp. **L'art et les artistes.** 2nd ed. Paris, Hachette, 1961. 343p. illus. index.

Classified trade bibliography of some 5,000 books in French on the fine arts. Lists chiefly general and popular books; gives a physical description of the book, place of publication, publisher (but not date of publication), and price. Although it is now out of date, it is still a useful compilation for the reference librarian.

4   Donati, Lamberto. **Bibliografia della miniatúra.** Florence, Olschki, 1972. 2v. (Biblioteca di Bibliografia Italiana, LXIX).

Classified bibliography of books, periodical articles, and museum and exhibition catalogs on all aspects of manuscript illumination. Reviews of major books are also given. Basic reference tool for the study of manuscript illumination.

5   Dove, Jack. **Fine Arts.** London, Clive Bingley, 1966. 88p. index. (The
     Readers Guide Series).
Classified and annotated bibliography of a small selected group of books. Title
and subject index. Good basic bibliography for the general reader and the art
collector.

6   Lasch, Hanna. **Architekten-Bibliographie.** Leipzig, Seemann, 1962. 215p.
     index.
Classified bibliography of books written in German on architects of all nations.
Arranged by architect. Author index. A valuable bibliography of nearly 4,000
monographs on important architects.

7   Lucas, Edna Louise. **Art Books: A Basic Bibliography of the Fine Arts.**
     Greenwich, Conn., New York Graphic Society, 1968. 245p. index. LC
     68-12364.
Classified bibliography of fine arts books covering basic reference tools, period
and medium histories, and monographs on artists. Author, artist, and title index.
Based on the author's *Harvard List of Books on Art* (last published in 1952) and
designed as a selection guide for college libraries. As such it includes only the
books then readily obtainable, so there are many important omissions, particularly
in reference categories. Its most useful feature is its bibliography of artist
monographs.

8   Lucas, Edna Louise. **Books on Art: A Foundation List.** 2nd ed. Cambridge,
     Mass., Fogg Museum, Harvard University, 1938. 84p. index. (Harvard-
     Radcliffe Fine Arts Series).
Classified list of books selected for the needs of a small college library. Now out
of date. Author index.

9   Lucas, Edna Louise. **Guides to the Harvard Libraries, No. 2: Fine Arts.**
     Cambridge, Mass., Harvard University Library, 1949. 54p.
Guide to the Fine Arts collections of the Harvard libraries. Useful list of basic
reference tools in the appendix.

10   McColvin, Eric Raymond. **Painting: A Guide to the Best Books with
     Special Reference to the Requirements of Public Libraries.** London,
     Grafton, 1934. 216p. index.
Annotated and classified bibliography of books on Western painting. Thoroughly
indexed by subject, schools, and artists. Although much out of date, it is still useful to the librarian for its evaluations of older popular literature on painting.

11   Mayer, Leo A. **Bibliography of Jewish Art.** Ed. by Otto Kurz. Jerusalem,
     Hebrew University Press, 1967. 374p. index. LC B 67-14948.
Bibliography of books and periodical articles that treat art by Jews between 70
and 1830 A.D. and that were published up to 1965. The 3,016 entries are arranged
alphabetically. Subject, artist, and author index.

12   Podszus, Carl O. **Art: A Selected Annotated Art Bibliography**. New York, n.p., 1960. 111p. LC 60-1621.
General bibliography of approximately 1,000 items covering all aspects of the visual arts, with particular emphasis on studio practice. Small section on history of art. Intended for schools, it should be useful for beginning students interested in the practice and the history of the fine arts.

13   Reisner, Robert G. **Fakes and Forgeries in the Fine Arts: A Bibliography**. New York, Special Libraries Association, 1950. 58p. index.
Bibliography of books and periodical articles on fine arts fakes and forgeries published from 1848 to 1948. Special feature is the list of articles on fakes published in the *New York Times* from 1897 to 1950.

14   Rosenthal, T. G. **European Art History**. Cambridge, Cambridge University Press, 1960. 32p. (Reader's Guide Fourth Series, No. 4).
Classified bibliography of books on European art, exclusive of architecture, for the general reader. Includes only books then in print.

15   Schlosser, Julius von. **La letteratura artistica: Manuale delle fonti della storia dell'arte moderna**. 3 ed. italiana aggiornata da Otto Kurz. Florence, "La Nuova Italia," 1964. 766p.
Originally published as *Die Kunstliteratur* (Vienna, Schroll, 1924). Scholarly classified bibliography of books on art published up to the early nineteenth century. Basic reference tool for advanced students of art history. Additions by Kurz are in brackets. Artist and author index.

16   Timmling, Walter. **Kunstgeschichte und Kunstwissenschaft: Kleine Literaturführer**. Leipzig, Koehler & Volckmar, 1923. 303p.
Classified and annotated bibliography of German books and periodical articles on all aspects of art history. The annotations are directed to the needs of the student; at the time it was published, it was most useful. A supplement, *Die Kunstliteratur der neuesten Zeit*, was published in Leipzig, 1928.

III. GENERAL SERIES BIBLIOGRAPHIES

17   **Art/Kunst: International Bibliography of Art Book[s]**, 1972– . Basel, Helbing & Lichtenhahn, 1973– . index.
Classified list of in-print art books submitted by major art book publishers. As a trade list, it is useful for the librarian and the beginning student.

18   **Bibliographie zur kunstgeschichtlichen Literatur in slawischen Zeitschriften**, 1960– . Munich, Zentralinstitut für Kunstgeschichte, 1964– .
Classified annual bibliography of articles on the history of art in Slavic language periodicals. Extremely useful guide to otherwise nearly inaccessible material in Slavic periodicals.

19   Delogu, Giuseppe, comp. **Essai d'une bibliographie internationale d'histoire de l'art, 1934/35.** Bergamo, Ist. Ital. d'Arti Grafiche, 1936. index. 176p.
Published by the Comité Internationale d'Histoire de l'Art. Defunct. Intended to be a classified bibliography of books on art and music published in German, French, English, Spanish, Italian, Polish, Czech, Romanian, Swedish, and Hungarian. Thorough coverage of exhibition and sales catalogs. Author index.

20   **Internationale Bibliographie der Kunstwissenschaft**, 1902-1917/18. Berlin, Behr, 1903-1920. index. 15v. in 14.
Classified bibliography of books, periodical articles, and book reviews published in all major languages. Outline of classification given at the beginning. Although defunct, it is a most thorough and comprehensive bibliography of the period 1903 to 1918. Author and subject indexes.

21   **Kunstgeschichtliche Anzeigen.** Neue Folge. Jahrg. 1– , 1955– . Graz, Cologne, Böhlaus, 1955– .
Continues *Kunstgeschichtliche Anzeigen* (Innsbruck, 1904-1913) and *Kritische Berichte zur kunstgeschichtlichen Literatur* (Leipzig, 1927-38). Published by the Kunsthistorisches Institut der Universität Wien. This is a periodical devoted to the scholarly criticism of art historical literature. Each issue is devoted to one or more periods or fields of art historical research. A basic reference tool for all serious students of art history. The important issues are listed in this volume under the appropriate period and civilization headings.

22   **Répertoire d'art et d'archéologie; dépouillement des périodiques et des catalogues de ventes, bibliographie des ouvrages d'art français et étrangers.** T. 1– . 1910– . Paris, Morancé, 1910– . index.
Since 1965, there has been a Nouvelle Série with the title *Répertoire d'art et d'archéologie (de l'époque paléochrétienne à 1939).* Classified and annotated annual bibliography of books and periodical articles on all aspects of Western art. In the original series–that is, until 1965– antiquity was covered. In the new series the bibliography begins with Early Christian art. The material is arranged in large categories subdivided by nation. An outline of classification and a list of serials consulted are given at the beginning of each volume. A basic reference tool for serious study in the history of Western art. The only international, annual bibliography that attempts to cover both periodical articles and books as well as sale and exhibition catalogs. Except for American art, the *Répertoire* indexes more periodicals than does the *Art Index* (155), and it should be used in conjunction with the *Art Index* in any serious pursuit of a subject in European art. The *Répertoire* does not replace special subject and national bibliographies, but it is especially complete for French material.

23   **The Worldwide Art Book Syllabus: A Select List of In-Print Books on the History of Art and Archaeology.** v. 1– . New York, Worldwide Books, 1966– .
Classified and annotated bibliography of fine arts books available from Worldwide Books. Gives book reviews and prices. Trade list useful to the librarian and general student.

24   **The Worldwide Art Catalogue Bulletin.** v. 1– . New York, Boston, Worldwide Books, 1963– .

List of museum and exhibition catalogs, annotated and listed by country. Prices are given. Useful trade list of art catalogs available through Worldwide Books.

25   **Zeitschrift für Kunstgeschichte.** Bd. 1– . Munich, Berlin, Deutscher Kunstverlag, 1932– .

Beginning with Vol. 12, this periodical publishes in its August issue a classified bibliography of books on art published in the previous year, covering all major Western languages. A most useful and thorough current bibliography.

IV. SPECIALIZED BIBLIOGRAPHIES

PREHISTORIC

26   **Bibliographie annuelle de l'âge de la pierre taillée (paléolithique et mésolithique).** No. 1– , 1955/56– . Paris, Bureau de Recherches Géologiques et Minières, 1958– .

Annual bibliography of books and periodical articles on all aspects of prehistoric civilization including prehistoric art. Succeeds *Old World Bibliography* (29).

27   **Bulletin Signalétique. Série 525: Préhistoire.** v. 24– . Paris, Centre National de la Recherche Scientifique, 1970– .

Annual bibliography of books and periodical articles on all aspects of prehistory, including prehistoric art. Titles are translated into French and abstracts in French are provided for the more complex entries. A valuable reference work for advanced students and scholars of prehistoric art.

28   Eppel, Franz. "In den Jahren 1954 bis 1959 erschienene Werke zur urgeschichtlichen Kunst," in: **Kunstgeschichtlichen Anzeigen**, Neue Folge, Jahrg. 4, 1959/60, pp. 57-105.

Critical examination of the major publications on prehistoric art published between 1954 and 1959. The works discussed are listed at the beginning of the article. See (21) for series annotation.

29   **Old World Bibliography: Recent Publications Mainly in Old World Palaeolithic Archaeology and Palaeo-Anthropology.** Cambridge, Mass., Peabody Museum, American School of Prehistoric Research, v. 1-8, 1948-1955.

Annual bibliography of books and periodical articles on all aspects of prehistoric archaeology and anthropology including prehistoric art. Defunct; succeeded by *Bibliographie annuelle de l'age de la pierre taillée* (26).

PRIMITIVE

30 **Bulletin Signalétique. Série 521: Sociologie-Ethnologie.** v. 21— . Paris,
   Centre National de la Recherche Scientifique, 1967— .
Annual bibliography of books and periodical articles on all aspects of sociology and
ethnology, including the arts of primitive peoples throughout the world. A valuable reference work for advanced students and scholars of primitive art.

31 Haselberger, Herta. "In den Jahre 1961 bis 1964 erschienene Werke zur
   ethnologischen Kunstforschung," in: **Kunstgeschichtliche Anzeigen,**
   Neue Folge, Jahrg. 7, 1965/66, pp. 62-92.
Critical examination of the major works on primitive art published between 1961
and 1964. The works discussed are listed at the beginning of the article. See (21)
for series annotation.

32 New York City. Museum of Primitive Art. Library. **Primitive Art
   Bibliographies.** New York, Museum of Primitive Art, 1963— .
Series of separate classified bibliographies of books and periodical articles on the
art of various primitive cultures. To date they include:

   No. 1, Douglas Fraser, *Bibliography of Torres Strait Art* (New York,
   1963; 6p.)
   No. 2, Julie Jones, *Bibliography of Olmec Sculpture* (New York, 1963;
   8p.)
   No. 3, Herbert M. Cole, and Robert F. Thompson, *Bibliography of
   Yoruba Sculpture* (New York, 1964; 11p.)
   No. 4, Douglas Newton, *Bibliography of Sepik District Art, Annotated for
   Illustrations, Part 1* (New York, 1965; 20p.)
   No. 6, Paula Ben-Amos, *Bibliography of Benin Art* (New York, 1968;
   17p.)
   No. 8, Allen Wardwell and Lois Lebov, *Annotated Bibliography of
   Northwest Coast Indian Art* (New York, 1970; 25p.)
   No. 9, Valerie Chevrette, *Annotated Bibliography of the Pre-Columbian
   Art and Archaeology of the West Indies* (New York, 1971; 18p.)

EUROPE

Periods of Western Art History

Ancient

33 **Annual Egyptological Bibliography,** 1947— . Leiden, Brill, 1948— .
Bibliography of books and periodical articles on all aspects of ancient Egyptian
civilization including the fine arts. Straight alphabetical listing. Entries have full
annotations, some by leading specialists. Standard reference work for all serious
study of ancient Egyptian art and architecture.

34   Archäologische Bibliographie: Beilage zum Jahrbuch des Deutschen
      Archäologischen Instituts, v. 1– . 1932– . Berlin, 1932– .
Preceeded by *Bibliographie zum Jahrbuch des Archäologischen Instituts* (Berlin,
1913-1931) and *Archäologischer Anzeiger zum Jahrbuch des Archäologischen
Instituts* (Berlin, 1889-1912). Classified bibliography of books and periodical
articles on all aspects of classical archaeology, including art. With its predecessor
series, the *Archäologische Bibliographie* is the most important bibliographical tool
for specialists in the history of ancient art.

35   Berghe, Louis van den. **Bibliographie analytique de l'Assyriologie et de
      l'archéologie du Proche-Orient**, v. 1– . Leyden, Brill, 1956– .
Comprehensive, classified, and annotated bibliography of books and periodical
articles on all aspects of the ancient civilizations of the Near East. Does not cover
Egypt. Contains a valuable section on art and architecture. Basic reference tool for
advanced students and scholars of Ancient Near Eastern art and archaeology.

36   **Fasti Archaeologici . . . Annual Bulletin of Classical Archaeology**, v. 1– ,
      1946– . Florence, Sansoni, 1948– .
Published by the International Association of Classical Archaeology. Issued
annually. Classified bibliography of books and periodical articles on all aspects of
classical archaeology, including art, from prehistoric to Early Christian times;
includes works in English, French, German, and Italian. Also contains bulletins of
archaeological discoveries throughout the ancient classical world. A basic reference
tool for specialists in ancient art. Author index at the end of each volume.

37   Kenner, Hedwig. "In den Jahren 1957 bis 1959 erschienene Werke zur
      griechischen Kunst," in: **Kunstgeschichtliche Anzeigen**, Neue Folge,
      Jahrg. 4, 1959/60, pp. 140-59.
Critical examination of the major works on Greek art published between 1957 and
1959. The works discussed are listed at the beginning of the article. See (21) for
series annotation.

38   Kenner, Hedwig. "In den Jahren 1957 bis 1959 erschienene Werke zur
      keltischen und etruskischen Kunst," in: **Kunstgeschichtliche Anzeigen**,
      Neue Folge, Jahrg. 4, 1959/60, pp. 160-64.
Critical examination of the major works on Celtic and Etruscan art published from
1957 to 1959. The works discussed are listed at the beginning of the article. See
(21) for series annotation.

39   Kenner, Hedwig. "In den Jahren 1957 bis 1959 erschienene Werke zur
      provinzialrömischen Kunst," in: **Kunstgeschichtliche Anzeigen**, Neue
      Folge, Jahrg. 4, 1959/60, pp. 178-84.
Critical examination of the major works on Roman provincial art published from
1957 to 1959. The works discussed are listed at the beginning of the article. See
(21) for series annotation.

40   Kenner, Hedwig. "In den Jahren 1957 bis 1959 erschienene Werke zur
      römischen Kunst," in: **Kunstgeschichtliche Anzeigen**, Neue Folge,
      Jahrg. 4, 1959/60, pp. 165-77.
Critical examination of the important publications on Roman art appearing from
1957 to 1959. The works discussed are listed at the beginning of the article. See
(21) for series annotation.

41   Kenner, Hedwig. "In den Jahren 1957 bis 1959 erschienene Werke zur
      spätantiken Kunst," in: **Kunstgeschichtliche Anzeigen**, Neue Folge,
      Jahrg. 4, 1959/60, pp. 185-94.
Critical examination of the major works on late Roman art published from 1957
to 1959. The works discussed are listed at the beginning of the article. See (21)
for series annotation.

42   Lopez Pegna, Mario. **Saggio di bibliografia etrusca**. Florence, Sansoni,
      1953.
Classified bibliography of books and periodical articles on all aspects of Etruscan
art.

43   Porter, Bertha, and Rosalind L. B. Moss. **Topographical Bibliographical
      Bibliography of Ancient Egyptian Hieroglyphic Texts, Reliefs and Paint-
      ings**. 2nd ed. Oxford, Clarendon, 1960. 7v.
Comprehensive classified bibliography of books and periodical articles dealing with
ancient Egyptian hieroglyphic inscriptions, reliefs, and paintings. Does not cover
architecture or free-standing sculpture. Contents:
    I.   *Theban Necropolis*
    II.   *Theban Temples*
    III. *Memphis*
    IV.   *Lower and Middle Egypt*
    V.   *Upper Egypt: Sites*
    VI.   *Upper Egypt: Temples*
    VII. *Nubia, the Deserts and Outside Egypt*
A basic reference tool for advanced study in ancient Egyptian painting and relief
sculpture.

44   Sarne, Berta. "In den Jahren 1955 bis 1961 erschienene Werke zur
      kretisch-mykenischen Kunst," in: **Kunstgeschichtliche Anzeigen**, Neue
      Folge, Jahrg. 7, 1965/66, pp. 7-61.
Critical examination of the major works on Aegean art published from 1955 to
1961. The works discussed are listed at the beginning of the article. See (21) for
series annotation.

45   Swoboda, K. M. "In den Jahren 1950 bis 1956 erschienene Werke zur
      griechischen Kunst," in: **Kunstgeschichtliche Anzeigen**, Neue Folge,
      Jahrg. 3, 1958, pp. 9-44.

Critical examination of the major works on ancient Greek art published from 1950 to 1956. The works discussed are listed at the beginning of the article. See (21) for series annotation.

46   Swoboda, K. M. "In den Jahren 1950 bis 1957 erschienene Werke zur Kunst der Spätantike," in: **Kunstgeschichtliche Anzeigen**, Neue Folge, Jahrg. 3, 1958, pp. 80-137.

Critical examination of the major works on late Roman art published from 1950 to 1957. The works discussed are listed at the beginning of the article. See (21) for series annotation.

47   Swoboda, K. M. "In den Jahren 1950 bis 1957 erschienene Werke zur römischen Kunst," in: **Kunstgeschichtliche Anzeigen**, Neue Folge, Jahrg. 3, 1958, pp. 57-79.

Critical examination of the major literature on Roman art published from 1950 to 1957. The works discussed are listed at the beginning of the article. See (21) for series annotation.

48   Swoboda, K. M. "In den Jahren 1950 bis 1954 erschienene Werke zur Kunst der prähistorie und alten Orients," in: **Kunstgeschichtliche Anzeigen**, Neue Folge, Jahrg. 1, 1955/56, pp. 3-77.

Critical examination of the major works on prehistoric art and the art of the Ancient Near East published from 1950 to 1954. The works discussed are listed at the beginning of the article. See (21) for series annotation.

Medieval and Byzantine

49   **Bibliographie de l'art byzantin et post-byzantin, 1945-1969.** Athens, Comité National Hellenique de l'Association Internationale d'Etudes du Sud-Est Européen, 1970. 115p. LC 72-318821.

Classified bibliography of books and periodical articles on all aspects of Byzantine and derivative art forms in Eastern Europe published between 1945 and 1969. Brings up to date the various special bibliographies published in *Orient et Byzance* and *Byzantion* in the 1930s and 1940s.

50   Bonser, Wilfrid. **An Anglo-Saxon and Celtic Bibliography (405-1087).** Berkeley and Los Angeles, University of California Press, 1957. 2v. index.

A general classified bibliography of Anglo-Saxon and Celtic culture. Includes a good section (pp. 480-574) on art, which includes books and periodical articles published up to 1953. Author and subject indexes in Vol. 2.

51   **Dumbarton Oaks Bibliographies Based on Byzantinische Zeitschrift. Series I: Literature on Byzantine Art 1892-1967, Volume 1: By Location.** Ed. by Jelisaveta S. Allen. London, Mansell, 1973. 2v.

Classified and annotated bibliography of books and periodical articles on all aspects of Byzantine art. The entries are derived from the annual bibliography published since 1892 in the periodical *Byzantinische Zeitschrift*, the leading scholarly journal for Byzantine studies. Volume 1 presents the material by country; part 1 includes Africa, Asia, and Europe (Italy-Yugoslavia). Volume 2 (in preparation) will be arranged by subject. Basic reference tool for all serious students of Byzantine art.

52   Filov, B. "Die Erforschung der altbulgarischen Kunst seit 1914," in: **Zeitschrift für slavische Philologie**, VIII, 1931, pp. 131-43.
Critically annotated bibliography of scholarly literature on the history of medieval Bulgarian art which appeared between 1914 and 1930. Of interest to students of Byzantine art.

53   Grabar, André, and K. Mijatev. "Bibliographie de l'art byzantin: Bulgarie," in: **Orient et Byzance**, IV, 2, 1930, pp. 417-26.
Classified bibliography of books and periodical articles on the Byzantine phase of art in Bulgaria. Part of a series of bibliographies in this periodical covering most Slavic schools of Byzantine art.

54   Millet, Gabriel, and N. A. Il'in. "Bibliographie de l'art byzantin chez les Russes," in: **Orient et Byzance**, V, 1932, pp. 439-90.
Classified bibliography of books and periodical articles on the Byzantine phase of Russian art. Part of a series of specialized bibliographies in this periodical covering the major Slavic schools of Byzantine art.

55   Sotiriou, G. A. "Bibliographie de l'art byzantin; Bulgarie, Serbie, Roumanie," in: **Orient et Byzance**, IV, 1930, pp. 417-54.
Classified bibliography of books and periodical articles on the Byzantine phase of art in Bulgaria, Serbia, and Rumania. Part of a series of specialized bibliographies in this periodical covering the major Slavic schools of Byzantine art.

56   Stein, Frauke. "In den Jahren 1957 bis 1962 erschienene Werke zur Kunst der frühen Mittelalters," in: **Kunstgeschichtliche Anzeigen**, Neue Folge, Jahrg. 6, 1963/64, pp. 105-133.
Critical examination of the major works on early medieval art published from 1957 to 1962. The works discussed are listed at the beginning of the article. See (21) for series annotation.

57   Swoboda, K. M. "In den Jahren 1950 bis 1961 erschienene Werke zur byzantinischen und weiteren ostchristlichen Kunst-Figurenkunst," in: **Kunstgeschichtliche Anzeigen**, Neue Folge, Jahrg. 5, 1961/62, pp. 9-183.
Critical examination of the major works on Byzantine art exclusive of architecture published from 1950 to 1961. The works discussed are listed at the beginning of the article. See (21) for series annotation.

58   Swoboda, K. M. "In den Jahren 1950 bis 1956 erschienene Werke zur Kunst des frühen Mittelalters," in: **Kunstgeschichtliche Anzeigen**, Neue Folge, Jahrg. 3, 1958, pp. 138-94.

Critical examination of the major works on early medieval art (i.e., pre-Carolingian) published from 1950 to 1956. The works discussed are listed at the beginning of the article. See (21) for series annotation.

59   Swoboda, K. M. "In den Jahren 1950 bis 1957 erschienene Werke zur byzantinischen und weiteren ostchristlichen Kunst-Architektur," in: **Kunstgeschichtliche Anzeigen**, Neue Folge, Jahrg. 4, 1959/60, pp. 34-56.
Critical examination of the major works on Byzantine and East Christian architecture published from 1950 to 1957. The works discussed are listed at the beginning of the article. See (21) for series annotation.

60   Swoboda, K. M. "In den Jahren 1950 bis 1957 erschienene Werke zur Kunst der karolingische Zeit," in: **Kunstgeschichtliche Anzeigen**, Neue Folge, Jahrg. 4, 1959/60, pp. 1-33.
Critical examination of the important literature on Carolingian art published from 1950 to 1957. The works discussed are listed at the beginning of the article. See (21) for series annotation.

61   Wulff, Oscar K. **Bibliographisch-Kritischer Nachtrag zu altchristliche und byzantinische Kunst.** Potsdam, Athenaion, 1937. 88p.
Classified bibliography of books and periodical articles on all aspects of early Christian and Byzantine art. Supplement to the author's *Altchristliche und byzantinische Kunst* . . . (Berlin, Athenaion, 1918) in the series "Handbuch der Kunstwissenschaft."

Modern (19th and 20th Centuries)

62   **Art Bibliographies Modern**, v. 1– . Santa Barbara, ABC-Clio Press, 1969– .
Annual bibliography of books and periodical articles on twentieth century art. Volume 1 was titled *L.O.M.A. Literature on Modern Art*; it was published in London by Lund and Humphries and was based on material in the Victoria and Albert Museum Library, Courtauld Institute Library, and the Library of the Lanchester Polytech. Subsequent volumes have been greatly expanded. First section is arranged alphabetically by artist, second section by subject. A valuable bibliographical tool for modern art.

63   Leitzmann, Hilda. **Bibliographie zur Kunstgeschichte des 19. Jahrhunderts: Publikationen der Jahre 1940-1966.** Munich, Prestel, 1968. 234p. illus. index. (Studien zur Kunst des neunzehnten Jahrhunderts, Bd. 4). LC 68-133420.
Classified bibliography of books and periodical articles on all aspects of nineteenth century art published from 1940 to 1966. General index. A thorough bibliography basic to serious research in European art of the nineteenth century.

64   Sharp, Dennis. **Sources of Modern Architecture.** New York, Wittenborn, 1967. 56p. illus. LC 67-19697. (Architectural Association Paper, No. 2).

Classified bibliography of books on modern architecture from art nouveau to the early 1960s. First part is a bio-bibliography of modern architects, giving a brief life, list of major works, and a comment on writings by and about the architect. Second part lists books on modern architecture by subject and nation. There is a helpful list of selected periodicals (p. 51). Basic reference tool for librarians and advanced students.

European National and Area Bibliographies

Belgium

65 Feyaerts, Monique. **La peinture en Belgique des origines à nos jours; bibliographie choisie et commentée d'ouvrages en langue française à l'usage de la bibliothèque du second degré.** Bruxelles, Commission Belge de Bibliographie, 1960. 462p. (Bibliographica Belgica, 47). LC 60-28509.

Classified and annotated bibliography of painting in Belgium from the Middle Ages to the present.

Denmark

66 **Bibliografi over Dansk Kunst**, 1971– . Copenhagen, Kunstakademiets Bibliotek, 1972– .

Annual, classified bibliography of books and periodical articles on all aspects of Danish fine arts. Includes foreign language literature as well as literature in Danish. Does not include works on archaeology, folk art, costume, numismatics, or photography. A retrospective bibliography covering the literature on Danish art published between 1933 and 1970 is planned to fill the gap between the *Bibliografi over Dansk Kunst* and Bodelsen and Marcus (67). A basic reference tool for any serious study of Danish art.

67 Bodelsen, Merete, and Aage Marcus. **Dansk Kunsthistorisk Bibliografi.** Copenhagen, Reitzel, 1935. 503p.

Classified bibliography of books and periodical articles on Danish art. Includes both Danish and foreign language publications.

France

68 Lebel, Gustave. **Bibliographie des revues et périodiques d'art parus en France de 1746 à 1914.** Paris, New York, 1951. (Gazette des Beaux-Arts, janv.-mars 1951, 6e per. t. 38).

List of periodicals of art published in France between 1746 and 1914 by title. Gives date of first issue, frequency, editors, and the location of copies (either

Bibliothèque Nationale or University of Paris Libraries). Some are annotated. Chronological index. Useful tool for students of eighteenth and nineteenth century French art history.

German-Speaking Countries

General Works

69 **Schrifttum zur deutschen Kunst**. Jahrg. 1— . Berlin, Deutscher Verein für Kunstwissenschaft, 1934— .
Published by the Deutscher Verein für Kunstwissenschaft and, since 1961, "zusammengestellt von der Bibliothek des Germanischen Nationalmuseums" in Nuremberg. One of the most thorough and comprehensive of national art bibliographies. Classified and annotated bibliography of books, periodical articles, exhibition catalogs, and book reviews on all aspects of art in German-speaking countries. Author, artist, and place indexes.

Austria

70 **Bibliographie zur Kunstgeschichte Österreichs**. Zusammengestellt im Kunsthistorischen Institut der Universität Wien. Lehrkanzel für Österreichische Kunstgeschichte. 1965— . Vienna, Schroll, 1966— .
Classified bibliography of books and periodical articles on all aspects of Austrian art. Issued as a supplement to *Österreichische Zeitschrift für Kunst und Denkmalpflege*, XX-XXV (1966-1971). Continues the bibliographic coverage of Austrian art in *Mitteilungen der Gesellschaft für vergleichende Kunstforschung in Wien*, I (1948)— XV (1963).

Germany

71 Beyrodt, Wolfgang. **Westfälische Kunst bis zum Barock: Ein Literaturverzeichnis**. Bielefeld, Stadtbibliothek Bielefeld, 1970. 63p.
Classified bibliography of books and periodical articles on all aspects of art in Westphalia from the early Middle Ages through the baroque.

72 Deutsche Akademie der Wissenschaft zu Berlin, Arbeitsstelle für Kunstgeschichte. **Schriften zur Kunstgeschichte**. Berlin, Akademie-Verlag, 1960— .
Bibliography of books and periodical articles on all aspects of art in the German Democratic Republic (East Germany) issued in volumes devoted to separate regions. To date the following have appeared: No. 4, *Bibliographie zur sächsischen Kunstgeschichte*, von Walter Hentschel (1960; 273p.). No. 7, *Bibliographie zur brandenburgischen Kunstgeschichte*, von Edith Neubauer und Gerda Schlegelmilch (1961; 231p.). No. 8, *Bibliographie zur Kunstgeschichte Mecklenburg und*

Vorpommern (1962; 123p.). No. 9, *Bibliographie zur Kunstgeschichte von Sachsen-Anhalt*, von Sibylle Harksen (1966; 431p.). No. 13, *Bibliographie zur Kunstgeschichte von Berlin und Potsdam*, von Sibylle Badstübner-Groger (1968; 320p.). With the completion of a volume on Thuringia, this series will comprise one of the most comprehensive retrospective national bibliographies in the field of the visual arts. Basic reference tool for serious study in the history of German art.

73   Deutscher Kunstrat. **Schrifttum zur deutschen Kunst des 20. Jahrhunderts: eine Bibliographie des deutschen Kunstrates e.V.** Bearb. von Ernst Thiele. v. 1– . Cologne, Oda 1960– . LC 61-47348.
Classified and annotated bibliography of books, periodical articles, exhibition catalogs, and book reviews published in Germany on German art of the twentieth century. Supplements *Schrifttum zur deutschen Kunst* (69), which does not include art after art nouveau.

74   Gruhn, Herbert. **Bibliographie der schlesischen Kunstgeschichte.** Breslau, Korn, 1933. 357p. (Schlesische Bibliographie, 6, 1).
Classified bibliography of books and periodical articles on all aspects of art and architecture in the former German province of Silesia.

75   Krienke, Gisela. **Bibliographie zu Kunst und Kunstgeschichte; Veröffentlichungen im Gebiet der Deutschen Demokratischen Republik.** V. 1, 1945-1935; V. 2, 1945-1957. Berlin, VEB, 1956, 1961. index.
Classified bibliography of books and periodical articles published in the German Democratic Republic (East Germany). Includes unpublished dissertations. Vol. 2 has supplement to Vol. 1. Indexes by periodical, artist, place, names, subjects, and authors.

76   Kügler, Hans Peter. **Schrifttum zur deutsch-baltischen Kunst.** Berlin, Deutscher Verein für Kunstwissenschaft, 1939. 42p.
Issued as a supplement to the *Schrifttum zur deutschen Kunst* (69). Classified bibliography of books and periodicals on German art in the former German Baltic provinces.

77   **Schrifttum zur rheinischen Kunst von den Anfängen bis 1935.** Berlin, Deutscher Verein für Kunstwissenschaft, 1949. 284p.
Classified and annotated bibliography of books and periodical articles on all aspects of the fine arts in the Rhineland. Covers material published up to 1935, when the *Schrifttum zur deutschen Kunst* (69) takes over the indexing of literature on Rhenish art.

78   Sepp, Hermann. **Bibliographie der bayerischen Kunstgeschichte bis Ende 1905.** Strasbourg, Heitz, 1906. 345p. index. (Studien zur deutschen Kunstgeschichte, Bd. 67). **Nachtrag für 1906-1910.** Strasbourg, Heitz, 1912. 208p. index. (Studien zur deutschen Kunstgeschichte, Bd. 67/155).

Classified and annotated bibliography of books and periodical articles on all aspects of art in Bavaria. Covers material published up to 1905, with the Nachtrag treating the literature between 1906 and 1910. Continued by Wichmann (79); together, they ensure that Bavaria is the most thoroughly bibliographized fine arts region in the world.

> 79 Wichmann, Hans. **Bibliographie der Kunst in Bayern.** Wiesbaden, Harrassowitz, 1961-1973. 4v.

Classified and annotated bibliography of books and periodical articles on all aspects of art in Bavaria. Covers only works published in the twentieth century, hence it complements Sepp (78). The most thorough of regional bibliographies thus far produced for the fine arts; includes nearly 70,000 items. Matthias Mende's *Sonderband: Dürer-Bibliographie*(Wiesbadan, Harrassowitz, 1971), classifies and annotates over 10,000 items dealing with the art of Albrecht Dürer, is also a model of an exhaustive artist bibliography.

Great Britain

> 80 London. University. Courtauld Institute of Art. **Annual Bibliography of the History of British Art**, v. 1- 6, 1934-1948. Cambridge, University Press, 1936-1957. index.

Classified bibliography of books and periodical articles. Includes Celtic and Viking but not Roman art. Index in each volume. Useful tool for the study of British art, unfortunately discontinued.

Hungary

> 81 Biró, Béla. **A Magyar Müsvészettörténeti Irodalom Bibliográfiája; Bibliographie der ungarischen kunstgeschichtlichen Literatur.** Budapest, Képzömüvészeti alap Kiadóvállata, 1955. 611p. index.

Classified bibliography of books and periodical articles on Hungarian art and Hungarian writings on art history from the eighteenth century to 1954. Table of contents and foreword are in Hungarian and German. Author and artist indexes.

> 82 Boskovits, Miklos, ed. **L'art du gothique et la Renaissance, 1300-1500: Bibliographie raisonnée des ouvrages publiées en Hongrie.** Budapest, Comité National Hongrois d'Histoire de l'Art, 1965. 2v. index. LC 68-37621.

Classified and annotated bibliography of books and periodical articles on Gothic and Renaissance art published in Hungary. Contains 2,858 entries. Author index.

Italy

83   **Bibliografia del libro d'arte italiano**, v. 1– , 1940– . Rome, Bestetti, 1952– .
       LC A-53-9809 rev.
Classified bibliography of books on Italian art including congresses, catalogs, and
guides. Vol. 1, "Cura die Erardo Aeschlimann." Author, title, artist indexes.

84   Borroni, Fabia. **"Il Cicognara": Bibliografia dell'archeologia classica e
       dell'arte italiana**, v. 1, t.1-v.2, t.7– . Florence, Sansoni, 1954-1967.
       (Biblioteca Bibliografica Italica, v. 6–).
Classified and annotated bibliography of books on classical and Italian art.
Arranged in classes and listed chronologically. Illustrates the title pages of earlier
works. A basic reference tool for students of classical and Italian art.

85   Ceci, Giuseppe. **Bibliografia per la storia delle arti figurative nell'Italia
       meridonale** . . . Naples, Presso la R. Deputazione, 1937. 2v. index.
Comprehensive classified bibliography of books and periodical articles on south
Italian art. Arranged chronologically, Volume 1 lists works published before 1742,
Volume 2 those published after that date. Material is best located by means of the
author, artist, and place indexes in Volume 2. An excellent regional fine arts
bibliography.

86   Geck, Francis J. **Bibliography of Italian Art** . . . , v. 5-10. Boulder, Colo.,
       University of Colorado Book Store, 1932-1941.
Volumes 1-4 were never published. Classified bibliography of books on Italian
history, customs, and literature as well as art and architecture. Emphasis is on
books in English. Contents:
       Vol. 5   *Italian Gothic Art 1200-1420*
       Vol. 6   *Italian Early Renaissance Art–Quattrocento*
       Vol. 7   *Italian High Renaissance Art–Cinquecento*
       Vol. 8   *Italian Late Renaissance Art–Cinquecento*
       Vol. 9   *Italian Baroque Art–Il Seicento*
       Vol. 10 *Italian Rococo Art*
Popular work for the general reader and beginning student.

87   Istituto Nazionale per le Relazioni Culturali con l'Estero. **Archeologia,
       arti figurative, musica**. Rome, I.R.C.E., 1941. 498p. (Bibliografie del
       Ventennio). index.
Classified bibliography covering archaeology, art, theater, cinema, and music in
Italy. Books and exhibition catalogs published between 1922 and 1941. Author
index. Supplements Bestetti (83).

Netherlands

88   "Bibliografisch Overzicht van in Nederland in 1966-verschenen
       Publicaties op het Gebied van de Kunstgeschiedenis en Enkele
       Aanverwante Wetenschappen," in: **Simiolus**, Jaargang 1– , 1966/67– .

Annual, classified bibliography of books and periodical literature published in the Netherlands on all aspects of the history of art.

89   Hall, H. van. **Repertorium voor de Geschiedenis der Nederlandsche Schilder- en Graveerkunst sedert het Begin der 12de Eeuw . . .** 's Gravenhage, Nijhoff, 1936-1949. 2v. index.
Classified bibliography of books and periodical articles on Dutch painting and engraving from the twelfth century to 1946. Belgian painting and engraving until 1500 included. Author index.

90   Netherlands. Rijksbureau voor Kunsthistorische Documentatie. **Bibliography of the Netherlands Institute for Art History.** v. 1– , 1943– . The Hague, 1943– .
Classified bibliography of books and periodical articles on Dutch painting and graphic arts. Continuation of Hall (89).

91   **Repertorium betreffende Nederlandse Monumenten van Geschiedenis en Kunst.** The Hague, 1940-1962. 3v. index.
Classified bibliography of periodical articles on all aspects of art and architecture in the Netherlands from the early Middle Ages to the present. The period from 1901 to 1940 is covered in the first two volumes; the period 1941 to 1950 is in the last volume. Subsequent volumes are planned. A basic reference tool for all serious study of Dutch art and architecture.

92   **Repertorium van Boekwerken betreffende Nederlandse Monumenten van Geschiedenis en Kunst.** The Hague, 1950. 169p. index.
Classified bibliography of books on all aspects of art and architecture in the Netherlands from the early Middle Ages to the present. Entries are short and give neither the place of publication, number of pages, nor illustrations. Edited by the Koninklijke Nederlandse Oudheidkundige Bond. Includes books published to 1940. Periodical literature is treated in (91). A basic reference tool for any serious study of Dutch art and architecture.

Russia

93   Alpatov, Mikhail V., and Nikolai I. Brunov. "Die altrussische Kunst in der wissenschaftlichen Forschung seit 1914," in: **Zeitschrift für slavische Philologie**, II, 1925, pp. 474-505; III, 1926/27, pp. 387-408.
Classified bibliographies of books and periodical articles on Russian medieval art, published between 1914 and 1925.

Spain and Portugal

94   "Aportaciones recientes a la historia del arte español," in: **Archivo español del Arte**, Tomo 22– , 1949– .

Annual, classified bibliography of books and periodical articles on all aspects of Spanish art. Appears at the end of the "Bibliografía" section in last number in each year. The basic bibliographical tool for the study of Spanish art.

95   López Serrano, Mathilde. **Bibliografía de arte español y americano 1936-1940** . . . Madrid, Gráficas Uguina, 1942. 243p. index.

Classified bibliography of books and periodical articles on art and archaeology of Spain, Latin America, and the Philippines published from 1936 to 1940.

96   Oliveira, Arnaldo Henriques de. **Bibliografia artistia portuguesa**. Lisbon, 1944. 320p.

Classified bibliography of books on all aspects of Portuguese art in the library of Luiz Xavier da Costa. Lists 2,930 titles.

97   Zamora Lucas, Florentino, and Eduardo Ponce de Leon. **Bibliografía española der arquitectura (1526-1850)** . . . Madrid, Asoc. de Libreros y Amigos del Libro, 1947. 205p. illus. index.

Classified bibliography of books on Spanish architecture from the period 1526 to 1850. Arranged chronologically by centuries.

Sweden

98   Lundqvist, Maja. **Svensk Konsthistorisk Bibliografi: Sammanställd ur den Tryckta Litteraturen till och med år 1950. Bibliography to Swedish History of Art: Literature Issued up to and including 1950.** Stockholm, Almqvist and Wiksell, 1967. index. 432p. (Stockholm Studies in History of Art, 12). LC 67-103402.

Classified bibliography of books and periodical articles on Swedish art and writings on art history in Swedish. Preface and table of contents in Swedish and English index.

99   "Svensk Konsthistorisk Bibliografi," 1959– , in: **Konsthistorisk Tidskrift**, XXIX, 1960) .

Classified bibliography of books and periodical articles on Swedish art and writings in Swedish on art history in general. Compiled by Gunhild Osterman and Karin Melin-Fravolini. With (98), the standard bibliographical tool for study of Swedish art history.

ORIENT

General Works

100   "Bibliography," in: **Oriental Art**, XVI, No. 3 (Autumn, 1970–).

Classified bibliography of books and periodical articles on all aspects of Oriental art and architecture. Divided into sections (Islamic and India, China and Japan) that reflect separate quarterly issues. Not annotated and not classified within the subsections. A valuable serial bibliography for students of Oriental art and architecture. For serious study, it should be used with *Bulletin Signalétique, Série 526* (101).

101   **Bulletin Signalétique. Série 526: Art et Archéologie: Proche-Orient, Asie, Amérique.** v. 25— . Paris, Centre National de la Recherche Scientifique, 1971— .

Annual bibliography of books and periodical articles on all aspects of the art and archaeology of the Near East, Asia, and the Americas. Covers those areas not treated in the *Répertoire* (22). Most entries have annotations or abstracts in French. A valuable reference work for all serious study of Oriental art and architecture.

102   Rowland, Benjamin, Jr. **The Harvard Outline and Reading Lists for Oriental Art**. 3rd ed. Cambridge, Harvard University Press, 1967. 77p. LC 67-22872.

Classified bibliography of books on Oriental art. Periodical articles included when no books on a particular subject exist. Useful to the beginning student of Oriental art.

Islamic World

103   Creswell, Keppel A. C. **A Bibliography of the Architecture, Arts and Crafts of Islam to 1960**. New York, Oxford University Press, 1961. 1330p. LC 62-3352.

Classified bibliography of books and periodical articles on all aspects of Islamic art with the exception of numismatics. Part 1 lists works on architecture classified by country; Part 2 treats arts and crafts, each subdivided by country. A most thorough and comprehensive bibliography. A basic research tool for any serious study of Islamic art. Incorporates the material in the author's *A Provisional Bibliography of Mohammadan Architecture in India* (1922) and *A Bibliography of Painting in Islam* (1953).

104   Ettinghausen, Richard, ed. **A Selected and Annotated Bibliography of Books and Periodicals in Western Languages Dealing with the Near and Middle East with Special Emphasis on Medieval and Modern Times.** Washington, D.C., Middle East Institute, 1952. 111p.

General classified and annotated bibliography on the Islamic world with a section on art and archaeology. Useful to the beginning student and general reader.

105   Mayer, L. A. **Annual Bibliography of Islamic Art and Archaeology, India Excepted . . .**, v. 1-3. Jerusalem, Divan Pub. House, 1935-37.

Classified bibliography of books and periodical articles on all aspects of Islamic art, with the exception of Islamic art in India.

106   Swoboda, K. M. "In den Jahren 1950 bis 1955 erschienene Werke zur
       Kunst Asiens vor den Islam," in: **Kunstgeschichtliche Anzeigen**, Neue
       Folge, Jahrg. 1, 1955/56, pp. 81-142.
Critical examination of the major works on Near and Middle Eastern art before the
time of Islam published from 1950 to 1955. The works discussed are listed at the
beginning of the article. See (21) for series annotation.

107   Swoboda, K. M. "In den Jahren 1950 bis 1956 erschienene Werke zur
       Kunst Islams," in: **Kunstgeschichtliche Anzeigen**, Neue Folge, Jahrg. 2,
       1957, pp. 63-112.
Critical examination of the major works on Islamic art published from 1950 to
1956. The works discussed are listed at the beginning of the article. See (21)
for series annotation.

India and Ceylon

108   **Annual Bibliography of Indian Archaeology** . . . , 1926– . Leyden, Brill,
       1928– . illus.
Classified and annotated bibliography of books and periodical articles on all
aspects of Indian archaeology, including art. Each volume has a useful introduction describing recent excavations. Basic reference tool for students of Indian art.

109   Coomaraswamy, Ananda K. **Bibliographies of Indian Art**. Boston, Museum
       of Fine Arts, 1952. 54p.
Classified bibliography of books on Indian art drawn from the catalog of the
Indian collection of the Museum of Fine Arts; 1,250 entries. Useful to the begin-
ning student and the general reader.

110   Mitra, Haridas. **Contribution to a Bibliography of Indian Art and
       Aesthetics**. Santiniketan, Visva-Bharati, 1951. 240p.
Classified bibliography of writings in Sanskrit on Indian architecture, sculpture, and
painting. Introduction has useful chapter on iconography and a chronology of the
masters of Indian art.

111   Rau, Heimo. "In den Jahren 1960 bis 1965 erschienene Werke zur indischen
       Kunst," in: **Kunstgeschichtliche Anzeigen**, Neue Folge, Jahrg. 7, 1965/
       66, pp. 93-108.
Critical examination of the major works on Indian art published from 1960 to
1965. The works discussed are listed at the beginning of the article. See (21) for
series annotation.

Central Asia

112   Bernier, Ronald M. **A Bibliography of Nepalese Art**. Khatmandu, Voice of
       Nepal, 1970. 46p. LC 74-915230.

Classified bibliography of books and periodical articles on art of Tibet, Sikkim, Bhutan, and Nepal.

113   Jettmar, Karl. "In den Jahren 1955 bis 1962 erschienene Werke zur frühen nomaden Kunst der asiatischen Steppen," in: **Kunstgeschichtliche Anzeigen**, Neue Folge, Jahrg. 5, 1961/62, pp. 184-97.
Critical examination of the major works on Central Asiatic nomadic art published from 1955 to 1962. The works discussed are listed at the beginning of the article. See (21) for series annotation.

114   Rau, Heimo. "In den Jahren 1955 bis 1960 erschienene Werke zur Kunst Indiens und Zentralasiens," in: **Kunstgeschichtliche Anzeigen**, Neue Folge, Jahrg. 4, 1959/60, pp. 122-39.
Critical examination of the major literature on the art of India and Central Asia published between 1955 and 1960. Works discussed are listed at the beginning of the article. See (21) for annotation of the series.

Far East

115   Borton, Hugh, comp. **A Selected List of Books and Articles on Japan in English, French and German**. Rev. and enl. ed. Cambridge, Mass., Harvard-Yenching Institute, 1954. 272p. index.
Books and periodical articles on art are listed on pages 195 to 222. Classified bibliography. Author, title, and subject indexes.

116   Dittich, Edith. "In den Jahren 1956 bis 1964 erschienene Werke zur Kunst Ostasiens/Japan," in: **Kunstgeschichtliche Anzeigen**, Neue Folge, Jahrg. 6, 1963/64, pp. 61-82.
Critical examination of the major works on Japanese art published between 1956 to 1964. The works discussed are listed at the beginning of the article. See (21) for series annotation.

117   Dittich, Edith. "In den Jahren 1957 bis 1962 erschienene Werke zur Kunst Ostasiens/China," in: **Kunstgeschichtliche Anzeigen**, Neue Folge, Jahrg. 6, 1963/64, pp. 1-37.
Critical examination of the major works on Chinese art published from 1957 to 1962. The works discussed are listed at the beginning of the article. See (21) for series annotation.

118   Kokusai Bunka Shinkokai, ed. **K.B.S. Bibliography of Standard Reference Books of Japanese Studies with Descriptive Notes**. Tokyo, 1959.
Volume 3, A: Arts and Crafts.
Volume on the fine arts in a ten-volume guide to reference works on Japanese studies. A classified and annotated retrospective bibliography of major works on Japanese fine arts and crafts. The titles are romanized and the annotations are in English. Useful guide to major works in Japanese and other languages on Japanese art and architecture for the advanced student.

119   Swoboda, K. M. "In den Jahren 1950 bis 1956 erschienene Werke zur
       Kunst Ostasians," in: **Kunstgeschichtliche Anzeigen**, Neue Folge, Jahrg. 2,
       1957, pp. 5-46.
Critical examination of the major literature on the art of East Asia published from
1950 to 1956. The works discussed are listed at the beginning of the article. See
(21) for series annotation.

NEW WORLD

Pre-Columbian America

120   Bernal, Ignacio. **Bibliografia de arqueologia y etografia: Mesoamérica y
       Norte de Mexico.** Mexico City, Instituto Nacional de Antropologia e
       Historia, 1962. 634p.
Comprehensive, retrospective bibliography of books and periodical articles on all
aspects of the archaeology and ethnology of Central America and Mexico, including art and architecture. Covers material published between 1514 and 1960.
Standard reference tool for the serious student of pre-Columbian art and
architecture.

North American Indian

121   Dawdy, Doris O. **Annotated Bibliography of American Indian Painting.**
       New York, Museum of the American Indian, 1968. 27p. (Contributions
       from the Museums of the American Indian Heye Foundation, vol. 21,
       pt. 2).
A useful bibliography of books and periodical articles on North American Indian
painting.

122   Harding, Anne, and Patricia Bolling. **Bibliography of Articles and Papers
       on North American Indian Art.** Washington, D.C., 1938. 365p.
Classified bibliography of periodical articles and scholarly papers on North American Indian art, with 1,500 entries. An important source for the early scholarly
literature on this field.

Latin America

General Works

123   **Handbook of Latin American Studies**, v. 1– . Cambridge, Mass., Harvard
       University Press, 1936– .
Each volume contains a classified and annotated bibliography of books on Latin
American art compiled by a specialist in the field.

124   Smith, Robert Chester, and Elizabeth Wilder. **A Guide to the Art of Latin America** . . . Washington, D.C., U.S. Govt. Printing Office, 1948. 480p. (U.S. Library of Congress Latin American Series, No. 21).

Classified and annotated bibliography of a selective list of books and periodical articles on Latin American art published before 1943. Source library given for each entry. Although old, it is still a valuable reference tool for the study of Latin American art.

Argentina

125   Buschiazzo, Mario José. **Bibliografía de arte colonial argentino.** Buenos Aires, 1947. 150p.

Classified and annotated bibliography of the colonial arts in Argentina. Entries for 843 books.

Brazil

126   Valladares, José. **Estudos de arte Brasileira publicações de 1943-1958: Bibliografia selectiva e comentada.** Salvador, 1960. 193p. (Museu do Estado da Bahia. Publicação No. 15). LC 64-43893.

Classified and annotated bibliography of books on Brazilian art published from 1943 to 1958. 693 entries.

Colombia

127   Giraldo Jaramillo, Gabriel. **Bibliografía selecta del arte en Colombia.** Bogota, Editorial A B C, 1956. 147p.

Classified and annotated bibliography of books on art in Colombia.

Mexico

128   Ocampo, María Luisa, and María Mediz Bolio. **Apuntes para una bibliografía del arte en Mexico.** Mexico, Secretaria de Educacion Publica, 1957. 194p. LC 68-43120.

Classified bibliography of books on Mexican art, with 1,031 entries.

Santo Domingo

129   Florén Lozano, Luis. **Bibliografía de las bellas artes en Santo Domingo.** Bogotá, Antares, 1956. 53p.

Classified bibliography of books and periodical articles on the art of Santo Domingo.

United States

130   The American Association of Architectural Bibliographers. **Papers.**
       William B. O'Neal, ed. v. 1— . Charlottesville, Va., University of Virginia
       Press, 1965— .
Each volume contains several classified bibliographies on architects, regions, and
buildings. Many bibliographies carry over into subsequent volumes. Includes both
American architects and architects working in the United States.

131   Chase, Frank H. **A Bibliography of American Art and Artists Before 1835.**
       Boston, 1918. 32p.
Short bibliography of 600 titles, chiefly periodical articles on the colonial and
federal periods of art in the United States. Still useful to the specialist.

132   Garrett, Wendell D., and Jane N. Garrett. **The Arts in Early American
       History.** Chapel Hill, University of North Carolina Press, 1965. 170p.
       index. LC 65-53132.
Classified and annotated bibliography of books and periodical articles on American
art up to 1826. Introductory essay, "An Unexploited Historical Resource," by
Walter Muir Whitehill.

133   Hitchcock, Henry Russell. **American Architectural Books: A List of
       Books, Portfolios, Pamphlets on Architecture and Related Subjects
       Published in America before 1895.** Minneapolis, University of Minnesota,
       1962. 130p.
Reprint of the third revised edition (1946). Classified bibliography giving location of copies in 130 libraries.

134   McCausland, Elizabeth. "A Selected Bibliography on American Painting
       and Sculpture from Colonial Times to the Present," in: **American Art
       Journal**, v. 36, 1947, pp. 611-53.
Classified bibliography of books and periodical articles on American painting and
sculpture. Most useful for access to artist monographs.

135   Roos, Frank J., Jr. **Bibliography of Early American Architecture: Writ-
       ings on Architecture Constructed before 1860 in Eastern and Central
       United States.** New ed. Urbana, University of Illinois Press, 1968. 389p.
       index. LC 68-24624.
Classified bibliography of books and periodical articles, with occasional
annotations.

AFRICA

136   Gaskin, Guy. **A Bibliography of African Art Compiled at the Interna-
        tional African Institute.** London, International African Institute, 1965.
        120p. index.
Classified bibliography of 4,827 books on African art, arranged by region. Author,
geographical, ethnic, and subject indexes.

137   Hassel, Herta. "In den Jahren 1954 bis 1960 erschienene Werke zur Kunst
        der ethnologischen Völker, besonders Negerafrikas," in: **Kunstgeschicht-
        liche Anzeigen**, Neue Folge, Jahrg. 4, 1959/60, pp. 106-121.
Critical examination of the major works on primitive art, particularly the art of
Black Africa. The works discussed are listed at the beginning of the article. See
(21) for series annotation.

138   Mirvish, Doreen Belle. **South African Artists, 1900-1958: Bibliography.**
        Cape Town, University of Cape Town, 1959. 41p. LC 61-21936.
Bibliography of books and periodical articles on South African artists published
between 1900 and 1958.

CHAPTER TWO

LIBRARY CATALOGS

A decade ago library catalogs were not important reference tools in the study of the fine arts. Only a few European libraries had issued printed catalogs and most of these were not kept up to date. With the improvement of the photomechanical process of reproducing actual library catalog cards, however, this situation changed rapidly. Today the majority of major fine arts libraries have had their card catalogs reproduced and made available to libraries around the world, with supplements issued regularly to keep them up to date.

It is essential for those who use these catalogs to be aware of the limitations of the photomechanically reproduced library catalogs. Since the cards as they exist in the libraries' files are simply reproduced and bound in pages as they are filed, without any attempt at further or supplementary classification, the user must be familiar with the system used in the original library catalog. Classification systems differ from library to library, and many of the older European libraries follow systems unfamiliar to the average American user. This seldom poses a problem with author listings. But if one wants to use these catalogs for their subject listings—and it is their potential use as subject bibliographies that is a most worthwhile aspect of these catalogs—the idiosyncracies and limitations of the subject classifications become a major restriction. But with perseverance and knowledge of classification (and occasionally of paleography as well), the modern catalogs can be very valuable bibliographic tools.

139   American School of Classical Studies at Athens. Genadius Library.
       Catalogue. Boston, Hall, 1968. 7v. LC 70-3154.
Photomechanical reproduction of the author and subject card catalogue of the
Genadius Library at the American School of Classical Studies at Athens, a library
of some 50,000 volumes devoted to the history of Greek culture from earliest
times to the present.

140   Amsterdam, Netherlands. Rijksmuseum. Kunsthistorische Bibliotheek. **Catalogus der Kunsthistorische Bibliotheek in het Rijksmuseum te Amsterdam**. Amsterdam, Dept. van Onderwijs, 1934-36. 4v.

A classified list of the books and periodicals in this important center for the research of Dutch art history. Outline of the classification at the beginning of each volume. Volume 4 contains author, artists, subject, place, collectors, and dealers indexes.

141   **Annuario bibliografico di storia dell'arte**. Anno 1– , 1952– . Modena, Soc. Tipo. Modenese, 1952– . index.

A classified list of the books and periodicals acquired by the Biblioteca dell' Istituto Nazionale d'Archeologia e Storia dell'Arte in Rome. Short abstracts are given for most entries. Index of names. Very useful bibliographical tool for the study of Italian art. Material arranged in three chief classes: I, Arte; II, Artisti; III, Paesi.

142   Columbia University. Avery Architectural Library. **Catalog of The Avery Memorial Architectural Library of Columbia University**. 2nd ed., enl. Boston, Hall, 1968. 19v.

Columbia University. Avery Architectural Library. **Catalog of The Avery Memorial Architectural Library of Columbia University**. First Supplement, 1972. 4v.

A union list of books and periodical titles on art and architecture in the extensive Columbia University Library system, as well as 10,000 original drawings in library collections. The catalog of an important American art library, especially strong in architecture.

143   Florence, Italy. Harvard University Center for Italian Renaissance Studies. **Catalogues of the Berenson Library of the Harvard University Center for Italian Renaissance Studies at Villa I Tatti, Florence, Italy**. Boston, Hall, 1972. 4v.

The total holdings of about 70,000 volumes are disposed in a two-volume author catalog and a two-volume subject catalog. The photomechanically reproduced cards are old and lack reliable orthography.

144   Florence, Italy. Kunsthistorisches Institut. Bibliothek. **Catalog of the Institute for the History of Art, Florence, Italy. Katalog des Kunsthistorischen Instituts in Florenz**. Boston, Hall, 1964. 9v. First Supplement, 1968, 2v. Second Supplement, 1972, 2v.

Photomechanical reproduction of the alphabetical catalog (author and key word). The Institut is the most important center for Italian Renaissance studies in Europe. Thus, the holdings of its library are of great interest to students of Italian Renaissance art. The handwritten cards are a formidable obstacle to its use by the inexperienced.

145   Harvard University. **Catalogue of the Harvard University Fine Arts Library**. The Fogg Art Museum. Boston, Hall, 1971. 16v.

Photomechanical reproduction of the author-subject card catalog of the combined holdings in the fine arts of the Widener Library and the Fogg Museum Library. Volume 16 is a separate catalog of the collection of sales catalogs. Harvard has one of the largest fine arts libraries in the United States; consequently, this reproduction of the card catalog with its thorough subject classification is a basic bibliographical tool.

146   London, England. Royal Institute of British Architects. Library.
        Catalogue of the Library. London, Royal Institute of British Architects, 1937-38. 2v.
Volume 1 (1138p.) is an author catalog of books and manuscripts in the collection. Volume 2 (514p.) contains a classified index and an alphabetical subject index.

147   London, England. Victoria and Albert Museum. **National Art Gallery Library Catalogue**. Boston, Hall, 1972. 11v. LC 73-153208.
The author catalog of a great art reference library. Volume 10 lists titles written before 1890; Volume 11 lists 50,000 exhibition catalogs.

148   National Gallery of Canada. **Catalogue of the Library of the National Gallery of Canada, Ottawa**. Boston, Hall, 1973. 8v.
Photomechanical reproduction of the author-subject card catalogue of the more than 35,000 volumes in the Canadian National Gallery Library. Useful tool for research into the visual arts in Canada.

149   New York City. Metropolitan Museum of Art. Library. **Library Catalog**. Boston, Hall, 1960. 25v. First Supplement, 1962; Second Supplement, 1965; Third Supplement, 1968; Fourth Supplement, 1970.
Photomechanical reproduction of the dictionary card catalog of this important collection. Vols. 1-23: books and periodical holdings; Vols. 24-25: sales catalogs. Supplements list accessions since 1960.

150   Paris, France. Bibliothèque Forney. **Catalogue des catalogues de ventes d'art, Bibliothèque Forney, Paris**. 2v. Boston, Hall, 1972. LC 72-226228.
Photomechanical reproduction of the card catalog of the important collection of sales catalogs in the Bibliothèque Forney in Paris.

151   Paris, France. Bibliothèque Forney. **Catalogue Matières: arts-decoratifs, beaux-arts métiers, techniques**. Paris, Société des Amis de la Bibliothèque Forney. 1970-74. LC 75-574191. 4v.
Photomechanical reproduction of the subject catalogue of this famous French library of nearly 100,000 volumes and 1,350 periodicals devoted to the applied arts. Particularly valuable for bibliographical information on art techniques.

152   Rome, Italy. Deutsches Archäologisches Institut. **Kataloge der Bibliothek des Deutschen Archäologischen Instituts, Rom**. Boston, Hall, 1969. 13v.

Photomechanical reproduction of the card catalogs of books and card index to periodical articles in the German Archaeological Institute in Rome. Part one is author and periodical title catalog; Part two, the subject catalog; Part three, the special author index to periodical articles, begun in 1956. The holdings of this famous archaeological library cover the ancient civilizations of the entire Mediterranean basin from prehistory through the early Christian period.

153   Smithsonian Institution, Freer Gallery of Art. **Dictionary Catalogue of the Library of the Freer Gallery of Art, Smithsonian Institution, Washington, D.C.** Boston, Hall, 1967. 6v.

Photomechanical reproduction of the dictionary catalog of books, pamphlets, and periodicals in this important research library (40,000 volumes) devoted to Far Eastern art. Part one lists works in Western languages; Part two, works in Chinese and Japanese.

CHAPTER THREE

INDEXES

I. INTRODUCTION

Included in this section are all reference works that index a limited body of material. In the fine arts these fall into two broad categories: indexes of literature on the fine arts and indexes to illustrations. In both categories there are important works for the general reader and the advanced student; illustration indexes comprise some of the reference librarian's most used tools.

Like library catalogs, indexes in the fine arts have increased substantially in the past decade, and the trend appears to be binal. There are the indexes to illustrations in popular periodicals and books, directed to the needs of librarians. And there are the indexes to special bodies of scholarly literature, made possible through the photomechanical process used to reproduce library card catalogs; these are designed for the advanced student of the history of art. These bibliographical indexes are especially important and deserve to be singled out. *The Art Index* (155) is one of the oldest and most used of bibliographical tools in the fine arts. It indexes a large number of art periodicals and gives special attention to the more accessible and popular English language journals. It is one of the mainstays of reference librarians. It has been supplemented by the reproduction of the Ryerson Library index (156) and, for specialized periodical literature, by the Avery Architectural Library index (159) and the most valuable catalog of the Bibliothèque Forney (163), which indexes the often ignored articles on the decorative arts.

II. INDEXES TO LITERATURE

154   **Art Bibliographies Current Titles.** v. 1— . Santa Barbara, ABC-Clio Press, 1972— .
Monthly index to the articles in approximately 250 current fine arts periodicals. Consists of photomechanical reproductions of the periodicals' tables of contents.

Since 1973, it no longer appears in July and August. List of periodicals indexed is given in each number, and a complete list is published twice a year. The selection of periodicals is international and includes some museum bulletins and annuals. A useful index for keeping up with current periodical literature. Produced by the American Bibliographical Center in Santa Barbara. Unfortunately, does not index the articles by subject.

155   **Art Index: A Cumulative Author and Subject Index to a Selected List of Fine Arts Periodicals and Museum Bulletins.** v. 1– , 1929– . New York, Wilson, 1933– .
Issued quarterly with annual and three-year cumulations. Classified bibliography of periodical articles and articles in museum bulletins. Coverage varies; museum bulletins included only through 1957. Periodical articles are listed under author and subject, book reviews under the author reviewed and subject, exhibitions under artist. A basic reference tool, especially for material in English-language periodicals. Should be supplemented with the Ryerson index (156) for more complete coverage.

156   Chicago. Art Institute, Ryerson Library. **Index to Art Periodicals.** Boston, Hall, 1962. 11v.
Photomechanical reproduction of the library's card file, which was begun in 1907. Over 300 periodicals are indexed, covering serial titles not indexed in Wilson's *Art Index* (155). Arranged by subject and artist.

157   Clapp, Jane. **Art Censorship: A Chronology of Proscribed and Prescribed Art.** Metuchen, N.J., Scarecrow, 1972. 582p. illus. LC 76-172789.
An index to acts of censorship against art recorded in 641 selected sources. The acts of censorship are arranged chronologically; each entry gives the date of the incident, reference to one of the sources, and a brief quotation from the source. General index (pp. 425-582).

158   Clapp, Jane. **Museum Publications. Part I: Anthropology, Archaeology and Art.** New York, Scarecrow, 1962. 434p.
A classified list of publications available from 276 museums in the United States and Canada, including books, pamphlets, and other monographs and some serial reprints. Now out of date.

159   Columbia University, Avery Architectural Library. **Avery Index to Architectural Periodicals.** Boston, Hall, 1963. 12v.
Photomechanical reproduction of the card index to articles in the architectural periodicals held by the Avery Library. The index, begun in 1934, covers architecture in the widest sense so as to include interior decoration, city planning, housing, etc. Articles are listed by subject. Supplements were issued yearly from 1965 to 1968, every two years since then. The Avery index is the most comprehensive index to periodical literature on architecture.

160   Columbia University, Avery Memorial Architectural Library. **Avery Obituary Index of Architects and Artists.** Boston, Hall, 1963. 338p. LC 64-7017.

Photomechanical reproduction of the card index to obituaries of architects and artists published in periodicals and newspapers. A valuable source for biographical material on many lesser-known architects.

161   Lugt, Frits. **Répertoire des catalogues de ventes publiques intéressant d'art ou la curiosité** . . . v. 1— . The Hague, Nijhoff, 1938— .

Chronological list of catalogs of art sales held throughout Europe from circa 1600 to 1860. Each entry gives date of the sale, place of the sale, name of the collector, artist or merchant, the contents of the sale, number of lots, names of auctioneers, number of pages in the sales catalog, and library source for copies of the catalog. Volume 1 covers period from 1600 to 1825; volume 2, 1826 to 1860. Index of collectors and names of collections. Basic reference work for the history of art sales.

162   **Museum Media. A Biennial Directory and Index of Publications and Audiovisuals Available from United States and Canadian Institutions.** Detroit, Gale Research, 1973. 455p. index. LC 73-16335.

Alphabetical listing of 732 museums of all kinds in the United States and Canada, with the publications and audiovisual materials currently available from them. Gives complete citations and prices for publications. Provided with an exhaustive title and keyword index. A most useful reference tool for the librarian.

163   Paris, Bibliothèque Forney. **Catalogue d'articles des périodiques—arts décoratifs et beaux-arts. Catalog of Periodical Articles—Decorative and Fine Arts.** Boston, Hall, 1972. 4v.

Photomechanical reproduction of the card index to articles dealing with the decorative arts in the Bibliothèque Forney in Paris. Articles are arranged by subject. Analyzes the articles on the decorative arts in 1,347 periodicals, 325 of them current. The most comprehensive index of its kind; supplements the other major periodical indexes (155, 156).

164   Rave, Paul O. **Kunstgeschichte in Festschriften.** Berlin, Mann, 1962. 314p.

Classified index of art historical essays that appear in *Festschriften* published up to 1960. Thoroughly indexed by title, author, artist, and place. For serious students of art history, an extremely valuable reference tool to give access to important material not usually included in other bibliographies.

III. INDEXES TO ILLUSTRATIONS

165   **A.L.A. Portrait Index to Portraits Contained in Printed Books and
       Periodicals** . . . Washington, D.C., Library of Congress, 1906. 1601p.
An index to portraits illustrated in a large set of books and periodicals published
before 1905. Arranged by subject. 120,000 portraits of nearly 45,000 persons.
Entries give dates of the subject, name of artist and/or engraver, and source for
illustrations.

166   Bertran, Margaret. **A Guide to Color Reproductions.** 2nd ed. Metuchen,
       N.J., Scarecrow, 1971. 625p.
Index of separate-sheet color reproductions of works of art. Lists only those
available in the United States, giving the source and price. Part I lists the reproductions by artist; Part II, by title or subject.

167   Cirker, Hayward, and Blanche Cirker. **Dictionary of American Portraits:
       4045 Pictures of Important Americans from Earliest Times to the
       Beginning of the Twentieth Century.** New York, Dover, 1967. 756p.
       illus. LC 66-30514.
An illustrated index of portraits of Americans, arranged by subject. A short caption
to each illustration gives artist and/or source. Index by profession.

168   Clapp, Jane. **Art in Life.** New York, Scarecrow, 1959. 504p. LC
       65-13552.
Index to pictures of art published in *Life* magazine from 1936 to 1956. Arranged
by artist, title, and/or subject. Supplement (covering years 1957 to 1963)
published in 1965.

169   Clapp, Jane. **Art Reproductions.** New York, Scarecrow, 1961. 350p.
       LC 61-8714.
Index to art reproductions available from 95 sources in the United States and
Canada. Arranged by medium. Entries give the dates of the artist, subject, dimensions, price, and source. Useful source for popular and easily accessible fine art
reproductions.

170   Clapp, Jane. **Sculpture Index.** 2v. in 3. Metuchen, N.J., Scarecrow, 1970.
Index to illustrations of sculpture in 950 selected sources, mostly books commonly
found in smaller libraries. Volume 1 indexes European and contemporary Middle
Eastern sculpture; Volume 2 deals with sculpture of the Americas, the Orient,
Africa, and Oceania. Emphasis is on American and European sculpture since 1900.
Arranged alphabetically by artist and subject depicted. Basic biographical data
given in artist entries.

171   Ellis, Jessie Croft. **Index to Illustrations.** Boston, F. W. Faxon, 1966.
       682p.

General index to illustrations of almost everything except nature. Uses a small group of illustration sources, mostly popular magazines.

172   Havlice, Patricia Pate. **Art in Time**. Metuchen, N.J., Scarecrow, 1970.
       350p. illus. LC 76-14885.
Index to all pictures in the art section of *Time* magazine arranged by artist, title, and/or subject. Entries give the dates of the artist, the medium of the work, whether the illustration is in black and white or color, and the source in *Time*. Useful for ready access to important reviews and criticisms of modern art.

173   Lee, Cathbert. **Portrait Register**, v. 1– . Asheville, N.C., Biltmore Press,
       1968– .
Index to some 8,000 painted portraits in private and public collections in the United States. Listed by subject and painter.

174   Morse, John D. **Old Masters in America: A Comprehensive Guide; More
       than Two-Thousand Paintings in the United States and Canada by Forty
       Famous Artists**. Chicago, Rand McNally, 1955. 192p.
Index of paintings by 40 famous "old masters" in American collections, arranged by artist. A short biographical note is given with each entry. Index by state and city. Handy tool for quick location of famous paintings.

175   Munro, Isabel Stevenson, and Kate M. Munro. **Index of American Paint-
       ings**. New York, Wilson, 1948. 731p. First Supplement, 1964.
       480p.
Index to illustrations of American paintings in a group of easily accessible books and periodicals; indexed by artist, title, and subject. Basic biographical data and location of the paintings are given.

176   Munro, Isabel Stevenson, and Kate M. Munro. **Index to Reproductions of
       European Paintings**. New York, Wilson, 1956. 668p. LC 55-6803.
Index to illustrations in 328 books and periodicals by artist, title, and subject. Entries give the dates of artists and the locations of the paintings. A valuable reference tool for easy access to illustrations of major European paintings. The sources used are generally available in small libraries.

177   Reinach, Salomon. **Répertoire de la statuaire grecque et romaine** . . .
       Paris, Leroux, 1897-1930. 6v. in 8. illus.
An illustrated index to ancient Greek and Roman statues, arranged by subject. Index at end of each volume and general index in Vol. 5. Still a useful tool for the study of classical iconography.

178   Reinach, Salomon. **Répertoire de reliefs grecs et romains** . . . Paris,
       Leroux, 1909-12. 3v. illus.
An illustrated index to ancient Greek and Roman reliefs, arranged by subject. General index in Vol. 3. Still a useful tool for the study of classical iconography.

179   **Fine Art Reproductions, Old and Modern Masters.** 9th ed. Greenwich,
         Conn., New York Graphic Society, 1972. 550p. illus. index. LC 72-85864.
Index of the reproductions marketed by the New York Graphic Society, one of the
largest manufacturers of fine art reproductions in the United States. Each entry is
illustrated and has a caption giving size, reproduction medium, and price.

180   Singer, Hans W. **Allgemeiner Bildniskatalog.** Leipzig, Hiersemann, 1930-
         1936. 14v. LC 31-15244. **Neuer Bildniskatalog** . . . Leipzig, Hiersemann,
         1937-38. 5v. index. LC AC 37-1659 rev.
Index to engraved portraits of all times and countries represented in 17 public
collections in Germany. The approximately 180,000 portraits, arranged by subject,
give the name of the artist, medium, and location. Separate artist and profession
indexes in each volume, general index in Volume 14.
         The *Neuer Bildniskatalog* is an index to painted and sculptured portraits
and some early photographic portraits. Same format as the earlier index. Volume 1
has list of sources and Volume 5 has general index by artist and profession.
These two Singer indexes are the most comprehensive guides to portraits made
up to 1929.

CHAPTER FOUR

DIRECTORIES

181   **American Architects Directory**. 3rd ed. New York, Bowker, 1970. 1126p.
Directory of registered architects in the United States, listed alphabetically and by
state and city. Also gives the membership of the American Institute of Architects
and an appendix listing the National Council of Architectural Registration Boards.

182   **American Art Directory**. 45th ed. New York, Bowker, 1974. 455p. LC
       99-1016.
Directory of American art organizations covering museums, foundations, organizations, university and college art departments, and art schools.

183   **Internationales Kunst-Adressbuch. International Directory of Arts.**
       Annuaire international des beaux-arts. 11th ed., 1971/72. Berlin, Deutsche
       Zentraldruckerei, 1972. 2v.
Directory of addresses of museums, art galleries, art libraries, art associations,
universities, colleges and art academies, auctioneers, restorers, art dealers, book-
sellers, art publishers, and collectors. Arranged by country. The standard address
directory for the fine arts.

184   **International Who's Who in Art and Antiques.** Cambridge, London and
       Dartmouth, Melrose Press Ltd., 1972. 679p. illus. LC 79-189269.
Directory of artists, art educators, gallery and museum directors, heads of art
associations, art and antique dealers, auctioneers, art publishers, and restorers in
58 countries. Five appendices list art schools, museums and galleries, art publishers,
art associations, and art scholarships and grants by country. Not as thorough as
(183), but it has the advantage of a single alphabetical list of persons.

185   Kloster, Gudrun B. **Handbook of Museums: Germany, Austria, Switzer-**
       land. Munich, Verlag Dokumentation, 1972. 2v. index.
Comprehensive directory of some 3,050 museums in Germany, Austria, and
Switzerland. Entries give address, telephone numbers, names of the professional
staff, hours of opening, entrance fees, summary history of the museum, description
of the buildings, collections, archives, and library, and sketch of the future plans of

development and bibliography. Introduction in German and English, entries in German. Very thorough and useful directory.

186   **Museums of the World/Museen der Welt: A Directory of 17,000 Museums in 148 Countries, Including a Subject Index.** Eleanor Braun, comp. Pullach bei München, Verlag Dokumentation; New York, Bowker, 1973. 762p. index.

A geographically arranged listing of all kinds of museums. Contains a useful classified subject index and an alphabetical listing by name.

187   **Official Museum Directory 1973: United States and Canada.** New York, National Register, 1973. 1173p. index. LC 79-144808.

Lists, by state and province, over 6,000 museums of all kinds in the United States and Canada. Gives names and specialties of museum curatorial staff, address of the museum, and a list of the museum's publications. Thorough alphabetical index. Standard American museum directory. Revised every two years.

188   Ploetz, Gerhard. **Bildquellen-Handbuch; der Wegweiser für Bildsuchende.** Wiesbaden, Chmielorz, 1961. 611p. illus. index.

Directory of photographic illustrations and their sources. Part I is an index of photographs by subject, country, place, persons, artists, etc., giving reference to sources in the approximately 4,000 photographic archives listed by country in Parts II-V. A useful directory with emphasis on sources of original photographs.

189   UNESCO. **Répertoire international des archives photographiques d'oeuvres d'art. International Directory of Photographic Archives of Works of Art.** 2v. Paris, 1950-1954.

Directory of photographic archives throughout the world. The archives are arranged by place; descriptions include subject specialty if any, size of the collection, nature or purpose of the archive, hours of opening, and the price charged for copies. Useful, although no longer current.

190   **Who's Who in American Art.** v. 1– . New York, Bowker, 1936– .

Issued by the American Federation of Arts. Directory of artists, art historians, art critics, art editors, museum personnel, art educators, and lecturers in the United States and Canada. Gives short biography and address. Geographical index and necrology at end of each volume. Standard directory for fine arts in America. Back issues are useful source for biographical information of lesser American modern artists.

191   **Who's Who in Art.** v. 1– . London, Art Trade Press, 1927– .

Directory of artists, designers, craftsmen, critics, writers, teachers, collectors, and museum personnel. Appendices with necrology and list of artists' marks and signatures. Useful chiefly for Great Britain.

CHAPTER FIVE

DICTIONARIES AND ENCYCLOPEDIAS

I. INTRODUCTION

There is no better testimony to the increased interest in the fine arts than the prodigious growth in dictionaries, both serious and popular, since World War II. Most of this activity has been concentrated in the production of biographical dictionaries. It would appear that the completion of the magnum opus of Thieme and Becker (232) in 1950 was a signal for, and in many cases the basis for, the publishing of numerous national biographical dictionaries, so that today the majority of European countries and several Western hemisphere nations have competent dictionaries of their artists. There are notable exceptions. France, for example, still lacks a national biographical fine arts dictionary. So does Spain, and the United States still awaits a comprehensive dictionary of its artists. But in some countries the coverage is so broad that specialized biographical dictionaries have appeared concentrating on small periods and, in some cases, on regions.

In contrast, the production of general dictionaries of the fine arts—in particular, those dealing with terminology—has lagged. Only very recently has the German-French *Glossarium Artis* (216) begun to replace our dependence on such old-fashioned works as Adeline's dictionary (215). In part this lack has been alleviated by smaller dictionaries restricted to periods and media. Architecture has always been well endowed with comprehensive dictionaries that give strong attention to terminology; painting has recently received its due in an excellent Swiss dictionary (213). But for sculpture and the graphic arts one must be content with bits and pieces culled from general dictionaries.

Encyclopedias devoted exclusively to the fine arts are very recent phenomena. Although general encyclopedias dealing with various epochs or periods of history have existed for well over a century, the first art historical encyclopedia was begun in 1937 with the publication of the first volume of the *Reallexikon zur deutschen Kunstgeschichte* (273), a work of truly encyclopedic scope and scholarly exactness that has in the intervening 44 years reached the letter "F" in six double-column volumes. In the past 20 years others have appeared, most notably the Italian-American *Encyclopedia of World Art* (193). With the possible exception of the advent of national bibliographies in the fine arts, these works have become the most important contributions to the field of fine arts reference tools since the last war. They provide the general reader and the student with access to a vast array of information and expert opinion that was previously known only to specialist-scholars. Since most provide excellent bibliographies, encyclopedias in the fine arts are now the first step in any serious study. Because of the close association of art history and archaeology in the study of the fine arts of prehistoric, ancient, and medieval cultures, the standard general encyclopedias and dictionaries for these periods have been included.

II. GENERAL DICTIONARIES AND ENCYCLOPEDIAS

GENERAL WORKS

192   **Das Atlantisbuch der Kunst; eine Enzyklopädie der bildenden Künste.**
       Zürich, Atlantis, 1952. 897p. illus. index.
One-volume encyclopedia of the visual arts; articles are signed and include bibliographies. Arranged by broad subject areas: 1, Vom Wesen der Kunst; 2, Die Künstlerischen Techniken und ihre Anwendung; 3, Epochen der Kunst in Europa; 4, Die Kunst der aussereuropäischen Völker; 5, Kunstpflege. Well illustrated. Particularly useful are the sections devoted to European styles and periods and the art of non-Western peoples.

193   **Encyclopedia of World Art.** New York, McGraw-Hill, 1959-1968. 15v.
       illus. index (v. 15). LC 59-134333.
Comprehensive encyclopedia of the art and architecture of all peoples and periods. Signed articles cover major artists, styles, periods, countries, civilizations, and media. Articles range in length from moderately long biographies of major artists to long articles on civilizations, countries, and periods. All have extensive bibliographies, classified and arranged by date of publication, covering books and periodical articles in all languages. Each volume has a corpus of excellent plates, and the articles are liberally provided with plans and diagrams. First appeared in an Italian edition (Florence, Sansoni), which has adversely affected the alphabetical arrangement in the English edition. In compensation, it is necessary to use the index volume. Only major artists are included; for secondary artists consult Thieme-Becker (232) or Myers (197). A standard reference work in the fine arts, although the quality of the entries varies with the contributor. The bibliographies are excellent guides to further study.

194   **Harper's Encyclopedia of Art: Architecture, Sculpture, Painting, Decorative Arts** . . . New York, Harper, 1937. 2v. illus.

Short-entry encyclopedia of the visual arts covering artists, styles, and periods. Some entries have short bibliographies. Based on the French encyclopedia of Louis Hourticq (Paris, 1925). Older, popular art encyclopedia.

195   Jahn, Johannes. **Wörterbuch der Kunst.** 6th ed. rev. and enl. Stuttgart, Kröner, 1962. 749p. illus.
General fine arts dictionary of artists, terms, styles, periods, and civilizations. Illustrated with line drawings. Short but excellent bibliographies given at the end of the larger entries. Thoroughly cross referenced. One of the best one-volume art dictionaries.

196   Murray, Peter, and Linda Murray. **Dictionary of Art and Artists.** New York, Praeger, 1966.
General fine arts dictionary containing artist biographies, definitions of terms and techniques, and articles on styles, periods, and schools of art. Excellent illustrations, but no bibliographies. Good general dictionary for the beginning student and general reader. Particularly useful for terms and techniques. Does not deal with non-Western art.

197   Myers, Bernard S., and Shirley D. Myers, eds. **McGraw-Hill Dictionary of Art.** New York, McGraw-Hill, 1969. 5v. illus. LC 68-26314.
Comprehensive dictionary of the visual arts covering artists, periods, styles, terms, monuments, museums, places, and countries. Articles range in length from short entries defining terms to long articles on major artists, styles, periods, etc. Larger articles are signed. The larger entries have separate bibliographies. Well illustrated. One of the best all-purpose art encyclopedias in English for the general reader and beginning student.

198   **New International Illustrated Encyclopedia of Art.** New York, Greystone, 1967-1971. 23v. illus. LC 67-24201.
Pictorial dictionary of the art and architecture of all peoples and periods. Entries cover artists, countries, media, and such subjects as urban planning. All illustrations are in color. No bibliography. For the general reader.

199   Osborne, Harold. **The Oxford Companion to Art.** New York, Oxford University Press, 1970. 1277p. illus.
A comprehensive general dictionary of the visual arts. Articles range in size from short definitions of terms and brief biographies of major artists to lengthy articles on periods, styles, civilizations, and special aspects of the study of the fine arts (such as preservation and conservation). Also includes places, major buildings, and museums. Entries have bibliographical references to the nearly 3,000 items in the general bibliography at the end of the volume. The best all-round fine arts dictionary in English.

200   Parow, Rolf, and H. E. Pappenheim. **Kunststile: Lexikon der Stil Begriffe.** 2nd ed. Munich, Kunst und Technik, 1958. 332p. illus. LC 58-19045.

General dictionary of art styles, schools, movements, and forms. Second part is a polyglot dictionary of the terms in German, English, and French. Bibliography (pp. 149-50). Useful dictionary for students confronted with the task of reading German art historical literature.

201   **Praeger Encyclopedia of Art**. New York, Praeger, 1971. 5v. illus. index. LC 75-122093.
Comprehensive encyclopedia-dictionary covering the art and architecture of all nations, civilizations, and periods. Covers artists, styles, schools, movements, and some terms. Most entries are short, but there are some 1,000 longer survey articles that cover major styles and periods. Based on the *Dictionnaire universel de l'art et des artistes* published by Hazan in Paris (1967), the work of a number of Continental specialists. A good reference work for the general reader and student.

202   Schaffran, Emerich. **Dictionary of European Art**. New York, Philosophical Library, 1958. 283p.
General fine arts dictionary of artists, terms, techniques, periods, styles, etc. No bibliographies. Popular dictionary with very short entries, uneven in coverage. Restricted to European art.

203   Sormani, Giuseppe. **Dizionario delle arti**. 2nd ed. rev. and enl. Milan, Sormani, c. 1953. 974p. illus.
General fine arts dictionary with entries arranged under broad subjects and movements. Index of names. The unusual arrangement is advantageous for quick reference to styles, schools and movements, particularly in Italian and modern art.

204   **Visual Dictionary of Art**. General editor, Ann Hill. Greenwich, Conn., New York Graphic Society, 1973. 640p. illus. index. LC 73-76181.
General dictionary of art, both Eastern and Western, covering civilizations, periods, styles, schools, movements, and artists as well as terms, techniques, and materials. Thoroughly illustrated. An unusual and useful feature is the collection of short essays on major periods and civilizations preceding the alphabetical entries. The brevity of the entries and the limited bibliography restrict its usefulness to the general reader.

ARCHITECTURE

205   Briggs, Martin S. **Everyman's Concise Encyclopaedia of Architecture**. London, Dent; New York, Dutton, 1959. 372p. illus.
General dictionary of architecture covering terms, periods, styles, and the biographies of major architects. Illustrated with numerous line drawings. An excellent one-volume dictionary of architecture.

206   Fleming, John, Hugh Honour, and Nikolaus Pevsner. **The Penguin Dictionary of Architecture**. Baltimore, Penguin, 1966. 248p. illus.

General dictionary of architecture with short biographies of architects, stylistic and technical terms, and short characterizations of major periods and styles of architecture. Illustrated with line drawings.

207 Harris, John, and Jill Lever. **Illustrated Glossary of Architecture, 850-1830**. New York, Potter, 1966. illus.
Concise dictionary of architecture covering styles, structures, decorations, materials, objects, etc. Brief definitions but excellent illustrations, with the pertinent features indicated by pointers.

208 Portoghesi, Paolo. **Dizionario enciclopedico di architettura e urbanistica**. Rome, Ist. Editoriale Romano, 1968-69. 6v. illus. LC 71-431738.
Comprehensive Italian encyclopedia of architecture and city planning. Entries, which have separate bibliographies, cover architects, structures, terms, styles, countries, and places. Well illustrated with plates, plans, and drawings. One of the most useful of the modern dictionaries and encyclopedias of architecture.

209 Saylor, Henry H. **Dictionary of Architecture**. New York, Wiley, 1952. 221p. illus. LC 52-8260.
Dictionary of architectural terms, materials, and styles. Illustrated with small selection of line drawings at the end. Too brief to be of much value for the complex subject; the entries dealing with architectural materials are the best feature.

210 Sturgis, Russell, ed. **A Dictionary of Architecture and Building, Biographical, Historical and Descriptive** ... New York, Macmillan, 1901-02. 3v. illus. index.
Comprehensive dictionary of architecture covering architects, styles, periods, major buildings, materials, structures, and decorations. Longer articles are signed. Illustrated with line drawings. Bibliography of sources consulted at end of Vol. 3. An old standard dictionary of architecture, still useful.

211 **Wasmuths Lexikon der Baukunst**. Berlin, Wasmuth, 1929-37. 5v. illus. LC 31-1582.
Comprehensive dictionary of architecture and the building arts. Covers architects, countries, places, buildings, terminology, decoration and furnishings, with information on constructional elements and engineering principles and details. Larger entries have separate bibliographies. Thoroughly illustrated with plates, plans, and diagrams. The standard reference tool for architecture, in spite of its age.

PAINTING

212 Gaunt, William. **Everyman's Dictionary of Pictorial Art**. London, Dent; New York, Dutton, 1962. 2v. illus.
General dictionary of painting with short biographies of major painters, definitions of terms, and descriptions of the main periods, styles, and schools of painting. Supplementary list of American and British artists.

213   **Kindlers Malerei Lexikon.** Zürich, Kindler, 1964-1971. 6v. illus. index.
Dictionary of painting covering all aspects of both Western and non-Western paintings. Volumes 1-5 devoted to biographies of painters; Volume 6 treats concepts, styles, subjects, and techniques. The biographies give basic biographical data, facsimiles of signatures and monograms, lists of selected works with locations, and fairly extensive bibliographies. There is at least one illustration for each painter, and some are in very fine color. The best all-round dictionary of painting. Many of the entries are by the greatest authority on the painter concerned.

214   Myers, Bernard S., ed. **Encyclopedia of Painting.** New York, Crown, 1955. 511p. illus.
This general dictionary of painting includes biographies of major painters, definitions of terms, and descriptions of styles, techniques, and movements in painting. Good illustrations. Reliable popular dictionary of painting.

III. DICTIONARIES OF TERMINOLOGY

215   Adeline, Jules. **Adeline's Art Dictionary.** New York, Appleton, 1927; repr. Ann Arbor, Mich., Edwards, 1953. 422p.
General fine arts dictionary with short definitions of terms, techniques, materials, subjects, and objects. Illustrated with line drawings. Although old, it is still useful for definitions of many terms, especially those encountered in antiquarian literature.

216   **Glossarium Artis. Deutsch-Französisches Wörterbuch zur Kunst.** fasc. 1– . Tübingen and Strasbourg, Niemeyer, 1972– . illus.
German-French dictionary of art terms arranged in fascicles by types of art works. To date, the following fascicles have appeared:
   1.   *Der Wehrbau. L'Architecture militaire.* 152p.
   2.   *Liturgische Geräte, Kreuze und Reliquiare der christlichen Kirchen. Objets liturgiques, croix et reliquaires des églises chrétiennes.* 159p.
   3.   *Bogen und Arkaden. Arcs et arcades.* 167p.
   4.   *Paramente und liturgische Bücher der christlichen Kirchen. Parements et livres liturgiques des églises chrétiennes.* 203p.
Each term is illustrated by a line drawing and briefly defined. Arranged under the German name with the French equivalent at the end of each entry. Synonyms and homonyms given as well. Each fascicle contains a comprehensive bibliography of the subject. General indexes are planned. The most scholarly and comprehensive dictionary of art terms. When complete, it will be the standard work in the field.

217   Haggar, Reginald G. **Dictionary of Art Terms.** New York, Hawthorn Books, 1962. 415p. illus.

General dictionary of art terms. Illustrated with line drawings. General bibliography (pp. 411-15). Chiefly useful for succinct definitions of art techniques, styles, and subjects.

218   Masciotta, Michelangelo. **Dizionario di termini artistici.** Florence, Le
       Monnier, 1967. 269p.
General Italian dictionary of art terms consisting of brief definitions. No bibliography. Useful tool for students who are reading extensively in Italian art historical literature.

219   Mayer, Ralph. **A Dictionary of Art Terms and Techniques.** New York,
       Crowell, 1969. 447p. illus. index. LC 69-15414.
General fine arts dictionary of terms and techniques, intended chiefly for the practicing artist and general reader. Particularly useful for definitions of materials and techniques.

220   O'Dwyer, John, and Raymond Le Mage. **A Glossary of Art Terms.**
       London and New York, Nevill, 1950. 148p.
Popular dictionary of terms, techniques, styles, and schools of Western art. Includes some foreign terms with English translations. For the general reader.

221   Réau, Louis. **Dictionnaire polyglotte des termes d'art et d'archéologie.**
       Paris, Presses Universitaires de France, 1953; repr. Osnabruck, Ohms,
       1974. 247p.
Polyglot dictionary of fine arts terms, consisting of one alphabetical listing under the French name of the term. Equivalents are given in Greek, Latin, Italian, Spanish, Portuguese, Romanian, English, German, Dutch, Swedish, Czech, Polish, and Russian. Greek and Russian names are transliterated into Latin alphabet.

222   Walker, John A. **Glossary of Art, Architecture and Design since 1945.**
       London, Linnet Books, 1973. 240p. index. LC 73-3339.
Dictionary of terms relating to the fine arts since 1945. Brief entries give definition and source when known. General bibliography (pp. 213-15). Useful for brief definitions of the most avant-garde art terms.

IV. GENERAL BIOGRAPHICAL DICTIONARIES

GENERAL WORKS

223   Aeschlimann, Erardo, and Paola d'Ancona. **Dictionnaire des miniaturistes
       du moyen âge et de la Renaissance dans les différentes contrées de
       l'Europe.** 2nd ed. rev. and enl. Milan, Hoepli, 1949. 239p. illus.

Dictionary of miniature painters of the Middle Ages and the Renaissance in Europe. Bibliographical references. Index by periods, subdivided by country.

224   Bénézit, Emmanuel. **Dictionnaire critique et documentaire des peintres, sculpteurs, dessinateurs et graveurs** . . . Paris, Gründ, 1948-1955; repr. Paris, 1957. 8v. illus. index.

Dictionary of painters, sculptors, and graphic artists of all times and nations. Entries vary from a few lines to several paragraphs. In addition to the basic biographical data, longer entries list prizes won by the artist and museums where his works can be found. Facsimiles of signatures are given and monograms are listed at the end of each letter of the alphabet. Author index and general bibliography in Volume 8. Directed to the general reader and collector rather than the scholar.

225   Bryan, Michael. **Bryan's Dictionary of Painters and Engravers.** New ed. rev. and enl. London, Bell, 1926-1934; repr. New York, Kennikat Press, 1964. 5v. illus. LC 64-15534.

First published in 1816 and added to in several successive editions. General biographical dictionary of painters and graphic artists. Entries vary in length; longer ones are signed and give lists of the artists' works. A standard work for the general reader and collector.

226   Darmond, J. E. **Dictionnaire des peintres miniaturistes sur vélin, parchemin, ivoire et écaille** . . . Paris, Morancé, 1927. 123p.

General biographical dictionary of European miniature painters. Brief biographical entries, occasionally with list of works. Chiefly of interest to the collector.

227   Darmstaedter, Robert. **Künstlerlexikon: Maler, Bildhauer, Architekten.** Bern and Munich, Francke, 1961. 527p.

General dictionary of artists' biographies covering all periods and peoples. Each entry gives basic biography, characterization of the artist's style, list of his major works, and a separate bibliography. The most comprehensive and reliable one-volume dictionary of artists. The bibliographies are especially useful.

228   Errera, Isabelle. **Dictionnaire répertoire des peintres depuis l'antiquité jusqu'à nos jours.** Paris, Hachette, 1913. 716p. Supplément. Paris, Hachette, 1924. 245p.

Dictionary of painters, both Eastern and Western, from antiquity to 1882. The artists' names and biographical information are given in tabular form. Reference is made to a select list of sources. Useful for quick reference for basic biographical data.

229   Foster, Joshua J. **A Dictionary of Painters of Miniatures (1525-1850) with Some Account of Exhibitions** . . . London, Allan, 1926. 330p.

Biographical dictionary of painters of portrait miniatures.

230   Kaltenbach, Gustave Emile. **Dictionary of Pronunciation of Artists' Names.** 2nd ed. Chicago, The Art Institute of Chicago, 1938. 74p.

Alphabetical list of 1,500 artists' names with their birth and death dates, nationality, and pronunciation of their names. A useful and reliable guide.

231   Lodovici, Sergio. **Storici, teorici e critici delle arti figurative (1800-1940)**. Rome, E.B.B.I., Istituto Editoriale Italiano, 1942. 412p. illus. (Enciclopedia Biografia e Bibliographica "Italiana," ser. IV).
Dictionary of art historians, theoreticians, and critics active between 1800 and 1940. Each biography gives a list of the writer's major works and a discussion of his theories; a portrait of the writer is often included.

232   Thieme, Ulrich, and Felix Becker. **Allgemeines Lexikon der bildenden Künstler von der Antike bis zur Gegenwart** . . . Leipzig, Seemann, 1907-1950. 37v.
The most comprehensive biographical dictionary of artists from antiquiry to the present. Entries are signed and vary in length depending on the artist. All have separate bibliographies. Larger entries have thorough discussions of the stylistic development of the artist and lists of works with locations. Volume 37, entitled *Meister mit Notnamen und Monogrammisten*, contains biographies of anonymous artists known by substitute names or monograms. Artists active chiefly in the twentieth century are not included; equivalent biographies of these are found in Vollmer (265). A reference work of outstanding scope and scholarship. The standard biographical source for the fine arts.

DICTIONARIES OF MARKS AND SIGNATURES

233   Goldstein, Franz. **Monogrammlexikon: Internationales Verzeichnis der Monogramme bildender Künstler seit 1850**. Berlin, de Gruyter, 1964. 931p.
Dictionary of the monograms of artists active since 1850, arranged alphabetically by the initial letters. Entries give the dates of the artist, media he worked in, and bibliographical reference to either Thieme-Becker, Vollmer, Bénézit, or *Dresslers Kunsthandbuch.* The standard reference tool for the monograms of modern artists. Complements Nagler (235).

234   Lampe, Louis. **Signature et monogrammes des peintres de toutes les écoles; guide monogrammiste** . . . Brussels, Castaign, 1895-98. 3v.
Dictionary of signatures and monograms of Western painters of all periods and schools. Arranged by the subject depicted and then alphabetically by artists. Short biographical entries with facsimiles of signatures and monograms. Still a useful dictionary.

235   Nagler, Georg Kaspar. **Die Monogrammisten und diejenigen bekannten und unbekannten Künstler aller Schulen** . . . Munich, Franz, 1858-79. 5v. illus. index. **General-Index zu G. K. Nagler die Monogrammisten** . . . Munich, Hirth, 1920. 109p.(Reprint: Nieuwkoop, De Graaf, 1966. 6v. illus. index.)

Comprehensive dictionary of the monograms of artists in all media and from all periods. In addition, it includes printers' and collectors' marks and marks on metalwork and ceramics. Arranged by the chief initials in the monogram. Facsimiles of the marks are given, with a short biography of the artist and a discussion of where the mark is found. Each volume has a supplement (Nachtrag) and index at the end. Volume six contains a general index and bibliography. The standard work on monograms. For the monograms of modern artists—i.e., active since 1870—see Goldstein (233).

V. SPECIALIZED DICTIONARIES AND ENCYCLOPEDIAS

PREHISTORIC

236   Ebert, Max, ed. **Reallexikon der Vorgeschichte**. Berlin, de Gruyter, 1924-32. 15v. in 16. illus. index.
Comprehensive and scholarly encyclopedia of signed articles covering all aspects of prehistoric archaeology. The long articles are accompanied by separate and extensive bibliographies and many excellent illustrations. The standard reference tool for prehistoric archaeology.

237   Filip, Jan, ed. **Enzyklopädisches Handbuch zur Ur- und Frühgeschichte Europas**. Stuttgart, Kohlhammer, 1966-69. 2v. illus. LC 67-101201.
Encyclopedia covering all aspects of European civilization during prehistoric and early historic times. Articles cover objects, sites, regions, and styles that are directly related to the study of prehistoric, Germanic, and Celtic art. Articles are occasionally illustrated with line drawings and plans; each major article is accompanied with an extensive bibliography of specialized literature. A standard reference tool for all serious study of early European art.

EUROPE

Periods of Western Art History

Ancient

238   Avery, Catherine B., ed. **The New Century Handbook of Greek Art and Architecture**. New York, Appleton-Century-Crofts, 1972. 213p. illus. LC 72-187738.
Dictionary of ancient Greek art and architecture covering artists, objects, monuments, places, styles, and schools. The entries are derived from the *New Century*

Classical Dictionary and in some instances have been expanded to reflect more recent archaeological findings. For the general reader and beginning student.

239   Bandinelli, Ranuccio, ed. **Enciclopedia dell'arte antica; classica e orientale.** Rome, Istit. della Enciclopedia Italiana, 1958-1973. 8v. illus. index.
Comprehensive encyclopedia of ancient art covering the period from prehistory to 500 A.D. Long signed articles by specialists with separate bibliographies and good illustrations. Treats classical antiquity including the ancient civilizations of the Near East, Egypt, and the prehistoric cultures of Northern Europe. Volume 8 contains an atlas. Excellent reference tool for ancient art.

240   Daremberg, Charles V., and Edmond Saglio. **Dictionnaire des antiquités grecques et romaines d'après les textes et les monuments.** Paris, Hachette, 1873-1919. 5v. illus. index. Reprint: Graz, Akademische Druck und Verlagsanstalt, 1962-63. 5v. in 10. LC 64-44287.
Scholarly encyclopedia covering all aspects of classical culture including the visual arts. Long signed articles by recognized specialists with separate bibliographical references. Does not include biography. One of the standard reference tools for classical studies. For greater depth and for classical biography and literature see Pauly-Wissowa (247).

241   **Dictionary of Ancient Greek Civilization.** London, Methuen, 1967. 491p. illus.
General dictionary covering all aspects of ancient Greek civilization, with articles on artists, art centers, major buildings, and subjects.

242   Ebeling, Erich, and Bruno Meissner, eds. **Reallexikon der Assyriologie.** v. 1– ("A" through "Hazazu"). Berlin, de Gruyter, 1928– . illus.
Comprehensive encyclopedia covering all aspects of the ancient civilizations of the ancient Near East. Long signed articles illustrated with line drawings and plans, plus extensive bibliographies. Most of the entries are in German, but some are in French and English. A standard reference work for the advanced student and scholar of ancient Near Eastern art and architecture.

243   Hammond, N. G. L., and H. H. Scullard, eds. **The Oxford Classical Dictionary.** 2nd ed. Oxford, Clarendon, 1970. 1176p.
Comprehensive dictionary of all aspects of classical Greek and Roman civilizations. Entries are signed and supply separate bibliographies. Useful for students of ancient art for quick reference on places, major artists, religious and mythological subjects, and literary subjects. The standard classical dictionary in English.

244   Helck, Wolfgang, and Eberhard Otto, eds. **Lexikon der Ägyptologie.** Bd. I– . Wiesbaden, Harrassowitz, 1972– .
The first volume of a comprehensive encyclopedia covering all aspects of ancient Egyptian civilization. Six volumes are planned. Entries are signed and provide excellent bibliographies. Should become a standard reference work for advanced students and scholars of ancient Egyptian art and architecture.

245   Lamer, Hans. **Wörterbuch der Antike mit Berücksichtigung ihres Fortwirkens.** 6th completely reworked ed. Stuttgart, Kröner, 1963. 639p.
General dictionary of Greek and Roman civilization covering terms, persons, places, objects, and subjects. Major entries have separate bibliographies. One of the best pocket-sized classical dictionaries; particularly useful for its attention to the continuation of classical traditions in later periods.

246   **Lexikon der alten Welt.** Zürich and Stuttgart, Artemis, 1965. 3524 columns. LC 67-105898.
Comprehensive dictionary covering all aspects of ancient civilization. Long signed articles cover places, persons, objects, and subjects; there are excellent separate bibliographies. An excellent classical dictionary.

247   Pauly, August Friedrich von. **Pauly's Real-Encyclopädie der classischen Altertumswissenschaft; neue Bearbeitung begonnen von Georg Wissowa, unter Mitwirkung zahlreicher Fachgenossen Herausgegeben von Wilhelm Kroll und Karl Mittelhaus.** Stuttgart, Metzler, 1894-1968. 44v.
Appeared in two series and eleven volumes of supplements. Additional supplements are planned. Scholarly encyclopedia covering all aspects of classical civilizations. Long signed articles, with separate bibliographies, cover biography, antiquities, literature, mythology, religion, sites, and historical events. The standard classical encyclopedia. A basic reference tool for advanced students of classical art.

248   **Praeger Encyclopedia of Ancient Greek Civilization.** New York, Praeger, 1967. 491p. illus. LC 67-25162.
General dictionary with brief signed articles covering all aspects of ancient Greek civilization, including art and architecture. A useful reference work for the general reader and the beginning student.

Medieval and Byzantine

249   Aressy, Pierre. **Abrégé de l'art roman, suivi d'un lexique des termes employés en art roman.** Montpellier, Causse et Castelnau, 1967. 143p. illus. LC 68-76605.
Part II (pp. 85-121) is a dictionary of terms used in the history of Romanesque art. Part I gives a short but useful history of Romanesque art in France. Useful handbook for the student of medieval art.

250   Cabrol, Fernand. **Dictionnaire d'archéologie chrétienne et de liturgie . . .** Paris, Letouzey et Ané, 1907-53. 15v. illus.
Volumes 3-14 "publié par le Rme. dom Fernand Cabrol . . . et le R. P. dom Henri Leclercq." Illustrated with line drawings. Scholarly encyclopedia covering all aspects of Christian culture of the period from the early Christians through the Carolingians. The long signed articles have separate bibliographies and are of particular importance to students of Christian art seeking information on sites, archaeological

and liturgical artifacts, and iconographical subjects. In the latter category the work's usefulness extends far beyond its period of specialty.

251   Gay, Victor, and Henri Stein. **Glossaire archéologique du moyen-âge et de la Renaissance.** Paris, Société Bibliographique, 1887-1928; repr. Nendeln, Kraus, 1967. 2v. illus.

Dictionary of terms encountered in the study of medieval and Renaissance art. Major entries give quotations from literary or documentary sources. Illustrated with line drawings.

252   Klauser, Theodor. **Reallexikon für Antike und Christentum; Sachwörterbuch zur Auseinandersetzung des Christentums mit der Antiken Welt . . .** Bd. I– . Stuttgart, Hiersemann, 1950– . illus.

Scholarly encyclopedia covering all aspects of the culture of the late Roman and early Christian period. It is designed to investigate the interrelationship between Christianity and late antiquity. Consists of long signed articles with separate and exhaustive bibliographies on a broad variety of subjects, many of which are of direct interest to art historians of the period. Particularly valuable for information on iconography, architecture, sites, and personalities of the early Christian period. Each volume has a table of contents in German, English, French, and Italian.

253   Laag, D. Heinrich. **Wörterbuch der altchristlichen Kunst.** Kassel, Stauda, 1959. 166p. illus.

General dictionary of terms, persons, subjects, and places encountered in the study of early Christian art and architecture. Illustrated with line drawings. A very useful, pocket-sized dictionary for the student of early Christian art.

254   Vogüe, Melchior de, Jean Neufville, and Wenceslas Bugara. **Glossaire de terms techniques à l'usage des lecteurs de "La Nuit des Temps."** Paris, Zodiaque, 1965. 473p. illus. index.

Dictionary of art and architectural terms used in the study of Romanesque and Gothic art. Very thorough dictionary is accompanied by numerous plates, plans, and diagrams, many with the terms included. An excellent dictionary of French terms for the advanced student of medieval art and architecture.

255   Wessel, Klaus, ed. **Reallexikon zur byzantinischen Kunst.** v. 1– . Stuttgart, Hiersemann, 1966– . illus. LC 76-446105.

Comprehensive and scholarly encyclopedia of all aspects of Byzantine art and architecture. Recognized specialists prepared the lengthy articles, which are well illustrated with plans and drawings and which have extensive separate bibliographies. Standard reference tool for the study of Byzantine art.

Renaissance

256   Avery, Catherine B., ed. **The New Century Italian Renaissance Encyclopedia.** New York, Appleton-Century-Crofts, 1972. 978p. illus. LC 76-81735.

Comprehensive dictionary of all aspects of the Italian Renaissance including articles on artists and writers, résumés of literary works, subjects, and some terms dealing with the fine arts. The entries are brief, without bibliographies. Useful reference work for the general reader and the beginning student.

Modern (19th and 20th Centuries)

257   Berckelaers, Ferdinand L. **A Dictionary of Abstract Painting, with a History of Abstract Painting by Michel Seuphor.** New York, Tudor, 1957. 305p. illus.

Dictionary (pp. 117-294) of brief biographies of some 500 abstract artists. Features a chronological table of abstract art and a general bibliography.

258   Charmet, Raymond. **Dictionnaire de l'art contemporain.** Paris, Larousse, 1965. 320p. illus.

This pocket-sized dictionary of twentieth century art and architecture provides brief biographies of artists and architects, with entries on schools, styles, terms, and places relative to modern art. No bibliography.

259   Du Peloux de Saint Romain, Charles. **Répertoire biographique et bibliographique des artistes du XVIIIe siècle français** . . . Paris, Champion, 1930-41. 2v.

Biographical dictionary and bibliography on French artists of the eighteenth century. Volume 1 contains the dictionary; Volume 2, the bibliography of about 4,000 titles of books and periodical articles published in the decade between 1930 and 1940.

260   Edouard-Joseph, René. **Dictionnaire biographique des artistes contemporains, 1910-1930** . . . Paris, Art et Edition, 1930-34. 3v. illus. index. Supplément. Paris, 1936. 162p. illus.

Dictionary of artists active in France from 1910 to 1930. In addition to basic biographical data, it also lists when and where the artist exhibited and the awards won by each artist. List of important works given for major artists. Index of monograms at end of Vol. 3.

261   Hatje, Gerd, ed. **Encyclopedia of Modern Architecture.** London, Thames and Hudson, 1963. 336p. illus.

Translation of *Knaurs Lexikon der moderne Architektur.* Signed articles, many with separate bibliographies, on major architects, schools, styles, countries, terms, techniques, and materials relative to Western architecture since the mid-nineteenth century. Excellent reference tool for the general reader and the beginning student.

262   Lake, Carlton, and Robert Maillard, eds. **Dictionary of Modern Painting.** 3rd ed. rev. and enl. New York, Tudor, 1964. 416p. illus.

General dictionary of painting since Impressionism; covers artists' biographies, movements, styles, and schools.

263   Maillard, Robert, ed. **New Dictionary of Modern Sculpture.** New York,
       Tudor, 1971. 328p. illus. LC 70-153118.
Biographical dictionary of modern sculptors. Signed entries with illustrations, no
bibliographies. Index of photographers.

264   **Phaidon Dictionary of Twentieth-Century Art.** London and New York,
       Phaidon, 1973. 420p. illus. LC 72-86572.
General dictionary of twentieth century art, including artists' biographies, artists'
groups, schools, styles, and a few terms. There are short bibliographies for most
entries. Particularly useful for quick reference to modern art styles and movements.

265   Vollmer, Hans. **Allgemeines Lexikon der bildenden Künstler des
       XX. Jahrhunderts.** Leipzig, Seemann, 1953-62. 6v.
Biographical dictionary of twentieth century artists in all media. Conceived as a
supplement to Thieme-Becker (232), it emphasizes artists born after 1870. In the
case of those artists that are also treated in Thieme-Becker, Vollmer gives additional
information. Volumes 5 and 6 are supplement volumes; additional supplement
volumes are planned. The entries vary in length, are signed, and have separate
bibliographies. The standard biographical dictionary for twentieth century artists.

European National Dictionaries and Encyclopedias

Austria

266   Fuchs, Heinrich. **Die Österreichischen Maler des 19. Jahrhunderts.** v. 1– .
       Vienna, Fuchs, 1972– . illus.
Biographical dictionary of Austrian painters of the nineteenth century, giving basic
biographical data and facsimiles of signatures. Large but rather poor illustrations
of each painter's work. No bibliography. Useful for lesser known artists, particularly
those of the Biedermeier or Romantic schools.

Denmark

267   Gelsted, Otto. **Kunstner Leksikon, med 1100 biografier af Danske Billed-
       huggere, Malere, Grafikere og Dekorative Kunstnere fra 1900-1942.**
       Copenhagen, Jensen, 1942. 197p.
Short-entry biographical dictionary of Danish artists active between 1900 and
1942.

268   Weilbach, Philip. **Kunstnerleksikon; udgivet af en Komite med Støtte af
       Carlsbergfondet, Redaktion: Meret Bodelsen og Povl Engelstoft.**
       Copenhagen, Aschehoug, 1947-1952. 3v. illus. index.
Biographical dictionary of signed entries for Danish artists and foreign artists active
in Denmark. Good bibliographies at the end of each entry. Supplement at end of
Volume 3. Indexes. Standard reference tool for Danish artists.

France

269 **Dictionnaire des artistes et ouvriers d'art de la France.** Paris, Bibliothèque d'Art et d'Archéologie, 1912-1919. 3v. illus. index.
Unfinished series of biographical dictionaries intended to cover all the provinces of France. Each volume has an introduction outlining the art history of the region, a biographical dictionary of artists of the region who died before 1900, and a bibliography. Contents: *Franche-Comté*, par l'Abbé Paul Brunne (1912); *Lyonnais*, par M. Audin et E. Vial (1918-1919; 2v.).

270 Lami, Stanislas. **Dictionnaire des sculpteurs de l'école française.** Paris, Champion, 1898-1921. 8v.
Biographical dictionary of French sculptors arranged alphabetically within period groups: *Du Moyen-âge au règne de Louis XIV* (1898; 581p.); *Sous le règne de Louis XIV* (1906; 504p.); *Au 18e siècle* (1910-11; 2v.); *Au 19e siècle* (1914-21; 4v.). Each entry has a list of works and a separate bibliography. Basic reference tool for French sculptors.

271 Portal, Charles. **Dictionnaire des artistes et ouvriers d'art du Tarn du XIIIe au XXe siècle.** Albi, Chez l'Auteur, 1925. 332p. illus. index.
Biographical dictionary of artists of the Tarn region covering the period from the thirteenth to the twentieth centuries. Introduction gives the sources for the work.

Germany

272 Neumann, Wilhelm. **Lexikon baltischer Künstler.** Riga, Jonck & Poliewsky, 1908; repr. Hannover-Döhren, von Hirschheydt, 1972. 171p. LC 72-366260.
Biographical dictionary (in German) of Baltic artists of all media and times. Covers artists born and/or active in the former German province of East Prussia and in Estonia, Latvia, and Lithuania. Major entries have separate bibliographical references. Standard biographical dictionary of Baltic area artists.

273 Schmitt, Otto, ed. **Reallexikon zur deutschen Kunstgeschichte.** Bd. 1– . Stuttgart, Metzler, 1937– . illus.
Comprehensive and scholarly encyclopedia of German art history. Long signed articles by leading specialists are accompanied by many illustrations and extensive bibliographies. Covers all aspects except biography. Many subjects not covered in other reference tools are treated with impressive scholarly thoroughness. This is especially true in the areas of iconography, materials, structures, and objects. Although the work is progressing slowly (at present only the beginning of the letter "F" has been reached) and is technically limited to German art, the *Reallexikon* is of almost universal value. Information and bibliography on subjects that cut across periods (such as apse, altarpiece and brick architecture) can be quickly and confidently obtained from this work. One of the finest reference tools in the field of art history.

274   Zülch, Walther K. **Frankfurter Künstler, 1223-1700.** Frankfurt am Main, Diesterweg, 1935. 670p. index.
Biographical handbook of artists active in Frankfurt am Main from 1223 to 1700. Arranged chronologically, entries give archival sources as well as thorough reference to recent literature. List of artists by media (pp. 601-629); alphabetical list of artists (pp. 629-54). An excellent regional biographical dictionary.

Great Britain

275   Colvin, Howard M. **A Biographical Dictionary of English Architects, 1660-1840.** London, Murrary, 1954. 821p.
Biographical dictionary of more than 1,000 architects. Entries give list of buildings and bibliographical references. Index of persons and places. Although not as detailed, it complements Harvey (280), with a gap of one hundred years.

276   Foskett, Daphne. **A Dictionary of British Miniature Painters.** New York, Praeger, 1972. 2v. illus. LC 72-112634.
Biographical dictionary of painters of miniature portraits born in or active in Great Britain and Ireland between 1520 and 1910. Entries give basic biographical data, media worked in, museums where the artist's work is to be found and a description of the artist's signature or initials. Selected bibliography (pp. 595-96). Volume two contains an excellent collection of plates. Standard work on British portrait miniaturists.

277   Grant, Maurice H. **A Dictionary of British Sculptors from the XIIIth Century to the XXth Century.** London, Rockliff, 1953. 317p.
Short-entry dictionary of British sculptors. No sources or bibliography.

278   Gunnis, Rupert. **Dictionary of British Sculptors, 1660-1851.** London, Oldhams, 1953. 514p. illus. index.
Dictionary of short biographies. No bibliographies. Index of places and names.

279   Hall, Henry C. **Artists and Sculptors of Nottingham and Nottinghamshire, 1750-1950.** Nottingham, H. Jones, 1953. 95p.
Biographical dictionary of artists in Nottingham and surrounding region, arranged in three parts: Artists of the past (pp. 11-67); Contemporary artists (pp. 71-85); Sculptors (pp. 89-95). Brief biographical notes, bibliography.

280   Harvey, John H. **English Medieval Architects: A Biographical Dictionary down to 1550.** London, Batsford, 1954. 411p.
Biographical dictionary of some 1,300 architects, master masons, carpenters, carvers, etc. A detailed work that includes references to sources.

281   Strickland, Walter G. **A Dictionary of Irish Artists** . . . Dublin, Maunsel, 1913. 2v. illus. index.

Biographical dictionary of artists who were of Irish birth or who worked in Ireland. No bibliography. Old but still useful for lesser-known artists.

282   Ware, Dora. **A Short Dictionary of British Architects.** London, Allen and Unwin, 1967. 312p. illus. index.

Biographical dictionary of British architects from the Middle Ages to the present. Entries are brief, giving basic biographical data and lists of works and writings. No bibliography.

Italy

283   Bessone-Aurelj, Antonietta M. **Dizionario degli scultori e architetti italiani.** Genoa, Dante Alighieri, 1947. 523p.

General biographical dictionary of Italian sculptors and architects. Complements the author's dictionary of Italian painters. Very short entries. No bibliographies.

284   Colnaghi, Dominic E. **A Dictionary of Florentine Painters from the Eleventh to the Seventeenth Centuries.** London, Lane, 1928. 286p.

Specialized biographical dictionary of Florentine painters of special importance for the references to and occasional quotes from documentary sources. Useful tool for the specialist.

285   Comanducci, Agostino Mario. **Dizionario illustrato dei pittori, disegnatori e incisori italiani moderni e contemporanei.** 3rd ed. Milan, Patuzzi, 1962. 4v. illus. LC 63-37089.

Comprehensive biographical dictionary of nineteenth and twentieth century Italian painters, draftsmen, and graphic artists. Entries vary in length and give separate bibliographies and illustrations for the major artists. Standard reference tool for modern Italian painters.

286   **Dizionario enciclopedico Bolaffi dei pittori e degli incisori italiani . . .** v. 1— . Turin, Bolaffi, 1972— .

Comprehensive dictionary of Italian painters and graphic artists covering the period from the eleventh through the twentieth centuries. Well illustrated. Each entry provides a good bibliography listing books and periodical articles in all languages. Portends to be a standard biographical dictionary of Italian painters and graphic artists.

287   Galetti, Ugo, and E. Camesasca. **Enciclopedia della pittura italiana.** Milan, Garzanti, 1950. 2v. illus.

General biographical dictionary of Italian painters. Entries vary in length; the longer entries give lists of works, facsimiles of signatures, and separate bibliographies. Also covers foreign painters who were active in Italy or who influenced Italian painters.

Low Countries

288   Bernt, Walter. **The Netherlandish Painters of the Seventeenth Century.**
New York and London, Phaidon, 1970. 3v. illus. LC 76-105963.
Biographical dictionary of major Dutch and Flemish painters of the seventeenth
century. The thorough biographies are accompanied with facsimiles of signatures
and separate bibliographies. Excellent illustrations.

289   Scheen, Pieter A. **Lexicon nederlandse beeldende Kunstenaars, 1750-
1950.** s'Gravenhage, Scheen, 1969-70. 2v. illus.
Biographical dictionary of Dutch painters active between 1750 and 1950. Expansion of the same author's *Honderd Jaren Nederlandsche Shilder- en Teekenkunst
1750-1850* (The Hague, 1946). Separate bibliographies after each entry; general
bibliography at end of Volume 2. Supplement in Volume 2. Illustrations arranged
by subject.

290   Wurzbach, Alfred. **Niederländisches Künstler Lexikon** . . . Vienna, Halm,
1906-1911. 3v.
Biographical dictionary of Dutch and Flemish artists. Biographies give facsimiles
of signatures, lists of major works, and separate bibliographies. Volume 3 is
devoted to anonymous artists and monogrammists. Standard reference tool for
artists from the Netherlands.

Portugal

291   Pamplona, Fernando de. **Dicionário de pintores e escultores Portugueses
ou que trabalharam em Portugal.** Lisbon, Santo Silva, 1954-59. 4v. illus.
LC 55-28095 rev.
Biographical dictionary of Portuguese painters and sculptors. Entries include
facsimiles of signatures and separate bibliographies for major artists. Basic reference
tool for Portuguese artists.

Sweden

292   **Svensk Konstnärs Lexikon.** Malmö, Allhems, 1952-1967. 5v. illus.
Comprehensive biographical dictionary of Swedish artists. Larger entries are
signed and have separate bibliographies. Standard reference guide to Swedish
artists.

Switzerland

293   Brun, Carl. **Schweizerisches Künstler Lexikon; Dictionnaire des artistes
suisses.** Frauenfeld, Huber, 1905-1917. 4v.

Biographical dictionary of Swiss artists of all periods and all media as well as foreign artists active in Switzerland. Articles are signed, and longer entries have separate bibliographies. Volume 4 contains a supplement. A standard reference work on Swiss artists. For the twentieth century see Plüss (294).

294   Plüss, Eduard, and Hans C. von Tavel. **Künstler Lexikon der Schweiz XX. Jahrhundert.** Frauenfeld, Huber, 1958-67. 2v.
Comprehensive and scholarly dictionary of Swiss artists of the twentieth century. Thorough biographies include lists of exhibitions and works in museums, and very good separate bibliographies. Standard reference tool for modern Swiss artists.

ORIENT

295   **Encyclopaedia of Islam**, v. 1— . New ed. Leiden, Brill, 1960— .
Comprehensive encyclopedia of long signed articles covering all aspects of Islamic civilization both past and present. Articles have thorough bibliographies of specialized literature. Entries cover places, persons, objects, and subjects. Of great value to the advanced student and scholar of Islamic art and architecture.

296   Hansford, Sidney Howard. **A Glossary of Chinese Art and Archaeology.** 2nd rev. ed. London, China Society, 1961. 104p. illus. (China Society Sinological Series No. 4).
A general dictionary of terms pertaining to most media; particularly useful for technical terms related to ceramics, lacquer, and other minor arts. Terms are given in Chinese characters, with transliteration and English translation.

297   **Index of Japanese Painters.** Comp. by the Society of Friends of Eastern Art. 2nd ed. Rutland, Vt., Tuttle, 1958. 160p.
Biographical dictionary of Japanese painters first published in Tokyo in 1940. Listed by romanized form of their names, with Japanese equivalent given. Contains basic biographical data and reference to three basic sources of illustrations (all in Japanese).

298   March, Benjamin. **Some Technical Terms of Chinese Painting.** New York, Paragon, 1969. 55p. illus. (American Council of Learned Societies. Studies in Chinese and Related Civilizations, No. 2). LC 76-88188.
Dictionary of Chinese terms concerning painting. The terms, arranged by media categories, are given first in Chinese characters, then transliterated and defined. The illustrations demonstrate the techniques defined.

299   Mayer, Leo Ary. **Islamic Architects and Their Works.** Geneva, Kundig, 1956. 183p. index.
Dictionary of Islamic architects active in the Muslim world from Morocco to Baluchistan. Covers only those architects whose works still exist or whose works

were adequately described before destruction. The biographies are brief but include detailed bibliographies.Topographical index and general bibliography (pp. 137-83).

NEW WORLD

Latin America

300   **Enciclopedia de arte en América.** Buenos Aires, Bibliographica OMEBA, 1969. 5v. illus. LC 72-236036.
General encyclopedia of Latin American art and architecture, edited by Vicente Gesauldo. Volumes 1 and 2 provide a general history of Latin American art and architecture. Volumes 3 to 5 comprise a biographical dictionary of Latin American artists. Brief bibliographies given at the end of the major entries. A standard but popular encyclopedia of Latin American art and architecture.

301   Merlino, Adrián. **Diccionario de artistas plasticos de la Argentina, siglos XVIII-XIX-XX.** Buenos Aires, 1954. 433p. illus.
Biographical dictionary of artists in Argentina covering the period from the beginning of the eighteenth to the middle of the twentieth centuries. Each entry gives basic biographical data, list of prizes and exhibitions, and a list of museums owning the artist's work. Provides a general bibliography (pp. 408-414).

302   Pontual, Roberto. **Dicionário das artes plasticas no Brasil.** Rio de Janeiro, Civilização Brasileira, 1969. 559p. illus. LC 76-464169.
General biographical dictionary of Brazilian artists. Most entries are short and have abbreviated bibliographies. Illustrations are given for the most important artists. Basic reference tool for Brazilian art.

303   Vargas, Ugarte R. **Ensayo de un diccionario de artifices coloniales de la America meridional.** Lima, Baiocco, 1947. 391p. index. **Apendice.** Lima, Baiocco, 1955. 118p.
Biographical dictionary of Latin American artists arranged by centuries. No bibliography.

United States and Canada

304   **Britannica Encyclopedia of American Art.** Chicago, Encyclopaedia Britannica Educational Corp., 1973; distr. New York, Simon and Schuster. 669p. illus. LC 73-6527.
Dictionary covering architecture and all the arts in America from pre-Colonial times to the present. Respected specialists prepared the articles, which are signed. Numerous color and black and white illustrations. A list of entries according to the various arts (pp. 622-27), is an effective index by media. Contains a guide to major American museums and collections, a four-page glossary of terms, and a two-part

bibliography (pp. 638-68): Part I, a good general classified bibliography of American arts; and Part II, a bibliography according to entries in the main body of the work. A sound reference tool in the field of American art.

305   Cederholm, Theresa D., ed. **Afro-American Artists: A Bio-Bibliographical Directory**. Boston, Boston Public Library, 1973. 348p. LC 73-84951.
Biographical dictionary of some 2,000 Afro-American artists. Gives basic biographical data, education, exhibition awards, and bibliographical references. A very useful tool for an otherwise neglected area of art biography.

306   **Creative Canada: A Biographical Dictionary of Twentieth-Century Creative and Performing Artists**, v. 1— . Toronto and Buffalo, University of Toronto Press, 1971— .
Biographical dictionary of performing and visual artists in Canada in the twentieth century. Does not include architects and designers. Each volume covers about 500 visual artists, chiefly painters and sculptors. Uneven coverage.

307   Cummings, Paul. **Dictionary of Contemporary American Artists**. 2nd ed. New York, St. Martin's, 1971. 368p. illus. LC 65-20815.
Biographical dictionary of short entries. In addition to basic biographical data, it tells where the artist taught, his one-man and group shows, and the collections owning works. Good general bibliography (pp. 315-31). The best reference tool for modern American artists.

308   Fielding, Mantle. **Dictionary of American Painters, Sculptors and Engravers** . . . New York, Carr, 1965. 433p. illus.
Reprint of 1926 edition with addendum containing corrections and additional material. Short biographies of approximately 8,000 American artists. Bibliography (pp. 424-33).

309   Groce, George C., and David H. Wallace. **The New York Historical Society's Dictionary of Artists in America, 1564-1860**. New Haven, Yale University Press, 1957. 759p.
Biographical dictionary of approximately 10,000 artists (professional and amateur, native or foreign-born) active in the present continental limits of the United States between 1564 and 1860. Key to sources (pp. 713-59). Standard reference guide to early American artists.

310   Harper, J. Russell. **Early Painters and Engravers in Canada**. Toronto and Buffalo, University of Toronto Press, 1971. 376p.
Biographical dictionary of Canadian painters and graphic artists born before 1967. Entries give basic biographical data plus list of public exhibitions, museums where the artist's work can be found, and reference to a brief list of books for further information.

311   Mallett, Daniel T. **Mallett's Index of Artists: International and Biographi-cal** . . . New York, Bowker, 1935. 493p. Supplement. 1940. 319p. (Reprint: New York, Smith, 1948, 2v.).
Index to biographical information on painters, sculptors, and graphic artists in 24 standard reference books and 957 additional sources. Entries give nationality, birth and death dates, medium, residence (if artist was then living), and reference to sources for further information. Supplement concentrates on contemporary artists. Useful index for the general reader seeking further information on major artists and lesser-known American artists of the first half of the present century. Inaccuracies severely limit its value as a source for biographical data.

312   Smith, Ralph C. **A Biographical Index of American Artists** . . . Baltimore, Williams & Wilkins, 1930. 102p.
Alphabetical index of about 4,700 American artists giving basic biographical data and reference to a collection (listed on p. ix) of basic reference works. Useful for lesser-known American artists.

313   Withey, Henry F., and Elsie Rathburn Withey. **Biographical Dictionary of American Architects.** Los Angeles, New Age, 1956. 678p.
2,000 brief biographies of deceased American architects. Entries give bibliographi-cal references and list of major works. Should be used together with the *Avery Obituary Index of Architects* (160).

AFRICA

314   **Dictionnaire des civilisations africaines.** Paris, Hazan, 1968. 448p. illus.
General dictionary covering all aspects of sub-Saharan African civilization, including useful articles on places, media, objects, and subjects of importance to the study of African art. Thoroughly illustrated with plates of African art. No bibliography.

AUSTRALIA

315   McCulloch, Alan. **Encyclopedia of Australian Art.** New York, Praeger, 1969. 668p. illus. LC 69-17079.
One-volume encyclopedia of Australian art from 1770 to the present. Covers all aspects including biography. The majority of entries give separate bibliographies.

CHAPTER SIX

ICONOGRAPHY

I. INTRODUCTION

Questions concerning the subject matter depicted in the fine arts pose special problems for the student and the reference librarian. The general reader and beginning student are often looking for an accurate identification and succinct explanation of a theme or subject encountered in a painting or sculpture. The advanced student, particularly in medieval and ancient art, frequently also needs information about the literary sources for the subject and its significance and place in the historical development of iconography. Until fairly recently this need for iconographical information was poorly met by reference works, and in many areas it is still inadequately served. Christian iconography, the most complex and the most intensely studied field of iconography, has seen the appearance of two major reference tools in the last five years: G. Schiller's *Handbook of Christian Iconography* (341) and the *Reallexikon der christlichen Ikonographie*, produced under the editorship of the late Engelbert Kirschbaum (335). Both are products of German scholarship; the former is being translated into English, and the latter is not only well organized but also equipped with a polyglot index so that it is accessible to anyone with a modest knowledge of German. These two works should finally retire to the antiquarian shelves two old standards: Anna B. Jameson's *The History of Our Lord as Exemplified in Works of Art . . .*, 2nd ed. (London, Longmans, Green, 1865), and Adolphe N. Didron's *Christian Iconography . . .* (London, Bell, 1886; 2v.).

The field of classical iconography has been well served by comprehensive dictionaries and encyclopedias on classical civilization. Some recent works, like Hunger's dictionary (356), have condensed the subject into even more accessible form. Non-Western iconography—especially the subject matter of Chinese and Japanese art, which has become increasingly popular in recent years—is most inadequately served by reference tools. Here it is necessary to fall back on general dictionaries of Asiatic mythology, which are included in this section in order to avoid the shortcomings of the few dilettante specialized works that do exist. Mention should be made of the *Bibliographie zur Symbolkunde* (318), a work recently begun under the editorship of Manfred Lurker. An annual bibliography of books and periodical articles on all aspects of symbolism, including iconography, its annotations were written by major scholars from around the world, so it is a reference tool of great value to any serious study of iconography.

Included in this section are reference works—i.e., bibliographies, encyclopedias, dictionaries, and handbooks. Studies and histories of special subjects are not included.

II. BIBLIOGRAPHIES

316   **Iconoclass, an Iconographic Classification System,** devised by H. van de Waal, completed and edited by L. D. Couprie with R. H. Fuchs and E. Tholen. Amsterdam, North-Holland Publishing Co. for the Royal Netherlands Academy of Arts and Sciences, 1973– .

A system of classification of works of art by subject matter with accompanying bibliographies. Seventeen volumes are planned: seven volumes for the system, seven for the bibliographies, and three volumes of indexes. To date two classification volumes and two bibliography volumes have appeared. These cover subjects pertaining to nature and man. The bibliographies cover both books and periodical articles in all Western languages. The classification is of interest to slide librarians and others compiling lists of works of art by subject. The bibliographies will be very valuable to all advanced students and scholars interested in iconography.

317   Lurker, Manfred, ed. **Bibliographie zur Symbolik, Ikonographie und Mythologie.** Jahrg. 1– . Baden-Baden, Heitz, 1968– .

Classified and annotated bibliography of books and periodical articles on all aspects of symbolism, iconography, and mythology, including their manifestation in the visual arts. Each entry has a descriptive annotation in the language of the entry.

318   Lurker, Manfred. **Bibliographie zur Symbolkunde.** Baden-Baden, Heitz, 1964-1968. 3v. (Bibliotheca Bibliographica Aureliana, XII-XIV). index.

Classified and annotated retrospective bibliography of books and periodical articles on all aspects of symbolism, including the representation of symbols and subjects in the fine arts of all periods, nations, and cultures. Literature published since 1964 is indexed in the same author's annual bibliography on symbolism (317). Standard reference tool for all serious students and scholars of iconography. A work of amazing scope, containing more than 11,000 entries. Indexes by subject and author.

319   Pöschl, Viktor. **Bibliographie zur Antiken Bildersprache.** Heidelberg, C. Winter, 1964. 674p. (Heidelberger Akademie der Wissenschaften, Bibliothek der klassischen Altertumswissenschaften, N.F. 1. Reihe).

Classified bibliography of special studies of imagery in classical literature. Part I lists the studies by author; Part II is an index to the first part arranged according to imagery of themes. This will be of direct value to classicists and art historians who wish to find the literary sources for images that are common in classical art.

320   Warburg Institute. **A Bibliography of the Survival of the Classics.** London, Cassell, 1934-38. 2v.
Classified and descriptively annotated bibliography of books dealing with all aspects of the survival of the classics in European civilization after antiquity. Continues Richard Newald's bibliography, "Nachleben der Antike," in *Jahresbericht über die Fortschritte der klassischen Altertumswissenschaft*, 232 (1931) and 250 (1935). Valuable bibliography for the specialist.

III. GENERAL DICTIONARIES

321   Bernen, Satia, and Robert Bernen. **Myth and Religion in European Painting 1270-1700: The Stories as the Artists Knew Them.** New York, Braziller, 1973. 280p. illus. LC 72-96070.
Dictionary of short entries covering religious subject matter in European painting. A popular dictionary with very brief bibliography of sources and no reference to special iconographic literature.

322   Cirlot, Juan E. **A Dictionary of Symbols.** New York, Philosophical Library, 1962. 400p. illus.
General dictionary of sacred and profane symbols. Does not include narrative subjects. Bibliographical references are made to a list of 61 reference books. A popular work for the general reader and beginning student.

323   Daniel, Howard. **Encyclopedia of Themes and Subjects in Painting.** New York, Abrams, 1971. 252p. illus. LC 74-153493.
Dictionary of short entries covering all aspects of subject matter in Western painting. A well-illustrated, popular iconographic dictionary. Of limited usefulness to advanced students because it lacks bibliography and specific reference to literary sources.

324   Henkel, Arthur, and Albrecht Schöne. **Emblemata: Handbuch zur Sinnbildkunst des XVI. und XVII. Jahrhunderts.** Stuttgart, Metzler, 1967. 2196p. illus.
Comprehensive dictionary of sixteenth and seventeenth century emblems and their meanings. Classified by groups, illustrated with facsimiles of engraved emblems. There is a list of the emblem books used (pp. xlv-lxix) and an excellent bibliography (pp. xxix-xliii). The standard scholarly reference work on emblems.

325   Jobes, Gertrude. **Dictionary of Mythology, Folklore and Symbols.** New York, Scarecrow, 1962. 3v. index. LC 61-860.
Short definitions of a comprehensive range of symbolic figures, objects, and concepts. Third volume is an index in two parts. Part A is a tabular index of deities, heroes, and personalities; Part B is a tabular index of mythological affiliations, supernatural forms, values, and objects. A long but unclassified and unannotated bibliography at the end of Volume 2 (pp. 1736-59).

326   Koch, Willi A. **Musisches Lexikon: Künstler, Kunstwerke und Motive aus Dichtung, Musik und bildender Kunst.** 2nd ed. Stuttgart, Kröner, 1964. 1250p. illus. index.
Dictionary of music, literature, and the fine arts covering biography and works of literature, music, and art, as well as the subjects depicted in the three arts. Most useful for tracing parallel treatments of some major subjects in literature, music, and the fine arts.

327   Pigler, Andor. **Barockthemen, eine Auswahl von Verzeichnissen zur Ikonographie des 17. und 18. Jahrhunderts.** Budapest, Verlag der Ungarischen Akademie, 1956. 2v. illus. index. LC 57-46167.
A classified list of subjects, both secular and religious, depicted in seventeenth and eighteenth century art. Volume one lists religious subjects; Volume two, secular subjects. Useful for tracing and comparing baroque iconography.

328   Todd, Alden, and Dorothy Weisbord. **Favorite Subjects of Western Art.** New York, Dutton, 1968. 224p. illus.
Short-entry dictionary of secular and religious subjects commonly depicted in Western art. This popular work is of little use to the advanced student, since it lacks reference to literary sources and to further literature.

329   Whittlesey, E. S. **Symbols and Legends in Western Art: A Museum Guide.** New York, Scribner's, 1972. 367p. illus.
Dictionary of short entries covering religious and non-religious subject matter in Western art. Reference is made to works of art in collections in the United States. An inadequate one-page bibliography limits its usefulness to advanced students.

IV. CHRISTIAN ICONOGRAPHY

GENERAL WORKS

330   Aurenhammer, Hans. **Lexikon der christlichen Ikonographie.** v. 1– . Vienna, Hollinek, 1959– .

Comprehensive dictionary of Christian iconography arranged alphabetically by subject; to date, it has reached the entry "Christus und die vierundzwanzig Ältesten." Each entry gives a thorough description of the subject, discussion of the literary sources, a sketch of the development of the subject, and a thorough bibliography of specialized literature. No illustrations. A valuable, scholarly dictionary of Christian iconography. Unfortunately, it is progressing very slowly. For the advanced student and scholar.

331   Ferguson, George W. **Signs and Symbols in Christian Art, with Illustrations from Paintings of the Renaissance.** New York, Oxford University Press, 1954. 346p. illus. index.
Handbook of Christian symbols and subjects in classified arrangement. Illustrations of works of Renaissance painting in American museums. Popular work with no bibliography and few references to specific literary sources.

332   Forstner, Dorothea. **Die Welt der Symbole.** 2nd ed. Innsbruck, Vienna, and Munich, Tyrolia, 1961. 510p. illus. index.
Handbook of Christian symbolism in the fine arts. Subjects are arranged in broad classes and the entries refer to literary and biblical sources as well as to specialized iconographical literature. General bibliography (pp. 487-89). Indexed by subject. An excellent one-volume handbook of Christian symbols. More useful for information on small subjects and symbols than for its complicated biblical narratives.

333   Goldsmith, Elizabeth Edwards. **Sacred Symbols in Art.** 2nd ed. New York, London, Putnam, 1912. 296p. illus. index.
General handbook of Christian iconography, based largely on such nineteenth century works as Jameson and Didron. Subjects are discussed in broad categories. A popular work that is still useful to the beginning student.

334   Keller, Hiltgart I. **Reclams Lexikon der heiligen und der biblischen Gestalten.** Stuttgart, Reclam, 1968. 571p. illus.
Dictionary of short entries covering Christian subject matter, with special emphasis on the iconography of the saints. A good one-volume dictionary-handbook of Christian iconography. Its valuable appendixes include attributes of the saints, glossary of terms dealing with costume, a calendar of saints' days, and a good representative bibliography.

335   Kirschbaum, Engelbert, ed. **Lexikon der christlichen Ikonographie.** Freiburg im Breisgau, Herder, 1968– . 6v. to date. illus.
Comprehensive encyclopedia covering all aspects of Christian iconography. Signed entries, arranged alphabetically, range in size from short entries on simple symbols to lengthy and exhaustive articles on major subjects. All entries give a list of literary sources, description of the subject, history of the representation in Christian art, and a thorough bibliography listing special iconographical literature. Does not include the iconography of saints but does cover all other biblical personages. Volume four gives a list of entries for the entire work in English and French with the

German equivalents. Volumes 5 and 6 comprise the beginning of a comprehensive dictionary of iconography of Christian saints. This is now the standard work on Christian iconography.

336 Künstle, Karl. **Ikonographie der christlichen Kunst** . . . Freiburg im Breisgau, Herder, 1926-1928. 2v. illus. index.
A comprehensive handbook of Christian iconography. Volume two covers the iconography of the saints in dictionary form; all other Christian subjects are covered in Volume 1, where they are arranged in classes. Each chapter has a separate bibliography with many references to specific literature. A standard handbook on Christian iconography, although it is somewhat out-of-date in certain areas.

337 Lipffert, Klementine. **Symbol-Fibel: Eine Hilfe zum Betrachten und Deuten mittelalterlicher Bildwerke.** 4th ed. Kassel, Stauda, 1964. 159p. illus. index.
Handbook of Christian symbolism arranged by classes (i.e., animals, plants, colors, persons, inanimate objects, initials). Bibliography (pp. 158-60). Useful for quick reference on simple Christian symbols.

338 Lurker, Manfred. **Wörterbuch biblischer Bilder und Symbole.** Munich, Kösel, 1973. 434p. index.
Dictionary of biblical subjects and symbols. The thorough entries discuss the meaning of the subject with references to scriptural passages. Very useful bibliographies citing specialized literature follow each entry. General bibliography (pp. 386-91). Provides a comprehensive index of meanings and scriptural passages. A valuable tool for anyone seeking the meaning of biblical subjects found in the fine arts.

339 Molsdorf, Wilhelm. **Christliche Symbolik der mittelalterlichen Kunst.** 2nd ed. rev. and enl. Leipzig, Hiersemann, 1926; repr. Graz, Akademischen Druck-und Verlagsanstalt, 1969. 284p. illus. index.
Handbook of Christian subject matter found in medieval art, arranged by classes. Entries have reference to further illustrations and to specific literature. Still a useful one-volume handbook to Christian iconography. Well indexed.

340 Réau, Louis. **Iconographie de l'art chrétien** . . . Paris, Presses Universitaires de France, 1955-59. 3v. in 6. illus.
Comprehensive handbook of Christian iconography covering both Eastern and Western traditions. Arranged by classes. Volume one gives a general introduction; Volume two covers biblical subjects; Volume three, the iconography of the saints. A general bibliography is given (pp. 21-26 in Volume one), and separate bibliographies follow each chapter. A particularly useful feature is the list of examples at the end of each chapter or class of subject. A standard handbook; Schiller (341) and Kirschbaum (335) are now more thorough.

341 Schiller, Gertrud. **Ikonographie der christlichen Kunst**. v. 1— .
Gutersloh, Mohn, 1966— . English translation: **Iconography of Christian
Art**. v. 1— . Greenwich, Conn., New York Graphic Society, 1969— .
LC 76-132965. illus. index.
A comprehensive handbook of Christian iconography, arranged by broad categor-
ies. Volume one covers the subjects related to the childhood of Christ; Volume two,
His Passion; Volume three, His Resurrection and Ascension. Volumes four and
five will cover subjects related to the Virgin Mary, the Last Judgment, and the
Old Testament. A very thorough and scholarly treatment of Christian iconography.
When completed and translated, it will provide the best coverage available in
English. Very well illustrated. Each volume has a good selected bibliography that
partly compensates for the lack of separate bibliographies after the major sections.
The only index at present is to scriptural passages. Presumably the last volume will
have a subject index that will greatly increase the work's usefulness.

342 Timmers, J. J. M. **Symboliek en Iconographie der Christelijke Kunst** . . .
Roermond-Maaseik, Romen & Zonen, 1947. 1125p. illus. index.
Comprehensive handbook of Christian iconography. Subjects are arranged in
broad classes similar to Künstle (336). Bibliography (pp. 1015-30). Indexed by
subjects, people, and places. Excellent Dutch handbook of iconography, with a
good, concise history of Christian symbolism as an introduction.

DICTIONARIES OF SAINTS

343 Braun, Joseph. **Tracht und Attribute der Heiligen in der deutschen
Kunst**. Stuttgart, Metzler, 1943; repr. Stuttgart, Druckenmüller, 1964.
854p. illus. index.
Dictionary of the saints found in German art. First part lists the saints alphabetically; each entry gives a short life of the saint and a thorough description of
how the saint is represented in art, with reference to and occasional illustrations
of works of German art. Excellent references to literary sources and specific
iconographical literature. Second part deals with the costume and attributes of
the saints. One of the finest iconographical dictionaries of the saints.

344 Drake, Maurice, and Wilfred Drake. **Saints and Their Emblems** . . .
London, Laurie, 1916; repr. New York, Franklin, 1971. 235p. illus.
General dictionary of saints and their attributes. Part one is a dictionary of
saints, with brief biographies; Part two is a list of their attributes; Part three
lists and describes other religious personages. An excellent general dictionary of
the saints.

345 Kaftal, George. **Iconography of the Saints in Central and South Italian
Painting**. Florence, Sansoni, 1965. illus. index.
Specialized dictionary of saints found in Central and South Italian painting of
the fourteenth and fifteenth centuries. Follows the plan of the author's dictionary
of Tuscan saints (346). Scholarly reference tool for the specialist.

346   Kaftal, George. **Iconography of the Saints in Tuscan Painting.** Florence,
        Sansoni, 1952. 1274p. illus. index.
Specialized dictionary of saints found in Tuscan painting of the fourteenth and
fifteenth centuries. Each entry gives short life and a description of how the saint
is represented, with reference to specific works of Tuscan painting, literary
sources, and special bibliography. Thoroughly indexed by attribute, painters,
place, and saints. A scholarly dictionary of amazing thoroughness. A basic reference
tool for the study of Italian painting.

347   Menzies, Lucy. **The Saints in Italy: A Book of Reference to the Saints in
        Italian Art and Decoration** . . . London, Medici Society, 1924. 496p.
Dictionary of saints found in Italian art. Entries give dates, short life, and description of how the saint is represented in art. List of attributes and description of the
habits of the monastic orders (pp. 465-96). This popular dictionary is still useful for
quick reference, but it lacks sources and bibliography as well as reference to specific
works of art.

348   Ricci, Elisa. **Mille santi nell'arte** . . . Milan, Hoepli, 1931. 734p. illus. index.
A general dictionary of saints in art. Brief entries give description of the saint and
reference to works of art in which the saint is depicted. Index of attributes (pp.
687-99). A good, well-illustrated dictionary of the saints in art.

349   Roeder, Helen. **Saints and Their Attributes: With a Guide to Localities
        and Patronage.** London, Longmans, Green, 1955. 391p. illus. index.
General dictionary of saints arranged by their attributes. Death date, main locality
of veneration, and day of commemoration are given for each saint. Indexed by
saints and by localities. A good general dictionary of saints, but it lacks specific
bibliography and reference to works of art.

350   Wimmer, Otto. **Die Attribute der Heiligen.** Innsbruck, Vienna, and
        Munich, Tyrolia, 1966. 169p.
Dictionary of the saints in art, arranged in two lists: by the name of the saint, and
by the attribute of the saint. Gives a brief life of each saint. Popular pocket dictionary of the saints in art.

V. WESTERN PROFANE ICONOGRAPHY

351   Marle, Raimond van. **Iconographie de l'art profane au moyen-âge et
        à la Renaissance, et la décoration des demeures** . . . The Hague, Nijhoff,
        1931-32. 2v. illus.
Comprehensive handbook of secular iconography in the art of the Middle Ages
and the Renaissance. Arranged in broad classes; entries relating to everyday life

are grouped in Volume one, while Volume two covers secular allegories and symbols. A standard work on secular subject matter. Lack of an index makes it difficult to use for quick reference.

352   Tervarent, Guy de. **Attributs et symboles dans l'art profane, 1450-1600.** Geneva, Droz, 1958-1964. 3v.
Dictionary of symbols and subjects found in works of non-religious art between 1450 and 1600. Entries give literary sources for the subject and references to specific works of art that depict the symbol or subject. Although restricted essentially to the Renaissance period, many of the secular subjects treated in this dictionary occur in earlier and later periods. Should be consulted by any serious student pursuing a secular subject.

VI. CLASSICAL MYTHOLOGY AND ICONOGRAPHY

353   Brommer, Frank. **Denkmälerlisten zur griechischen Heldensage.** Marburg, Elwert, 1971. LC 78-592151.
Alphabetical list of personages, objects, and subjects from ancient Greek mythology with references to works of ancient Greek and Roman art that depict the subjects. Gives location of the works, short description of the object, and references to sources of illustrations and further information. Does not include works of ancient vase painting, which are indexed in a separate list (354). A very useful index for advanced students interested in classical iconography.

354   Brommer, Frank. **Vasenlisten zur griechischen Heldensage.** 2nd ed. Marburg, Elwert, 1960.
Index to subjects from Greek mythology depicted in works of ancient Greek vase painting. Follows the arrangement of (353). A very useful index for advanced students interested in classical iconography.

355   Grimal, Pierre. **Dictionnaire de la mythologie grecque et romaine.** 3rd ed. Paris, Presses Universitaires de France, 1963. 578p. illus. index.
Dictionary of ancient Greek and Roman mythology. Each entry has a collection of bibliographical footnotes that refer chiefly to source material. A competent classical mythology dictionary, though it does not refer specifically to depiction of the subjects in the fine arts.

356   Hunger, Herbert. **Lexikon der griechischen und römischen Mythologie: Mit Hinweisen auf des Fortwirken antiker Stoffe und Motive in der bildenden Kunst, Literatur und Musik des Abendlandes bis zur Gegenwart.** 5th ed. Vienna, Hollinek, 1959. 387p. illus.
Comprehensive dictionary of ancient Greek and Roman mythological subjects in Western art, literature, and music to the present day. Each entry provides

numerous bibliographical references, a short account of the subject according to original sources, a discussion of the meaning of the subject, and a description of the subject's use in later Western art, literature, and music. Excellent general bibliography (pp. 383-87) with section on classical iconography. Very useful tool for students interested in classical mythology.

357   Roscher, Wilhelm H. **Ausführliches Lexikon der griechischen und römischen Mythologie.** Leipzig, Teubner, 1884-1927. 6v. plus Supplements (3v. in 5). illus.

Comprehensive dictionary of ancient Greek and Roman mythology. The entries give very thorough discussions of the myths, their literary sources and cult significance, and their representation in the fine arts. A standard dictionary of classical mythology; basic to all serious research on classical iconography.

VII. NON-WESTERN MYTHOLOGY AND ICONOGRAPHY

358   Bonnet, Hans. **Reallexikon der ägyptischen Religionsgeschichte.** Berlin, de Gruyter, 1952. 883p. illus. LC A52-9962.

Comprehensive dictionary of ancient Egyptian religion. Covers deities and other personages, places, objects, and subjects. Each entry has a separate bibliography of specialized works. Standard reference work on ancient Egyptian religion. Invaluable for all serious study of ancient Egyptian iconography.

359   Gordon, Antoinette K. **The Iconography of Tibetan Lamaism.** 2nd ed. New York, Paragon, 1967. 131p. illus. index. LC 67-711.

Little changed from first edition of 1938. Dictionary of subjects of Tibetan Lamaism. Arranged in classes with descriptions and illustrations. General bibliography (pp. 111-18). Popular work, yet still important to serious student.

360   Grey, Louis H., and John A. MacCulloch, eds. **Mythology of All Races.** Boston, Jones, 1916-1932. 13v. illus. index.

Comprehensive handbook of world mythology. Arranged by broad cultures with subject index in Vol. 13. Good bibliographies at the end of each volume. The most comprehensive dictionary of mythology in English. A valuable aid to the study of non-Western iconography.

361   Hackin, Joseph, *et al.* **Asiatic Mythology.** London, Harrap, 1932; repr. New York, Crowell, 1963. 459p. illus. index. LC 63-20021.

A collection of articles by specialists on the mythology of Persia, the Kafirs, Buddhism, Lamaism, Indochina, Central Asia, modern China, and Japan. Responsible collection of myths found in Oriental art, but the lack of bibliography and specific references to literary sources limits its usefulness for the serious student.

362   Haussig, Hans Wilhelm, ed. **Wörterbuch der Mythologie. I. Abteilung:**
        Die Mythologie der alten Kulturvölker. Lieferung 1— . Stuttgart,
        E. Klett, 1961— . illus. index.
Comprehensive dictionary of the mythology of all ancient cultures of the world.
Consists of a series of separate dictionaries of the mythologies, in five categories:
Ancient Near East (includes Egypt), Ancient Europe, the Iranian Peoples, Central
and East Asia, and Ancient America. Thus far the first and second parts have been
published. A second section, covering the mythology of primitive peoples, is being
planned.
        Each dictionary has a valuable introduction with an historical survey of
the mythology concerned. The entries cover gods, ideas, cults, etc., and have
thorough cross-references and excellent separate bibliographies attached to the
major entries. A collection of plates, maps, and chronological tables is provided.
The basic, scholarly reference tool for the study of mythology. Essential for any
serious study of non-Christian iconography; of special value to the specialist in
non-classical archaeology.

363   Joly, Henri L. **Legend in Japanese Art: A Description of Historical**
        Episodes, Legendary Characters, Folk-Lore, Myths, Religious Symbolism
        Illustrated in the Arts of Old Japan. Rutland, Vt., Tuttle, 1967. 623p.
        illus. LC 67-16411.
Reissue of 1908 edition. This dictionary of Japanese iconography explains the
mythology, but without specific reference to literary sources or specialized literature. Bibliography (pp. 596-609) lists, for the most part, works that are older and
that are in Japanese.

364   Lurker, Manfred. **Symbole der alten Ägypter: Einführung und kleines**
        Wörterbuch. Weilheim, O. W. Barth, 1964. 152p. illus. LC 66-93601.
Dictionary of ancient Egyptian symbols. The alphabetical part, covering signs,
signets, gods, and goddesses, is preceded by a brief account of ancient Egyptian
mythology and its representation in the visual arts. A useful dictionary for the
advanced student.

365   Ross, Nancy Wilson. **Three Ways of Asian Wisdom: Hinduism, Buddhism,**
        Zen and Their Significance for the West. New York, Simon & Schuster,
        1966. 222p. illus. index. LC 66-11065.
British edition titled *Hinduism, Buddhism, Zen: An Introduction to Their Mean-*
ing and Their Arts (London, Faber, 1968). A handbook of the subject matter of
Hinduism, Buddhism, and Zen religions. There are separate chapters for each
religion, with sub-sections on the representation of their subjects in the fine arts.
Adequate illustrations, with descriptive captions. Bibliography (pp. 199-207)
lists chiefly works on religion. A general and popular treatment, it is still useful
because of the lack of other substantial works in the field.

366   Werner, Edward T. C. **A Dictionary of Chinese Mythology.** New York,
        Julian Press, 1961. 627p. illus.

Reprint of 1932 edition. Comprehensive dictionary of characters, objects, and subjects of Chinese mythology. Longer entries have references to sources and occasionally to specialized literature. Bibliography (pp. 625-27) lists books in Chinese and Western languages. A standard dictionary of Chinese mythology. Essential for all serious study of Chinese pictorial art.

367   Williams, Charles Alfred S. **Encyclopedia of Chinese Symbolism and Art Motives: An Alphabetical Compendium of Legends and Beliefs as Reflected in the Manners and Customs of the Chinese Throughout History.** New York, Julian, 1960. 468p. illus. index.

Reissue of *Outlines of Chinese Symbolism and Art* (1931). Dictionary of Chinese iconography. Chinese characters are given after the main English heading. Very useful dictionary. Longer entries have bibliographies of specialized literature.

Part II

HISTORIES
AND
HANDBOOKS

INTRODUCTION

This section contains a selected list of comprehensive histories and topographical handbooks of the world's fine arts. To qualify as comprehensive they must treat two or more of the major arts of architecture, sculpture, and painting. Thus, books dealing solely with the painting or sculpture or architecture of a given period or country are not included. To include them would have more than tripled the length of this bibliography and frustrated the aim of providing the scholar-student and general reader with a critical bibliography of basic works. In any case, access to this important class of more specialized books can easily be obtained through the reference works listed in Part I and through the bibliographies noted in the annotations to the histories and handbooks in this section. Books in this section that have especially thorough bibliographies are marked with an asterisk (*) at the beginning of the entry.

Also excluded from this list are works of a non-historical or topographical nature, exhibition and museum catalogs, and cultural histories. It is also important to recall that books published before 1900 are not included and that those published before 1958, the date of Chamberlin's bibliography (2), have been subjected to a rigorous selection; of the pre-1958 titles, only those that have endured as classics or that are still standard studies have been included here.

As in the entire bibliography, the aim in this section has been to present the full spectrum of books on the fine arts, to include books for the general reader along with exhaustive works of interest to scholars and advanced students.

CHAPTER SEVEN

PREHISTORIC AND PRIMITIVE ART

I. GENERAL WORKS

368   *Adam, Leonhard. **Primitive Art**. New York, Barnes and Noble, 1963.
       250p. illus. index.
Actually covers both prehistoric and primitive art of Africa, Asia, Oceania,
Australia, and the arts of the American Indian. Introductory chapters cover
primitive art and the artists of the West, primitive art and psychoanalysis, etc.
Appendixes give a good annotated bibliography of general literature and a very
useful section on primitive art in museums.

369   Christensen, Erwin O. **Primitive Art**. New York, Crowell, 1955. 384p.
       illus. index. LC 55-11109.
Concise survey of the arts of the primitive peoples of Africa, Alaska, the American
Indian, the pre-Columbian societies of Central and South America, Oceania,
Australia, and prehistoric art of Europe. Provides maps, a fair selection of plates,
and a bibliography (pp. 367-76), which lists books and periodical articles chiefly
in English. A somewhat out-of-date survey for the general reader.

370   Lommel, Andreas. **Prehistoric and Primitive Man**. New York, McGraw-
       Hill, 1966. 176p. illus. index.
Survey of the arts of prehistoric and primitive cultures in Europe, Asia, Indonesia,
Oceania, the Americas, and Africa. Includes maps and a general reading list
(pp. 171-72). For the general reader and the beginning student.

371   *Pericot-Garcia, Luis, John Galloway, and Andreas Lommel. **Prehistoric
       and Primitive Art**. New York, Abrams, 1968. 340p. illus. index. LC
       68-26867.
Handbook of European prehistoric art to the Bronze Age and the arts of the primitive societies of Africa, Oceania, and the American Indian. Excellent bibliography
(pp. 326-33), which covers the major general works; numerous footnotes give
reference to more specialized literature. Well illustrated. A good survey for the
general reader and serious student.

372   Sydow, Eckhart von. **Die Kunst der Naturvölker und der Vorzeit. . .**
        Berlin, Propyläen, 1923. 569p. illus. index.
Covers prehistoric art of Europe, promitive art of Africa and Oceania, art of ancient
America, and Germanic art of the migrations and Viking periods. General bibliography (pp. 551-58). Still a useful one-volume handbook of primitive and prehistoric
art.

II. PREHISTORIC

373   Bandi, H. G., *et al.* **The Art of the Stone Age.** London and New York,
        World, 1961. 242p. illus. index.
Covers paleolithic art in Europe, north and south Africa, and Australia. Balanced
bibliography of general works and glossary of terms. Good survey directed to the
student rather than to the general reader.

374   Grand, Paule M. **Prehistoric Art: Paleolithic Painting and Sculpture.**
        Greenwich, Conn., New York Graphic Society, 1967. 103p. illus. index.
        (Pallas Library of Art, v. III). LC 67-28690.
Pictorial survey of paleolithic art in Europe, Africa, and Australia. Well illustrated
with plates, line drawings, and diagrams; also included are a useful selection of
maps and a select but well-chosen bibliography (p. 101) of basic books in all
languages. A good survey for the general reader and the beginning student.

375   *Graziosi, Paolo. **Palaeolithic Art.** New York, McGraw-Hill, 1960. 278p.
        (text); 306p. (illus.). index.
Comprehensive and scholarly study of European paleolithic sculpture and painting. One chapter is an excellent introduction to the study of paleolithic art.
Excellent selection of plates. Bibliography (pp. 221-36) is unclassified but is a
thorough list of books and periodical articles. A standard handbook for the
advanced student.

376   Hoernes, Moritz, and Oswald Menghin. **Urgeschichte der bildenden
        Kunst.** 3rd ed. Vienna, Schroll, 1925. 864p. illus. index.
Comprehensive handbook-history of prehistoric art, chiefly in Europe, from
neolithic through La Tène periods. Thorough reference to specialized literature
in the footnotes. Illustrated chiefly with line drawings. An old but classic history
of European prehistoric art. For the advanced student and scholar.

377   Kühn, Herbert. **Die Kunst Alteuropas.** 3rd ed. Stuttgart, Kohlhammer,
        1958. 251p. illus. index. LC 59-52274.
Concise history of art of Europe from the Ice Age through the early Middle Ages.
Attempts to trace a continuous stylistic development from prehistoric through
ancient and medieval times. Most useful for the earlier chapters on art up to the

first millenium. Good classified bibliography (pp. 235-42), with mention of additional literature in the notes to the plates. For the advanced student.

378   *Leroi-Gourhan, André. **Treasures of Prehistoric Art**. New York, Abrams, 1967. 543p. illus. index. LC 67-22851.
Comprehensive study of and handbook for paleolithic art. Provides chronological tables, maps, lists of works of art that are reliably dated, list of cave sites, analysis of cave art by style, etc. General bibliography (p. 527) is followed by specialized bibliography arranged by site (pp. 528-37). A standard work on paleolithic art; fully documented. For the advanced student.

379   Maringer, Johannes, and Hans Georg Bandi. **Art in the Ice Age**. London, New York, Praeger, 1953. 167p. illus. index.
Survey of paleolithic art in Europe. Bibliography (pp. 164-65) of major works. For the general reader and the beginning student.

380   Müller-Karpe, Hermann. **Das Vorgeschichte Europa**. Baden-Baden, Holle, 1968. 223p. illus. index. LC 74-497422.
Concise history of European prehistoric art. Provides a glossary, a chronological table, and a good, classified bibliography (pp. 194-99), which lists books and periodical articles in all languages. German edition of the series "Art of the World." A good survey of prehistoric art for the beginning student.

381   Nougier, Louis R. **L'art préhistorique**. Paris, Presses Universitaires de France, 1966. 186p. illus. LC 67-72072.
Survey of prehistoric art in Europe with a brief chapter on America and Africa. Good selection of plates; bibliography (pp. 185-86) lists books in all languages. For the beginning student.

382   Powell, Thomas George E. **Prehistoric Art**. New York, Praeger, 1966. 284p. illus. LC 66-12991.
Treats the art of prehistoric Europe through La Tène Celtic. Bibliography (pp. 263-69) lists only recent publications, chiefly those in English. Popular work for the general reader and beginning student.

383   *Sandars, Nancy K. **Prehistoric Art in Europe**. Harmondsworth, Penguin, 1968. 350p. illus. index. (Pelican History of Art Z30). LC 79-352957.
Art of prehistoric Europe through La Tène Celtic. Good bibliography of general works and extensive bibliographical footnotes to specialized literature. A standard work on prehistoric art for the advanced student and scholar.

384   Torbrügge, Walter. **Prehistoric European Art**. New York, Abrams, 1968. 260p. illus. index. LC 68-28390.
Concise history of prehistoric art in Europe from paleolithic times through La Tène. Well illustrated; provided with useful maps, chronological tables, and a bibliography (pp. 255-56) that lists major books in all languages. A good survey of European prehistoric art for the general reader and the beginning student.

385   Waage, Frederick O. **Prehistoric Art**. Dubuque, Iowa, W. C. Brown, 1967.
       113p. illus. index. LC 67-22709.
Survey of prehistoric art from paleolithic times through the Levant style of Spanish
rock art. Bibliography (pp. 109-110) provides a short list of books in English.
Designed as an inexpensive text for the beginning student.

III. PRIMITIVE

386   Batterberry, Michael, and Ariane Ruskin. **Primitive Art**. New York,
       McGraw-Hill, 1972. 192p. illus. index. LC 72-2295.
Pictorial survey of the arts of primitive Africa, Oceania, Australia, and pre-
Columbian America. No bibliography. For the general reader.

388   Boas, Franz. **Primitive Art**. New York, Dover, 1955. 372p. illus. index.
Reprint of 1927 edition. Conceptual study of primitive art, with emphasis on the
art of the Northwest Coast Indians of America. Bibliography in the footnotes. An
old but classic study, for the beginning and advanced student.

389   *Fraser, Douglas. **Primitive Art**. Garden City, N.Y., Doubleday, 1962.
       320p. illus. index. LC 62-13342.
Survey of the arts of the primitive cultures of Africa, Asia, Oceania, and America.
The American section covers both the pre-Columbian civilizations of Central and
South America and the arts of the North American Indian. Bibliography (pp. 313-
16) is a good selection of the major works in this broad field. A good survey for the
general reader and the beginning student.

390   Wingert, Paul S. **Primitive Art: Its Traditions and Styles**. New York,
       Oxford University Press, 1962. 421p. illus. index. LC 62-20161.
Treats the arts of the primitive societies of Africa, Oceania, and the American
Indian. Illustrated in black and white, with a selection of maps. Selected
bibliography (pp. 387-94). A good workmanlike handbook on the main aspects of
primitive art, for the general reader and the student.

CHAPTER EIGHT

PERIODS OF WESTERN ART HISTORY

I. ANCIENT

GENERAL WORKS

391   Byvanck, Alexander Willem. **De Kunst der Oudheid** . . . Leiden, Brill, 1946-65. 5v. illus. index.
Comprehensive Dutch history of art and architecture in the ancient world from Egypt to Mesopotamia through Rome. Well illustrated with plates, plans, and diagrams and provided with good bibliographies at the end of each volume. A good comprehensive history of ancient art. For the advanced student.

392   Curtius, Ludwig. **Die Antike Kunst.** Berlin and Potsdam, Athenaion, 1923, 1938; repr. Hildesheim, Olms, 1959. 2v. illus. index.
Comprehensive history of the art and architecture of ancient Egypt, the ancient Near East, and ancient Greece. Bibliographies are given at the end of each chapter. Once a standard handbook-history, it is still valuable for the force of the author's language and ideas. For the advanced student.

393   Groenewegen-Frankfort, Henriette A., and Bernard Ashmole. **Art of the Ancient World.** New York, Abrams, n.d. 529p. illus. index. LC 77-113722.
Survey history of the art and architecture of the major civilizations of the ancient Mediterranean from ancient Egypt and Mesopotamia through Roman civilization. Has a brief bibliography of selected English language works (pp. 509-514) , and the extensive footnotes give access to more specialized literature. Well illustrated. One of the best histories of ancient art in English. A standard textbook for advanced students.

394   Huyghe, René, ed. **Larousse Encyclopedia of Prehistoric and Ancient Art.** London, Hamlyn, 1966. 415p. illus. index. LC 67-85568.
Collection of essays by French experts on various aspects of the arts of prehistoric and primitive man, plus the art and architecture of ancient Egypt, the ancient Near

East, and Asia to 1000 A.D. Historical summaries are given at the end of each major section. Provides maps and chronology but no bibliography. For the general reader and beginning student.

395   Otto, Walter, ed. **Handbuch der Archäologie, im Rahmen des Handbuchs der Altertumswissenschaft** . . . Munich, Beck, 1939-1953. 4v. illus. index. (Handbuch der Altertumswissenschaft, 6.Abt.).
Comprehensive handbook of ancient art and archaeology. Volume one covers the ancient civilizations of Egypt and the Near East; Volume two, the Stone and Bronze Ages of Europe; Volumes three and four the ancient civilizations of Greece and Rome. *Die griechische Plastik*, by G. Lippold (v. 3, part 1), and *Malerei und Zeichnung*, by A. Rumpf (v. 4, part 1), are classics in the field. A scholarly work for the advanced student and scholar.

396   Powell, Ann. **The Origins of Western Art**. New York, Harcourt, Brace, 1973. 224p. illus. index. LC 74-183245.
General survey history of art in Europe from the Stone Age through the late Roman Empire. Glossary, chronological table, and a bibliography (pp. 219-20) that lists recent books in English. For the general reader and the beginning student.

EGYPTIAN

397   Abbate, Francesco, ed. **Egyptian Art**. London and New York, Octopus, 1972. 158p. illus. LC 72-172102.
Very brief pictorial survey of Egyptian arts from predynastic times through the Ptolemaic period. Includes a chronological outline. All color illustrations. For the general reader.

398   Aldred, Cyril. **The Development of Ancient Egyptian Art from 3200-1315 B.C.** 3v. New York, Transatlantic, 1952. One-volume ed.: London, Tiranti, 1962.
Survey history of the fine arts of ancient Egypt, excluding architecture, from predynastic times through the eighteenth dynasty. Suggestions for further reading at the end of each volume. Informative notes on the black and white plates. For the general reader and beginning student.

399   Capart, Jean. **Egyptian Art: Introductory Studies** . . . New York, Stokes, 1923. 179p. illus. index.
Concise handbook of ancient Egyptian art, with bibliographies at the end of each chapter. Once a standard work for the beginning student, it is now obsolete; nevertheless, it is still worthwhile because of its organization and its succinct language.

400   Capart, Jean. **L'art égyptien**. 2v. Brussels, Vromant, 1909-1911.
An illustrated handbook of the art and architecture of ancient Egypt from predynastic times through the Greco-Roman period. The notes to the plates offer

very thorough bibliographies. This old standard illustrated handbook is still useful to the advanced student because it provides access to older literature.

401   Driot, Étienne. **Egyptian Art**. New York, Arts, Inc., 1951. 161p. illus.
Brief survey of the fine arts in ancient Egypt from prehistoric times through the Greco-Roman period. A pictorial survey for the general reader.

402   Lange, Kurt. **Egypt**. Photographs by Max Hirmer. 4th ed., rev. and enl.
New York and London, Phaidon, 1968. 559p. illus. index.
The brief introductory survey of ancient Egyptian art is followed by many excellent photographs and informative notes. General bibliography (pp. 548-49). A standard illustrated handbook for the beginning and advanced student.

403   *Michalowski, Kazimierz. **The Art of Ancient Egypt**. New York, Abrams, 1969. 600p. illus. index. LC 68-26865.
A comprehensive and richly illustrated history of the fine arts in ancient Egypt. Useful chronological tables, glossaries, and bibliography of general works. Most useful parts are the section on archaeological sites arranged by regions and the bibliographies of specialized literature given at the end of the various chapters. A standard handbook-history for the advanced student.

404   Poulsen, Vagn. **Egyptian Art**. Greenwich, Conn., New York Graphic Society, 1968. 184p. illus. index. LC 69-15492.
Pictorial survey of ancient Egyptian art and architecture. Brief bibliography. Excellent illustrations. For the general reader.

405   Rachewiltz, Boris de. **An Introduction to Egyptian Art**. New York, Viking, 1960. 255p. illus. index. LC 60-11232.
Concise survey of the history of art and architecture in ancient Egypt from pre-dynastic times through the Roman period. Provides maps, a useful chapter on chronology, modest but intelligent selection of plates, diagrams and plans, and a well-classified and selected bibliography of major books and periodical articles in all languages (pp. 233-50). A good survey history for the general reader.

406   *Schäfer, Heinrich. **Von ägyptischer Kunst: eine Grundlage**. 4th ed.
Wiesbaden, Harrassowitz, 1963. 462p. illus. index. LC 65-49119.
History of ancient Egyptian art and architecture from predynastic times through the New Kingdom. Well illustrated and with excellent bibliography in the notes (pp. 368-94). A standard handbook-history for the advanced student.

407   Schäfer, Heinrich, and Walter Andrea. **Die Kunst des alten Orients**. 3rd ed. Berlin, Propyläen, 1942. 686p. illus. index. (Propyläen Kunstgeschichte, II).
A pictorial handbook of the art and architecture of ancient Egypt and Mesopotamia, and the Hittite and Aramaic cultures. Brief introductory essays precede the large collection of plates. No bibliography. Still a useful collection of illustrations,

although it will soon be superseded by the forthcoming volumes in the new *Propyläen Kunstgeschichte.*

408   *Smith, William S. **Art and Architecture of Ancient Egypt.** London, Penguin, 1958. 301p. illus. index. (Pelican History of Art, Z14).
Scholarly history of the fine arts in ancient Egypt from the predynastic period through the Saitic period. Bibliography of general works (pp. 289-90). Thorough coverage of specialized literature in the numerous footnotes. The standard history of Egyptian art and architecture for the advanced student.

409   *Vandier, Jacques. **Manuel d'archéologie égyptienne.** Paris, Picard, 1952-55. 6v. illus. index.
Handbook of ancient Egyptian art and architecture from predynastic times through the New Kingdom. Contents: Tome I, *Les époques de formation* (2v.); Tome II, *Les grandes époques: Ancien, Moyen et Nouvel Empire* (2v.); Tome III, *La statuaire* (2v.). Excellent bibliographies at the end of each tome and extensive bibliographical references in the text footnotes. A standard handbook of ancient Egyptian art and archaeology. For the advanced student.

410   Westendorf, Wolfhart. **Painting, Sculpture and Architecture of Ancient Egypt.** New York, Abrams, 1969. 260p. illus. index. LC 68-2839.
Survey history of fine arts in ancient Egypt from prehistoric times through the Coptic (12th century A.D.). Chronological table and brief bibliography (pp. 255-56). Designed for the general reader, this work discusses literature, religions, and history as well as the fine arts.

411   Woldering, Irmgard. **The Art of Egypt: The Time of the Pharaohs.** New York, Crown, 1963. 260p. illus. index. LC 62-20055.
Survey history of ancient Egyptian art and architecture from prehistory through the Ptolemaic period. Each period has a separate chapter on history and culture. Chronological table, glossary, and brief bibliography of general works (pp. 248-49). For the beginning student.

412   Woldering, Irmgard. **Gods, Men and Pharaohs: The Glory of Egyptian Art.** New York, Abrams, 1967. 275p. illus. index. LC 67-26468.
Survey of art and architecture in ancient Egypt from predynastic times to the end of the New Kingdom. Bibliography (pp. 247-50) lists major books in all languages. For the general reader and the beginning student.

413   Wolf, Walter. **The Origins of Western Art: Egypt, Mesopotamia, the Aegean.** New York, Universe, 1971. 207p. illus. index.
Survey history of ancient art and architecture of Egypt, Mesopotamia, and the Aegean Islands. Does not cover Iran or Asia Minor. Brief bibliography (pp. 202-203). Excellent condensation for the beginning student. There are many appropriate illustrations, with informative captions.

ANCIENT NEAR EASTERN

General Works

414   Bossert, Helmuth T. **Altsyrien: Kunst und Handwerk in Zypern, Syrien, Palästina, Transjordanien und Arabien von den Anfängen bis zum volligen Aufgehen in der griechisch-römischen Kultur.** Tübingen, Wasmuth, 1951. 407p. illus. index. LC A51-10617.
Illustrated handbook and history of the art and architecture of ancient Syria, Cyprus, Palestine, Jordan, and Arabia from prehistoric times to the second century B.C. Especially good coverage of the minor arts. A standard handbook and survey history concentrating on an area often slighted in other surveys of ancient Near Eastern art and architecture. For the advanced student.

415   *Frankfort, Henri. **The Art and Architecture of the Ancient Orient.** 4th rev. ed. Harmondsworth, Penguin, 1970. 465p. illus. (Pelican History of Art, PZ7). LC 70-128007. (Revised paperback edition of the 1954 hardcover edition.)
Comprehensive and scholarly history of art and architecture in the ancient Near East from Sumerian times to the end of the Achaemenian Empire. Covers Mesopotamia, Anatolia, Iran, and the Levant. Good selection of plates, many plans and diagrams. Bibliography (pp. 413-36) is an excellent classified list of books and periodical articles in all languages; it has been brought up to date by an additional bibliography edited by Helene Kanter. The standard history of ancient Near Eastern art and architecture. For the advanced student and scholar.

416   Garbini, Giovanni. **The Ancient World.** New York, McGraw-Hill, 1966. 176p. illus. index. LC 66-19270.
Historical survey of the art of Mesopotamia (Sumeria, Akkadia, Neo-Sumeria, Babylonia, the Kassites, Assyria, Neo-Babylonia), Palestine, Anatolia, plus the Hittites, Syria, Persia, Phoenicia, Egypt (pre-dynastic through Saite dynasty), Nubia, South Arabia, Ethiopia, and Carthage. Includes chronological tables, glossary, maps, and a general bibliography (p. 172). For the general reader and beginning student.

417   Lloyd, Seton. **The Art of the Ancient Near East.** New York, Praeger, 1961. 303p. illus. index. LC 61-15605.
Survey of the art and architecture of the ancient Near East covering Mesopotamia, Egypt, and Iran from prehistoric times to the Persian Empire. Architecture is surveyed in a separate chapter. Brief bibliography (p. 283). For the general reader.

418   *Potratz, Johannes M. H. **Die Kunst des alten Orient: Babylonien und Assyrien, Alt-Syrien, Alt Anatolien und das Alten Persien.** Stuttgart, Kröner, 1961. 438p. illus. index. LC 67-55551.

Concise history of art and architecture of the ancient Near East including Mesopotamia, Iran, Syria, and Anatolia. Covers the period from circa 3100 B.C. to 330 B.C. Although it is a pocket-sized book, it is well provided with plates, plans, diagrams, a useful chronological table, and an excellent classified bibliography (pp. 404-417), which lists books and periodical articles in all languages. An excellent handbook-history of ancient Near Eastern art and architecture for the advanced student.

419   Ry van Beest Holle, Carel J. du. **Art of the Ancient Near and Middle East.** New York, Abrams, 1970. 264p. illus. index. LC 78-92910.
Concise history of art and architecture in the Near and Middle East from 9000 B.C. to the third century A.D. Covers Mesopotamia, Anatolia, Iran, Syria, Jordan, Palestine, and Arabia. Good selection of color illustrations, maps, and chronological tables. Has a good chapter on the discovery of ancient Near Eastern civilization. Bibliography (pp. 258-60) lists major books in all languages. A good survey for the general reader and beginning student.

420   Woolley, Charles Leonard. **The Art of the Middle East Including Persia, Mesopotamia and Palestine**. New York, Crown, 1961. 259p. illus. index.
A survey history of the fine arts in the ancient Near East from Elam and Sumeria to the Greco-Roman period covering Mesopotamia, Iran, Anatolia, Syria, and Palestine. Provides maps, chronological tables, glossary, and brief bibliography (pp. 247-50). For the general reader and the beginning student.

Mesopotamia

421   Moortgart, Anton. **The Art of Ancient Mesopotamia: The Classical Art of the Near East**. London and New York, Phaidon, 1969. 356p. illus. index.
Comprehensive history of the art and architecture of ancient Mesopotamia from Sumerian through Neo-Babylonian times. General bibliography and notes (pp. 329-40). An excellent survey with emphasis on stylistic development. For the advanced student.

422   *Parrot, André. **The Arts of Assyria**. New York, Golden Press, 1961. 380p. illus. index. (The Arts of Mankind, 2). LC 61-11170.
Pictorial survey of the art and architecture of Mesopotamia and Iran from the Assyrian period through the Achaemenian period to the death of Alexander the Great. Part Two has an interesting section on Mesopotamian techniques, literature, and music. Provides maps, glossary-index, and good bibliography (pp. 343-59). Informative notes to the plates. Sequel to (423). For both the beginning and the advanced student.

423   *Parrot, André. **Sumer, the Dawn of Art**. New York, Golden Press, 1961. 396p. illus. index. (The Arts of Mankind, 1). LC 61-6746.

Pictorial survey of art and architecture in ancient Mesopotamia from prehistoric times through the Kassite and Elamite periods. Provides a glossary-index, maps, and good bibliography (pp. 361-70). Richly illustrated, there is often more information in the notes to the illustrations than in the overly condensed text. For the general reader and the beginning student.

424   Strommenger, Eva. **5000 Years of the Art of Mesopotamia.** New York, Abrams, 1964. 480p. illus. index. LC 64-15231.
A comprehensive illustrated handbook of the art and architecture of ancient Mesopotamia from the Sumerian through the late Babylonian periods. A concise and well-written introduction is followed by a section of 280 superlative plates and very informative notes on the plates with references to specialized literature. General bibliography (pp. 465-69) includes an excellent section on excavation reports. Standard illustrated handbook for ancient Mesopotamian art. For the advanced student.

Iran

425   *Ghirshman, Roman. **The Arts of Ancient Iran from Its Origins to the Time of Alexander the Great.** New York, Golden Press, 1964. 439p. illus. (The Arts of Mankind, 5). LC 64-13072.
History of art and architecture in Iran from the prehistoric period through Achaemenian times. In addition to Iranian art and architecture, it covers Irano-Urartian and Scythian art. Provides a glossary-index, maps, chronological table, and a good bibliography (pp. 405-417), which lists books and periodical articles in all languages. Well illustrated. For the advanced student.

426   *Ghirshman, Roman. **Persian Art: The Parthian and Sassanian Dynasties.** New York, Golden Press, 1962. 344p. illus. index. (The Arts of Mankind, 3). LC 62-19125.
Pictorial survey of the art and architecture of ancient Iran from 249 B.C. to 651 A.D. Provides a glossary-index, maps, and good annotated bibliography (pp. 369-77). Numerous plans, chronological tables, and reconstructions are used throughout. For the beginning and advanced student.

427   Porada, Edith. **The Art of Ancient Iran: Pre-Islamic Cultures.** New York, Crown, 1965. 279p. illus. index. LC 65-15839.
Concise history of the art and architecture of ancient Iran from the Elamites through the Sassanians. Provides useful glossary of terms, map, chronological table, and a good basic bibliography (pp. 262-67). An excellent survey history for the general reader as well as for the beginning and advanced student.

Anatolia

428   *Akurgal, Ekrem. **The Art of the Hittites**. New York, Abrams, 1962.
        315p. illus. index. LC 62-11624.
History of Hittite art and architecture from 2500 to 700 B.C. Excellent illustrations
and a good, comprehensive bibliography (pp. 306-312) of books and periodical
articles in all languages. A standard history of Hittite art and architecture. For the
beginning and advanced student. The latter should be aware of translation errors
and should consult the German original (Munich, 1961).

429   *Akurgal, Ekrem. **Die Kunst Anatoliens von Homer bis Alexander.**
        Berlin, de Gruyter, 1961. 350p. illus. index.
Scholarly history of art and architecture of the Greeks, Phrygians, Lydians,
Urartians, Persians, and other societies in Anatolia from circa 1000 B.C. to the
middle of the fourth century B.C. Extensive footnotes with reference to specialized
literature. Informative notes to the black and white plates, with further bibliography. Standard history of one phase of ancient Anatolian art.

430   Bossert, Helmuth T. **Altanatolien: Kunst und Handwerk in Kleinasien von
        den Anfängen bis zum volligen Aufgehen in der griechische Kunst.** Berlin,
        Wasmuth, 1942. 112p. (text); 160p. (illus). index. LC A47-2988.
Illustrated handbook of the art and architecture of ancient Asia Minor from prehistoric times to the middle of the fourth century B.C. A standard survey and handbook with emphasis on the minor arts. For the advanced student.

Scythia

431   Artamonov, M. I. **The Splendor of Scythian Art**. New York, Praeger,
        1966. 296p. illus. index. LC 68-31440.
Pictorial survey of the arts of the ancient Scythians from the sixth through the
fourth century B.C., with emphasis on the remains from Russian tombs. Bibliography is brief and listed by the various Russian barrows. For the general reader and
beginning student.

432   Charrière, Georges. **L'art barbare scythe**. Paris, Éditions Cercle d'Art,
        1971. 263p. illus.
Pictorial survey of the arts of the ancient Scythians. Provides a glossary of terms,
informative notes to the plates, and brief bibliography (p. 259). For the beginning
student.

433   *Jettmarr, Karl. **Art of the Steppes**. New York, Crown, 1967. 272p. illus.
        index. LC 67-17700.
Concise history of art of the ancient peoples of the Russian steppes. Covers the
Scythians, Sarmatians, and societies of Eastern and Central Soviet Union from
circa 900 B.C. to 200 A.D. Provides a valuable chronological table, maps, good
color plates and an excellent, classified bibliography of books in all languages

(pp. 242-58). An excellent history of this complex and slighted area of ancient art history. For the beginning and advanced student.

435 Rice, Tamara T. **The Scythians**. London, Thames & Hudson, 1957. 255p. illus. index.
Concise survey of the arts of the ancient Scythians, with emphasis on their relationship to the general culture of the Scythians. Provides a chronological table, list of major burial sites, and a useful bibliography of books (pp. 201-208), arranged by language. For the beginning and advanced student.

435 Rostovtsev, Mikhail I. **The Animal Style of South Russia and China . . .** Princeton, Princeton University Press, 1929. 112p. illus. (Princeton Monographs in Art and Archaeology, XIV).
A survey of the arts of the ancient Scythians and Sarmatians, with an exploration of the relationship of these arts to Chinese art of the Han and Chou dynasties. Bibliographical footnotes. An old but still influential study for the advanced student.

436 Rostovtsev, Mikhail I. **Iranians and Greeks in South Russia**. Oxford, Clarendon Press, 1922. 260p. illus. index.
History of the arts of the major ancient civilizations of Southern Russia including the Scythians, Cimmerians, Sarmatians, and Greeks from the eighth century B.C. through the Roman period. Good bibliography (pp. 223-38). A standard work for the advanced student.

AEGEAN

437 Boardman, John. **Pre-Classical: From Crete to Archaic Greece**. Harmondsworth, Penguin, 1967. 186p. illus. index.
Concise history of art and architecture of the ancient Mediterranean from circa 3000 to 500 B.C. Covers the art of the Minoans, Mycenaeans, Etruscans, Scythians, and Greeks from the Geometric period through the Archaic period. Modest but well-chosen selection of plates. Bibliography (pp. 183-84) lists and annotates major books in English. An excellent survey for the beginning and advanced student.

438 *Demargne, Pierre. **The Birth of Greek Art**. New York, Golden Press, 1964. 446p. illus. index. (The Arts of Mankind, 6). LC 64-21312.
Pictorial handbook-history of art and architecture in the Aegean including Minoan, Mycenaean, and Greek art of the early Archaic period. Richly illustrated and equipped with maps, plans, and reconstructions, plus a useful glossary-index and an extensive bibliography (pp. 421-30) with its own index. Excellent pictorial handbook for the beginning and advanced student.

439 Hafner, German. **Art of Crete, Mycenae and Greece**. New York, Abrams, 1969. 264p. illus. index. LC 68-28392.

Concise history of art and architecture in the ancient Aegean area and Greece from circa 2800 B.C. to 146 B.C. Covers Helladic, Cretan-Mycenaean, and Greek art and architecture. The introduction, which traces the main outlines of the development, is followed by a good collection of illustrations, arranged chronologically, and a brief introduction to the major periods. The illustrations have informative notes as well as captions. There are no plans for the architectural examples, but the work does provide a useful chronological table, a map, and a good, classified bibliography (pp. 258-60), which lists major books in all languages. For the general reader and the beginning student.

440   Higgins, Reynold A. **Minoan and Mycenaean Art**. New York, Praeger, 1967. 216p. illus. index. LC 67-27569.
Survey history of the art and architecture of ancient Crete, the Cyclades and mainland Greece to the late Bronze Age. Selected bibliography (pp. 195-96). A few brief bibliographical footnotes. For the general reader and the beginning student.

441   Marinatos, Spyridon. **Crete and Mycenae**. New York, Abrams, 1960. 177p. illus. index. LC 60-8399.
Survey history of the art and architecture of the ancient civilizations of Minoan Crete and Mycenaean Greece. Bibliography is found in notes to the plates and notes to the text. A good survey for the general reader and the beginning student.

442   Matz, Friedrich. **The Art of Crete and Early Greece: The Prelude to Greek Art**. New York, Crown, 1962. 260p. illus. index. LC 62-20056.
Survey history of art and architecture in the Aegean Islands and the Greek mainland from the Neolithic through the Mycenaean periods. Provides maps, glossary, chronological tables, and selected bibliography (pp. 248-50). For the general reader and the beginning student.

CLASSICAL

General Works

443   *Becatti, Giovanni. **The Art of Ancient Greece and Rome: From the Rise of Greece to the Fall of Rome**. New York, Abrams, 1967. 441p. illus. index. LC 67-12684.
Comprehensive history of the art and architecture of ancient Greece and Rome from the Archaic period through the late Roman period. Well illustrated with plates, plans, and reconstructions. Provides a glossary of terms and an excellent comprehensive bibliography (pp. 401-423). A standard history of classical art for the beginning and advanced student.

444   Bohr, Russell LeRoi. **Classical Art**. Dubuque, Iowa, W. C. Brown, 1967. 158p. illus. index. LC 67-21302.
Survey history of art and architecture of ancient Greece and Rome from the Stone Age through Constantinian Roman art. Provides maps on the end papers,

tables of major works of art (with phonetic spelling), and a brief bibliography of basic works in English (pp. 149-52). Designed for the beginning student.

445   Ducati, Pericle. **L'arte classica.** 3rd ed. Turin, Ed. Torinese, 1944. 829p. illus. index. (Storia dell'Arte Classica e Italiana, v. 1).
History of art and architecture in ancient Greece and Rome. Well illustrated, it provides a useful chronological table, list of major museums and collections of classical art, and a bibliography (pp. 789-802), which lists major works in all languages. A standard Italian history of classical art and architecture. For the beginning and advanced student.

446   Kjellberg, Ernst, and Gosta Säfflund. **Greek and Roman Art, 3000 B.C. to A.D. 550.** New York, Crowell, 1968. 250p. illus. index. LC 68-20758.
A survey history of art and architecture from the Aegean period through late Roman. Chronological table, glossary, and bibliography of major works in English (pp. 222-28). A general history and guide to classical art for the general reader and tourist as well as for the beginning student.

447   Ruskin, Ariane. **Greek and Roman Art.** Adapted by Ariane Ruskin and Michael Batterberry. New York, McGraw-Hill, 1968. 192p. illus. index. LC 73-96242.
Pictorial survey of the architecture, sculpture, and painting of the ancient world, from Crete and Mycenae through the Roman Empire. For the general reader.

448   Strong, Donald E. **The Classical World.** New York, McGraw-Hill, 1965. 166p. illus. index. LC 65-21594.
Survey of the architecture, painting, sculpture, and minor arts of Greek and Roman civilizations, from Bronze Age Crete through late Roman art. Includes glossary, general bibliography (p. 169), and chronological table. For the general reader and the beginning student.

449   *Zinserling, Gerhard. **Abriss der griechischen und römischen Kunst.** Leipzig, Reclam, 1970. 606p. illus. index. (Reclams Universal-Bibliothek, Band 435). LC 72-581110.
Concise history of art and architecture in ancient Greece and Rome from the second millennium B.C. to the middle of the fourth century A.D. A pocket-sized aid for students, it provides many useful assists: glossary of terms, chronological table, list of principal excavations, list of major museums of ancient art, and an excellent classified bibliography listing books and periodical articles. Additionally, there are special sections for periodicals and books of reference in fields relating to the study of ancient art and architecture. An excellent handbook for the advanced student.

Greek

450   Abbate, Francesco, ed. **The Art of Classical Greece and the Etruscans.**
London and New York, Octopus, 1972. 158p. illus. LC 72-17040.
Brief pictorial survey of painting, sculpture, and architecture in Greece from the
fifth century B.C. through Hellenistic times and of pre-Roman Italic and Etruscan
art. All color illustrations. Weak one-page bibliography. For the general reader, a
most summary introduction to the subject.

451   Akurgal, Ekrem. **The Art of Greece: Its Origins in the Mediterranean and
the Near East.** New York, Crown, 1968. 258p. illus. index. LC 75-548860.
A survey of the art and architecture of Archaic Greece and the neighboring cultures
(Neo-Assyrian, Babylonian, Aramaean, Neo-Hittite, Phoenician, and Syrian). Provides glossary of terms, chronological tables, maps, and general bibliography.
Useful survey of this otherwise slighted group of Eastern cultures that influenced
the early development of Greek art. For the advanced student.

452   *Arias, Paolo Enrico. **L'arte della Grecia.** Turin, Unione Torinese, 1967.
951p. illus. index. (Storia universale dell'Arte, v. 2, t. 1). LC 68-109179.
Comprehensive history of ancient Greek art and architecture from the Geometric
period through the Hellenistic period. Well illustrated and provided with a good,
classified bibliography (pp. 895-930) of books and periodical articles in all
languages. For the beginning and advanced student.

453   Boardman, John. **Greek Art.** New York, Praeger, 1964. 286p. illus. index.
LC 64-22936.
Concise survey of art and architecture in ancient Greece from the Geometric period
through the Hellenistic period. Chronological table and selected bibliography
(pp. 271-72). For the general reader and the beginning student.

454   Boardman, John, José Dörig, and Werner Fuchs. **The Art and Architecture
of Ancient Greece.** New York, Abrams, 1967. 600p. illus. index. LC
67-22850.
Comprehensive handbook of the art and architecture of ancient Greece richly
illustrated with photographs by Max Hirmer and numerous plans, maps, and reconstructions. Selected, general bibliography (pp. 587-88), and extensive bibliographical references in the notes to the text. An excellent handbook for the advanced
student.

455   Brilliant, Richard. **Arts of the Ancient Greeks.** New York, McGraw-Hill,
1973. 406p. illus. index. LC 72-14098.
Concise history of the art and architecture of ancient Greece from Mycenaean
times through the Hellenistic period. Excellent selection of plates, plans, and
diagrams. Bibliographies at the end of each chapter list major books and periodical
articles in all languages. An excellent survey for the general reader and the
beginning student.

456   Chamoux, François. **Greek Art**. Greenwich, Conn., New York Graphic
       Society, 1966. 97p. illus. index. LC 65-21746.
Concise survey of the art and architecture of ancient Greece from Mycenaean
times through Hellenistic. Excellent plates. Brief bibliography of recent works in
English. For the general reader.

457   *Charbonneaux, Jean, Roland Martin, and François Villard. **Archaic
       Greek Art (620-480 B.C.)**. New York, Braziller, 1971. 437p. illus. index.
       (The Arts of Mankind, 14). LC 78-13166.
Pictorial history of ancient Greek art and architecture during the Archaic period.
Provides a useful glossary-index, maps, plans, and reconstructions, and a very
thorough bibliography (pp. 385-95) with its own index. With the sequel volumes
(458 and 459) by the same authors, it forms a good pictorial handbook of ancient
Greek art and architecture for the beginning and advanced student.

458   *Charbonneaux, Jean, Roland Martin, and François Villard. **Classical
       Greek Art (480-330 B.C.)**. New York, Braziller, 1972. 422p. illus. index.
       (The Arts of Mankind, 16). LC 72-80015.
Pictorial history of art and architecture in ancient Greece during the classical
period. Richly illustrated. Provides useful chronological table, glossary-index, maps,
and good bibliography (pp. 367-77). Sequel to (457). Together with other volumes
in the series (457 and 459) it forms a valuable pictorial handbook for advanced
students of ancient Greek art. Yet the text is concise enough for the general reader
and beginning student.

459   *Charbonneaux, Jean, Roland Martin, and François Villard. **Hellenistic
       Art (330-50 B.C.)**. New York, Braziller, 1973. 421p. illus. index. (The
       Arts of Mankind, 18). LC 72-89850.
Pictorial history of art and architecture in ancient Greece during the Hellenistic
period. Richly illustrated. Provides chronological table, glossary-index, maps, and
good bibliography (pp. 371-82). Sequel to (458). Together with other volumes in
the series (457 and 458), it forms a valuable pictorial handbook for advanced
students, while the text is concise enough for the general reader and beginning
student.

460   Carpenter, Rhys. **Greek Art: A Study of the Formal Evolution of Style**.
       Philadelphia, University of Pennsylvania Press, 1962. 256p. illus. index.
       LC 61-6619.
Survey of art and architecture in ancient Greece from the Archaic through Hellenistic periods, with an emphasis on stylistic development. No bibliography. A good
stylistic survey for the general reader and the beginning student.

461   Cook, Robert M. **Greek Art: Its Development, Character and Influence**.
       New York, Farrar, Straus, Giroux, 1973. 277p. illus.
Handbook-history of ancient Greek art, arranged by media. Contains a brief but
usefully annotated bibliography (pp. 261-66). Good glossary and useful section
on Greek art in museums. Good workmanlike handbook similar to but more

up-to-date than Richter (466). For the serious general reader and the student. Lacks bibliographical references for more serious study.

462   Holloway, R. Ross. **A View of Greek Art.** Providence, R.I., Brown University Press, 1973. 213p. illus. index. LC 72-187947.
History of ancient Greek art and architecture, with an emphasis on the purpose or use. Covers the periods from Archaic through Hellenistic and deals chiefly with monumental art. A brief bibliographical note (p. 203), maps, and chronological table of the periods of ancient Greek art and architecture round it out. For the beginning student.

463   Homann-Wedeking, Ernst. **The Art of Archaic Greece.** New York, Crown, 1968. 224p. illus. index. LC 68-16898.
Concise survey of the art and architecture of ancient Greece during the Archaic period, circa 600-480 B.C. Provides a useful glossary, map, and chronological table. General bibliography (pp. 209-211) and further bibliographical references in the notes to the text. Together with the sequel volumes in the same series (451, 467, and 471), it forms a good history of the art and architecture of ancient Greece for the beginning and advanced student.

464   *Matz, Friedrich. **Geschichte der griechischen Kunst; I, Die geometrische und früharchaische Form.** Frankfurt/Main, Klostermann, 1949. 2v. illus. index.
The only volume to appear in a projected comprehensive history of ancient Greek art and architecture. Covers the Geometric and early Archaic periods. Volume one, text; volume two, plates (which are excellent). Thorough bibliography (pp. 511-38) lists books and periodical articles in all languages. Even though it is incomplete, it is a major work for the advanced student.

465   Pollitt, J. J. **Art and Experience in Classical Greece.** London, Cambridge University Press, 1972. 205p. illus. index. LC 74-160094.
A history of art and architecture in ancient Greece from circa 480 to 323 B.C., with emphasis on the interrelationship of the fine arts and the general cultural climate. Bibliography (pp. 199-202) is a useful commentary on the major scholarly interpretations of classical Greek art. A good cultural-historical introduction for the beginning student.

466   *Richter, Gisela M. A. **A Handbook of Greek Art: A Survey of the Visual Arts of Ancient Greece.** 6th ed. London and New York, Phaidon, 1969. 431p. illus. index.
Handbook-history of ancient Greek art from the Archaic period through the Hellenistic period. Treats the various arts separately by type with good attention to the minor arts. Provides glossary, maps, tentative chronology of Greek sculptural work, and a good bibliography of basic literature (pp. 399-410). Further reference to specialized literature in the notes. A standard handbook of Greek art and architecture for the beginning and advanced student.

467   Schefold, Karl. **The Art of Classical Greece.** New York, Crown, 1967.
       294p. illus. index. LC 67-17705.
Concise survey history of the art and architecture of ancient Greece during the
Classical period, circa 480-330 B.C. Provides a useful glossary of terms, a map, and
a chronological table. General bibliography (pp. 236-45) and further bibliography
in the notes to the text. Together with other volumes in the series (451, 463, and
471), it forms a good history of art and architecture in ancient Greece for the
beginning and advanced student.

468   *Schefold, Karl. **Die Griechen und ihre Nachbarn.** Berlin, Propyläen,
       1967. 372p. (text); 432p. (illus.). index.
Comprehensive illustrated handbook of the art and architecture of ancient Greece
from the Geometric period through the Hellenistic period, and the art and
architecture of the neighboring civilizations in the Near East (Phrygian, Lydian,
Scythian, Iranian to the Seleucids) and the western Mediterranean (Phoenician
and Iberian, and Italy before Rome). The introductory essay is by Schefold, and
there are additional essays on the development of the various arts by leading European specialists. Excellent illustrations, numerous plans and elevations in the notes.
Long, very informative notes to the illustrations (with references to specialized
literature) and a very good comprehensive bibliography (pp. 343-55). The finest
handbook for ancient Greek art. For the advanced student and the scholar.

469   Schoder, Raymond V. **Masterpieces of Greek Art.** Greenwich, Conn.,
       New York Graphic Society, 1965. 121p. illus. LC 65-6508.
Brief pictorial survey of ancient Greek art and architecture. Excellent illustrations.
For the general reader.

470   Schuchhardt, Walter H. **Greek Art.** New York, Universe, 1972. 189p.
       illus. index. LC 70-17860.
Concise history of art and architecture in ancient Greece from the Archaic
through the Hellenistic periods. Brief bibliography of major works (pp. 186-87).
Excellent condensed history for the beginning student, with many well-chosen
illustrations and informative captions.

471   Webster, Thomas Bertram L. **The Art of Greece: The Age of Hellenism.**
       New York, Crown, 1966. 243p. illus. index. LC 66-26188.
Concise history of the art and architecture of ancient Greece during the Hellenistic
period, circa 330-50 B.C. Provides a useful glossary of terms, a map, and a chronological table. General bibliography (pp. 224-32) and further bibliography in the
notes to the text. Together with other volumes in the series (451, 463, and 467),
it forms a good history of ancient Greek art for the beginning and advanced
student.

Etruscan

472 Bloch, Raymond. **Etruscan Art: A Study**. Greenwich, Conn., New York
      Graphic Society, 1966. 103p. illus. index. LC 65-22674.
Brief history of Etruscan art and architecture. Good illustrations. For the general
reader and beginning student.

473 Ducati, Pericle. **Storia dell'arte etrusca**. Florence, Rinascimento del Libro,
      1927. 2v. illus. index.
Comprehensive history of Etruscan art and architecture. Volume one is text;
volume two is plates. Good bibliographies given at the end of each chapter. Once
a standard history, it is now out of date. Nevertheless, it is still useful to the
advanced student for its plates and its bibliography of older literature.

474 Giglioli, Giulio Q. **Arte Etrusca**. Milan, Treves, 1935. 95p. illus. index.
Pictorial handbook to ancient Etruscan art and architecture. Still a valuable
collection of illustrations for the beginning and advanced student.

475 *Mansuelli, Guido Achille. **The Art of Etruria and Early Rome**. New
      York, Crown, 1965. 255p. illus. index. LC 65-24336.
Concise and well-illustrated history of Etruscan art and architecture and the art and
architecture of the Republican period of Rome. Provides a useful glossary of terms,
a map, a chronological table, and an appendix on the Etruscan tombs. General
bibliography (pp. 240-46) is excellent except that it does not note English translations of certain key titles. A good history for the beginning and advanced student.

476 Matt, Leonard von. **The Art of the Etruscans**. Photos by Leonard von
      Matt. Text by Mario Moretti and Guglielmo Maetzke. New York, Abrams,
      1970. 252p. illus. index. LC 70-125781.
Illustrated handbook of the art and architecture of the ancient Etruscans, arranged
by place. For the general reader, the beginning student, and the tourist.

477 Pallottino, Massimo. **The Etruscans**. Baltimore, Penguin, 1956. 295p.
      illus. index. LC 56-53.
History of Etruscan civilization, with strong emphasis on its art and architecture.
Good selection of plates. Brief bibliography (pp. 281-82) lists major books in all
languages. For the beginning and advanced student.

478 Pallottino, Massimo, and Martin Hürlimann. **Art of the Etruscans**. New
      York, Vanguard, 1955. 154p. illus.
Pictorial survey of the art and architecture of the ancient Etruscans. Emphasis is
on painting and sculpture; only tomb architecture is included. Brief but sensible
text is followed by a fine collection of plates with informative notes. Provides a
map, a chronological table, and a brief bibliography (p. 29) that lists major books in
all languages. A good survey for the general reader and the beginning student.

479   *Richardson, Emeline Hill. **The Etruscans, Their Art and Civilization.**
       Chicago, University of Chicago Press, 1964. 285p. illus. index. LC
       64-15817.
History of the arts and civilization of the ancient Etruscans from the prehistoric
period through the Hellenistic period. Good general bibliography (pp. 251-63) and
further reference to specialized literature in the notes to the plates. One of the best
surveys of Etruscan art.

480   Riis, Poul J. **An Introduction to Etruscan Art.** Copenhagen, Munksgaard,
       1941. 144p. illus. index.
Collection of lectures on various aspects of Etruscan art and architecture, some
out of date, others still useful to the beginning student. Bibliographical references
are given at the end of each chapter.

Roman

481   Abbate, Francesco, ed. **Roman Art.** London and New York, Octopus,
       1972. 158p. illus. LC 72-172341.
Brief pictorial survey of Roman painting, sculpture, and architecture from the
Republican era through the fourth century A.D. All color illustrations. Weak,
one-page bibliography. For the general reader.

482   *Bianchi Bandinelli, Ranuccio. **Rome, the Center of Power: Roman Art
       to A.D. 200.** New York, Braziller, 1970. 455p. illus. index. (The Arts of
       Mankind, 15). LC 79-526920.
Illustrated history of Roman art and architecture from Republican times to
200 A.D. Provides excellent illustrations, numerous maps, plans, reconstructions,
and chronological and genealogical tables. A good comprehensive bibliography
(pp. 391-96). Together with Vol. 16 in the series (by the same author), it forms
a good pictorial handbook-history for the advanced student.

483   *Bianchi Bandinelli, Ranuccio. **Rome, the Late Empire: Roman Art
       A.D. 200-400.** New York, Braziller, 1971. 463p. illus. index. (The Arts of
       Mankind, 17). LC 71-136167.
Illustrated history of the art and architecture of ancient Rome during the third and
fourth centuries A.D. Provides a glossary-index, a chronological table, numerous
plans and reconstructions, and a good bibliography (pp. 411-21). Together with
another volume in the series (482), it forms a good pictorial handbook-history of
ancient Roman art and architecture for the advanced student.

484   *Ducati, Pericle. **L'arte in Roma dalle origini al sec. VIII** . . . Bologna,
       Cappelli, 1938. 500p. illus. index.
History of art and architecture in ancient Rome from early Republican times
through the eighth century. Well illustrated and provided with a good annotated
bibliography (pp. 421-36). For the advanced student.

485   *Frova, Antonio. **L'arte di Roma e del mondo romano.** Turin, Unione
       Torinese, 1961. 947p. illus. index. (Storia universale dell'Arte, v. 2,
       t. 2). LC 61-49278.
Comprehensive history of Roman art and architecture from Etruscan times through
the fourth century A.D. Well illustrated and provided with a good classified bibliography (pp. 839-93) that lists books and periodical articles in all languages. For the
beginning and advanced student.

486   Hafner, German. **Art of Rome, Etruria and Magna Graecia.** New York,
       Abrams, 1969. 264p. illus. index. LC 71-92911.
Concise history of art and architecture of the Etruscans and ancient Romans from
the eighth century B.C. through the fourth century A.D. An introduction sketching the main outlines of the development is followed by a good selection of illustrations, arranged chronologically, and a brief introduction to the chief periods of
ancient Etruscan and Roman art. The plates are accompanied by informative notes
in addition to the captions. Unfortunately, there are no plans for the architectural
examples. Does have a good chronological table, maps, and a good, classified
bibliography (pp. 257-59) that lists books in all languages. For the general reader
and beginning student.

487   Heintze, Helga. **Roman Art.** New York, Universe, 1971. 200p. illus. index.
       LC 79-134759.
Concise history of art and architecture of the ancient Romans from 600 B.C. to
500 A.D. Good selection of plates, plans, and diagrams. Succinct and informative
text and illustration captions. Bibliography (pp. 193-95) lists major books in all
languages. A good survey of Roman art and architecture for the beginning student.

488   Kähler, Heinz. **The Art of Rome and Her Empire.** New York, Crown,
       1963. 262p. illus. index. LC 63-14558.
Concise history of art and architecture in ancient Rome from the time of Augustus
to that of Constantine. Provides a useful glossary of terms, a chronological table,
a map, and a bibliography of basic works (pp. 216-24). Mansuelli's volume (475)
in the same series treats earlier Roman art. A good basic history for the beginning
and advanced student.

489   Kaschnitz von Weinberg, Guido. **Römische Kunst.** Reinbek bei Hamburg,
       Rowohlt, 1961-1963. 4v. illus. index.
Comprehensive history of the art and architecture of ancient Rome, beginning with
Republican times and ending with the fourth century. Volume one is a general
introduction that explores the concept of Roman art, the problem of Roman art
form, the origins of Roman art, and the general historical background to Roman
art. Volume two is a history by types of Roman sculpture; Volumes three and four
cover the history of Roman architecture. Provides a chronological table, brief
bibliography at the end of each volume, and an index at the end of Volume four.
A basic work for advanced students. Emphasizes form in the tradition of Alois
Riegl.

490   Koch, Herbert. **Römische Kunst.** 2nd ed. Weimar, Böhlaus, 1949. 160p.
        illus. index.
Concise history of art and architecture in ancient Rome from early Republican
times through the fifth century. Chronological outline (pp. 151-54) and selected
bibliography (pp. 145-50). A brief but well-written general history of Roman art
and architecture. For the beginning and advanced student.

491   *Kraus, Theodor. **Das Römische Weltreich.** Berlin, Propyläen, 1967.
        336p. (text); 414p. (illus). index. (Propyläen Kunstgeschichte, 2).
Comprehensive illustrated handbook of the art and architecture of ancient Rome
and its dominions from late Etruscan times through the fifth century. Introductory
essay is followed by sections on the development of the various arts, written by a
number of specialists. Excellent illustrations, numerous plans and elevations, and
very informative notes to the illustrations, with references to specific bibliography.
Good comprehensive bibliography (pp. 305-319). The finest handbook of ancient
Roman art. For the advanced student.

492   Strong, Eugénie. **Art in Ancient Rome** . . . New York, Scribner's, 1928.
        2v. illus. index. Repr.: Westport, Conn., Greenwood Press, 1970. 220p.
        illus. index. LC 72-109858.
Handbook of ancient Roman art from the early Republican period through the
fifth century A.D. Does not cover architecture. Once a standard history, it is still
valuable for its succinct stylistic analysis and its organization.

493   Toynbee, Jocelyn M. C. **The Art of the Romans.** New York, Praeger, 1965.
        271p. illus. index. (Ancient People and Places, v. 43). LC 65-20080.
Concise history of the art but not the architecture of ancient Rome from the
sixth century B.C. to the end of the fifth century A.D. General bibliography (pp.
183-89) and further references to specialized literature in the footnotes and notes
to the plates. One of the best modern surveys of Roman art. For the general
reader and the beginning student.

494   Wheeler, Robert Eric Mortimer. **Roman Art and Architecture.** New York,
        Praeger, 1964. 250p. illus. index. LC 64-22933.
Concise history of art and architecture in ancient Rome from Republican through
late Roman times. The arts are surveyed separately by medium. Short bibliography
(p. 237). For the general reader and the beginning student.

GERMANIC AND CELTIC

495   *Déchelette, Joseph. **Manuel d'archéologie préhistorique celtique et
        gallo-romaine.** Paris, Picard, 1908-1934. 6v. illus. index.
Handbook of Celtic and Gallo-Roman archaeology. Useful information on the fine
arts. Volume one covers prehistoric archaeology; Volumes two through four,
Celtic archaeology; the remaining volumes, Gallo-Roman archaeology. Each volume has extensive bibliographies. A standard handbook for the advanced student
and scholar.

496   *Eggers, Hans J., *et al.* **Les Celtes et les Germains à l'époque paienne.**
       Paris, Michel, 1965. 263p. illus. index. LC 66-56194.
Concise history of the art of the ancient Celts and Germanic peoples from 500
B.C. through the fifth century A.D. Also covers provincial Roman art in Gaul.
Provides excellent color plates, a supplementary collection of black and white
plates, maps, diagrams, drawings, a chronological table, and a good classified
bibliography of major works in all languages (pp. 241-49). This is the French edition of the "Art of the World Series"; it may soon be translated into English. A
good survey history of a period otherwise neglected in the general literature. For
the advanced student.

497   Finlay, Ian. **Celtic Art: An Introduction.** London, Faber and Faber, 1973.
       183p. illus. index.
Concise history of Celtic art in Ireland, exclusive of architecture, from the Hallstatt
period through the fourteenth century. Good selection of plates and a brief,
unclassified bibliography (pp. 174-75). For the general reader and the beginning
student.

498   Grenier, Albert. **Manuel d'archéologie gallo-romaine.** v. 1– . Paris,
       Picard, 1931– . illus. index.
Comprehensive handbook of Gallo-Roman archaeology with much information on
Celtic and Gallo-Roman art and architecture. Continues Déchelette (495).
Contents: Tome 1, *Généralités: travaux militaires*; Tome 2, *Archéologie du sol*;
Tome 3, *L'architecture*; Tome 4, *Les monuments* (2v.). A basic handbook for the
advanced student and scholar.

499   Jacobsthal, Paul. **Early Celtic Art.** Oxford, Clarendon Press, 1970. 2v.
       illus. index. LC 73-16002.
Reissue of the 1944 edition. Comprehensive study of Celtic art of the third
through the early second century B.C. Does not cover Celtic art in Spain and
Portugal. The excellent selection of plates is accompanied by a catalog with
reference to specialized literature. A standard history-handbook of Celtic art for
the advanced student.

500   *Jenny, Wilhelm Albert von. **Die Kunst der Germanen im frühen
       Mittelalter.** Berlin, Deutsche Kunstverlag, 1940. 151p. illus.
History of the arts of the Germanic peoples from the first through the tenth
centuries. Covers the arts of the North Germans through the Viking period as well
as the arts of the various migrating Germanic tribes. Well illustrated. Good bibliography (pp. 77-86), which lists books and periodical articles in all languages. A
standard history of Germanic art. For the advanced student.

501   László, Gyula. **Steppenvölder und Germanen: Kunst der Völkerwander-
       ungszeit.** Vienna and Munich, Schroll, 1970. 152p. illus. LC 70-58275.
Pictorial survey of the arts of the pre-Christian Germans, Huns, Avars, Slavs, and
Hungarians during the period of the migrations. Well illustrated. Brief bibliography

(pp. 154-57) of books and periodical articles. One of the few recent surveys of the art of the migrations period. For the beginning and advanced student.

502   Megaw, J. V. S. **Art of the European Iron Age**. Bath, England, Adams and Dart, 1970. 195p. illus. index.
Concise history of the arts of barbarian Europe from the eighth century B.C. to the second century A.D. Concentrates chiefly on Celtic art but does not cover Celtic art in Iberia or the Iron Age cultures in the Balkans and East Hallstatt region. The catalog of plates provides excellent bibliographical references. A basic history for the advanced student.

503   Scheltema, F. Adama van. **Die altnordische Kunst: Grundprobleme vorhistorischer Kunstentwicklung**. 2nd ed. Berlin, Mauritius, 1924. 252p. illus. index.
Comprehensive history of the art of Europe from paleolithic times through the Iron Age art of the Germanic peoples. Illustrated with line drawings and a few plates. Extensive bibliography in the footnotes. In many aspects out of date and still controversial in approach, yet a classic study of the development and significance of prehistoric and migration art in Europe. For the advanced student.

II. MEDIEVAL AND BYZANTINE

GENERAL WORKS

504   *Focillon, Henri. **The Art of the West in the Middle Ages**. 2nd ed. New York, Phaidon, 1963. 2v. illus. index.
Comprehensive survey of art and architecture in Western Europe during the Romanesque and Gothic periods. Good collection of black and white plates; emphasis is on architecture, with less on sculpture and little on painting. Good bibliographies are at the end of the chapters, with further bibliography in the informative footnotes, some brought up-to-date by editor Jean Bony. Not strictly a factual history, but a highly individualistic interpretation of medieval art that emphasizes the metamorphosis of forms. For the beginning and advanced student.

505   Huyghe, René, ed. **Larousse Encyclopedia of Byzantine and Medieval Art.** New York, Prometheus, 1963. 416p. illus. index. LC 63-12755.
Collection of essays by French specialists on the art and architecture of the early Christian through the Gothic periods. Includes Asian art and architecture of the same time span. No bibliography. For the general reader and the beginning student.

506   Kidson, Peter. **The Medieval World**. New York, McGraw-Hill, 1967. 176p. illus. index. LC 67-11796.

Pictorial survey of the art and architecture of the Western Middle Ages from Hiberno-Saxon and Carolingian times through the Gothic. Provides a glossary, chronological tables, maps, succinct captions to the illustrations, and a brief list of books for further reading. For the general reader and the beginning student.

507   Lethaby, William R. **Medieval Art, from the Peace of the Church to the Eve of the Renaissance, 312-1350.** Rev. by David T. Rice. New York, Philosophical Library, 1950; repr. New York, Greenwood, 1969. 223p. illus. index. LC 71-97315.

Survey history of the art and architecture of the Middle Ages from 312 to 1350. Also covers Byzantine art and architecture. Few bibliographical references in the footnotes. Originally published in 1904 and long a standard history. This useful work has been brought up to date by Rice chiefly through the addition of supplementary footnotes. For the general reader and the beginning student.

508   Morey, Charles R. **Medieval Art.** New York, Norton, 1942. 412p. illus. index.

Survey of art and architecture from the early Christian through the late Gothic periods. Brief reading list (p. 395). Illustrated with black and white plates and line drawings. Some bibliographical references given in footnotes. Once a standard history of medieval art, it is now quite out-of-date. Nevertheless, it is still useful to the general reader and beginning student for its effective organization and succinct language.

509   Smith, Norris Kelly. **Medieval Art: An Introduction to the Art and Architecture of Europe, A.D. 300-A.D. 1300.** Dubuque, Iowa, W. C. Brown, 1967. 111p. illus. index. LC 67-22712.

Concise survey of the art and architecture in Eastern and Western Europe from 300 to 1300. Includes Byzantine art and architecture. General, unclassified bibliography (pp. 113-14). A survey text for beginning students.

510   Strong, Donald E., *et al.* **Origins of Western Art.** New York, Franklin Watts, 1965. 246p. illus. index.

Pictorial survey of the art and architecture of Europe from late Roman times through the thirteenth century. Consists of essays on late Roman, early Christian, Byzantine, early Medieval, Romanesque, and Gothic art and architecture by specialists. Well illustrated. Provides brief bibliography (p. 15) of books in English. A good survey of medieval art, with an emphasis on painting. For the general reader and the beginning student.

FRANCE

511   Evans, Joan. **Art in Medieval France, 987-1498.** 1st ed., 3rd impression with additional bibliography. Oxford, Clarendon Press, 1969. 325p. illus. index. LC 70-430545.

History of art and architecture in medieval France cast in the context of the cultural environment. Some bibliography in the text footnotes; unclassified bibliography (pp. 293-300). Useful and readable history of the arts and general culture of medieval France. Particularly valuable are the chapters on the monastic orders. For the general reader and the beginning student.

GERMANY

512   Schmitz, Hermann. **Die Kunst des frühen und hohen Mittelalters in Deutschland**. Munich, Bruckmann, 1924. 272p. illus.
Concise survey of the history of art and architecture in the German-speaking countries from prehistoric times through the late Romanesque (mid-thirteenth century). Includes a brief, unclassified bibliography of German books (pp. 268-69). Although now out of date in the details, it is still a well-written survey of German medieval art for the beginning and advanced student.

GREAT BRITAIN

513   Saunders, O. Elfrida. **A History of English Art in the Middle Ages**. Oxford, Clarendon Press, 1932; repr. Freeport, N.Y., Books for Libraries, 1969. 272p. illus. index. LC 70-103658.
Concise history of art (exclusive of architecture) in England beginning with Saxon period and ending with the late Gothic. General bibliography (pp. 260-62) in addition to the bibliographies at the ends of chapters. An old survey history that is still of interest to the general reader.

514   Stoll, Robert. **Architecture and Sculpture in Early Britain: Celtic, Saxon, Norman**. New York, Viking, 1967. 356p. illus. index.
Pictorial survey of architecture and sculpture in Britain during the early Middle Ages, from the seventh century through the Romanesque. The short introductory essay is followed by a collection of black and white plates (chiefly of architecture) and notes to the plates. No bibliography. For the general reader and the beginning student.

ITALY

515   *Lavagnino, Emilio. **L'arte mediaevale**. 2nd ed. Torino, Unione Tipografico Editrice Torinese, 1960. 942p. illus. index. (Storia dell'Arte Classica e Italiana, v. 2).
Survey of art and architecture in Italy from the early Christian through the Gothic periods. Gothic section includes the Trecento. Good annotated bibliography

(pp. 880-89). First published in 1936, still a good, well-illustrated history of medieval art and architecture in Italy. For the beginning and advanced student.

SCANDINAVIA

516   Anker, Peter, and Aron Andersson. **The Art of Scandinavia**. London, Hamlyn, 1970. 2v. illus. index. LC 79-21555.
Comprehensive history of art and architecture in Scandinavia during the Middle Ages. Well illustrated with plates, plans, and diagrams. Bibliographical footnotes. This is a translation of the French edition, titled *La Pierre-qui-vire* (Zodiaque, 1968-69). An excellent history of Scandinavian medieval art and architecture. The first volume is especially valuable as a thorough treatment of Viking art. For the beginning and advanced student.

517   Rácz, István. **Art Treasures of Medieval Finland**. New York, Praeger, 1967. 252p. illus. LC 67-15670.
Pictorial survey of art and architecture in Finland during the fourteenth and fifteenth centuries. Introduction and notes on the plates by Riitta Pylkkänen. No bibliography. For the general reader and the beginning student.

518   Rácz, István. **Norsk Middelalderkunst**. Oslo, Cappeln, 1970. 224p. illus. index. LC 79-574133.
Survey history of medieval art and architecture in Norway. Well illustrated. No bibliography. For the general reader and the beginning student.

EASTERN EUROPE

519   Grabar, André. **L'art du moyen âge en Europe orientale**. Paris, Michel, 1968. 243p. illus. index.
Concise history of the art and architecture in Eastern Europe covering the Balkans, Rumania, Russia, and Greece from the tenth to the seventeenth century. Provides maps, chronological tables, and a classified bibliography of books in all languages (pp. 229-31). A good survey history for the advanced student.

520   *Voyce, Arthur. **The Art and Architecture of Medieval Russia**. Norman, University of Oklahoma Press, 1966. 432p. illus. index. LC 66-13433.
History of art and architecture in Russia from the pre-Christian era (Scythians, etc.) to 1600. Provides a chronological table, a useful glossary of Russian art terms, maps, and good bibliography of general works (pp. 405-416). A standard history of medieval Russian art and architecture for the beginning and advanced student.

EARLY CHRISTIAN

521   Beckwith, John. **Early Christian and Byzantine Art**. Harmondsworth,
       Penguin, 1970. 211p. illus. index. (Pelican History of Art).
History of early Christian art from the early third century and Byzantine art to the
middle of the fifteenth century. Does not cover architecture, which is treated in
the same series by R. Krautheimer's *Early Christian and Byzantine Architecture*.
Provides a glossary of terms, maps, and a brief bibliography of general works
(pp. 191-92). Specialized literature is mentioned in the notes to the text. A basic
history of early Christian and Byzantine art for the advanced student.

522   *Du Bourguet, Pierre. **Early Christian Art**. New York, Reynal, 1971. 219p.
       illus. LC 77-151935.
Comprehensive history of early Christian art and architecture from circa 200 to
the end of the fourth century A.D. Excellent illustrations, useful plans and maps,
and a good classified bibliography (pp. 216-17), which lists books and periodical
articles in all languages. A good survey history for the beginning and advanced
student.

523   Francia, Ennio. **Storia dell'arte paleocristiana**. Milan, Martello, 1969.
       209p. illus. index. LC 78-434554.
Concise history of early Christian art and architecture from the early second century
A.D. through the fifth century. Good selection of plates. Bibliography (pp. 147-54)
lists books and periodical articles in all languages. For the beginning and advanced
student.

524   Gerke, Friedrich. **Spätantike und frühes Christentum**. Baden-Baden, Holle,
       1967. 279p. illus. index. LC 68-114559.
Concise history of early Christian art and architecture from the pre-Constantinian
art through the time of Heraclius. Provides a useful glossary of terms, a map, and
a brief bibliography (pp. 251-52). Useful survey for the advanced student.

525   Gough, Michael. **The Origins of Christian Art**. London, Thames &
       Hudson, 1973. 216p. illus. index.
Concise history of art and architecture in Europe from pre-Constantinian Christian
art of the third century A.D. through Hiberno-Saxon art and architecture of the
eighth century. Covers Byzantine art and architecture through the seventh
century. Good choice of illustrations, plans, and diagrams. Bibliography (pp. 203-
204) lists major books in Western languages. A good survey of early Christian and
early medieval art and architecture for the general reader and the beginning student.

526   *Grabar, André. **Early Christian Art: From the Rise of Christianity to
       the Death of Theodosius**. New York, Odyssey, 1969. 325p. illus. index.
       (The Arts of Mankind, 9). LC 68-100414.
British edition is titled: *The Beginnings of Christian Art, 200-395*. This is an illustrated history of the art and architecture of the early Christian period from circa

200 to 395 A.D. Provides chronological tables, maps, useful glossary, index, an excellent section on documents in translation, and good bibliography (pp. 307-313). For the general reader and the beginning student.

527   Hutter, Irmgard. **Early Christian and Byzantine Art.** New York, Universe, 1971. 191p. illus. index. LC 75-122018.
Concise survey history of the art and architecture of the early Christian and Byzantine periods beginning with the third century and ending with the thirteenth century. Balanced, well-chosen illustrations with informative captions. Brief bibliography (pp. 186-87). A good survey text for the beginning and advanced student.

528   Lassus, Jean. **The Early Christian and Byzantine World.** New York, McGraw-Hill, 1967. 176p. illus. index. LC 67-11797.
Survey of the architecture, mosaics, sculpture, and minor arts of these two epochs. Includes a chronological table, a glossary, maps, and a general bibliography (p. 172). For general readers and beginning students.

529   Lowrie, Walter. **Art in the Early Church.** 2nd rev. ed. New York, Harper, 1965. 229p. illus. index.
Survey of early Christian art and architecture beginning with the pre-Constantinian art of the catacombs and ending with a discussion of the influence of early Christian art on early medieval art. Provides a chronological table and a good selective and annotated bibliography of the older literature. An enthusiastic study and interpretation of early Christian art for the general reader and the beginning student.

530   Meer, Frederik van der. **Early Christian Art.** London, Faber, 1967. 149p. illus. index. LC 67-114396.
Concise survey of the art and architecture of the early Christian period from the catacombs through the sixth century. Good chapter on the discovery of early Christian art. No bibliography. Good, appreciative survey of early Christian art for the general reader and the beginning student.

531   Morey, Charles R. **Early Christian Art.** 2nd ed. Princeton, Princeton University Press, 1953. 282p. illus. index.
History of early Christian art beginning with the Hellenistic background and ending with the eighth century. Does not cover architecture. Informative notes to the plates. Bibliography is included in the footnotes. Once a standard history, it is now out-of-date; nevertheless, it is still useful to the advanced student because of the author's original approach in dealing with the origins of early Christian art and because of its bibliographical footnotes.

532   Syndicus, Eduard. **Early Christian Art.** New York, Hawthorn Books, 1962. 186p. illus. index. (Twentieth Century Encyclopedia of Catholicism, v. 121, Section 12: Catholicism and the Arts). LC 62-11412.
Concise history of art and architecture from the early third century A.D. to the end of the Carolingian period. Emphasis is on the content of early Christian art and

its interrelationship with the world of late antiquity. The selection of plates is modest, but the book is liberally provided with plans and diagrams. Brief bibliography (pp. 187-88) lists major books in all languages. A good survey written from the standpoint of the church. For the general reader and the beginning student.

533   Volbach, Wolfgang F. **Early Christian Art.** New York, Abrams, 1962. 363p. illus. index. LC 61-8333.

Illustrated handbook of early Christian art and architecture. Short introductory essay is followed by 258 excellent plates (with informative notes) containing plans, elevations, reconstructions, and references to specialized literature. A basic handbook for the beginning and advanced student.

534   *Wulff, Oskar K. **Altchristliche und byzantinische Kunst.** 2v. Berlin, Athenaion, 1918. illus. index.

Comprehensive history of the art and architecture of the early Christian period of Byzantium. Volume one covers early Christian art and architecture from pre-Constantinian times through the fifth century; Volume two, Byzantine art and architecture from the sixth through the fourteenth centuries. Extensive bibliographies are given at the end of chapters. A third volume, containing a critical bibliography, appeared in 1939 and is annotated elsewhere in this bibliography (61). This is an old standard handbook that is still useful to the advanced student and the scholar.

BYZANTINE

535   Beckwith, John. **The Art of Constantinople: An Introduction to Byzantine Art, 330-1453.** 2nd ed. New York, Phaidon, 1968. 184p. illus. index. LC 68-18908.

History of Byzantine art (but not architecture) from 330 to 1453, with emphasis on the contribution of Constantinople. Chronological table, glossary of terms, and thorough reference to and discussion of the literature of Byzantine art in the footnotes. Well-chosen illustrations. For beginning and advanced students.

536   Diehl, Charles. **Manuel d'art byzantin** . . . 2nd ed. Paris, Picard, 1925-26. 2v. illus. index.

History of Byzantine art and architecture from the sixth century through the middle of the fifteenth century. Extensive references to specialized literature in the footnotes; bibliographical note (pp. xiii-xv) discusses major works in all languages. Has a useful iconographical index. An old but still useful handbook for the advanced student.

537   Grabar, André. **The Art of the Byzantine Empire: Byzantine Art in the Middle Ages.** New York, Crown, 1966. 216p. illus. index. LC 66-21147.

Survey history of the art and architecture in the Byzantine Empire from the Iconoclastic period (mid-eighth century) to the fifteenth century. Provides a chronological table and a brief, general bibliography (pp. 209-210). A good survey history of later Byzantine art for the beginning and advanced student.

538   *Grabar, André. **The Golden Age of Justinian, from the Death of Theodosius to the Rise of Islam.** New York, Odyssey, 1967. 408p. illus. index. (The Arts of Mankind, 10). LC 66-29363.
British edition is titled: *Byzantium, from the Death of Theodosius . . .* Illustrated history of the art and architecture of Byzantium from the early sixth through the fifteenth century. Treats the various arts separately by type. Provides plans, maps, chronological tables, informative notes to the plates, and a good bibliography (pp. 383-92). For beginning and advanced students.

539   Peirce, Hayford, and Royall Tyler. **L'art byzantin** . . . Paris, Libraire de France, 1932-34. 4v. illus. index.
Illustrated handbook of Byzantine art, exclusive of architecture, from the fourth century through the sixth century. Each volume has a brief introductory essay sketching the development of the various media, followed by a good collection of plates with informative notes. No bibliography. Still valuable to the advanced student for its illustrations.

540   Rice, David T. **The Art of Byzantium.** London, Thames and Hudson, 1959. 339p. illus. index.
Illustrated handbook of Byzantine art and architecture from the time of Justinian to the middle of the fifteenth century. Brief introductory survey is followed by an excellent collection of plates; the informative notes to the plates include bibliographical references. A standard illustrated handbook for beginning and advanced students.

541   Rice, David T. **The Art of the Byzantine Era.** New York, Praeger, 1963. 286p. illus. index. LC 63-16444.
Survey history of art and architecture in Byzantium from the early sixth to the mid-fifteenth centuries. Includes Coptic, Palestinian, and Syrian art. Provides maps, a chronological table, and a brief bibliography of major works (pp. 267-68). Good survey for the general reader and the beginning student.

542   *Rice, David T. **Byzantine Art.** Rev. and expanded ed. Harmondsworth, Penguin, 1968. 580p. illus. index. LC 75-356968.
Survey of the art and architecture of Byzantium from the early sixth through the middle of the fifteenth century. The various arts are treated separately. Provides maps, an excellent selection of illustrations, and a good, annotated bibliography (pp. 563-70). An excellent survey for the general reader and the beginning student.

543   Schug-Wille, Christa. **The Art of the Byzantine World.** New York, Abrams, 1971. 263p. illus. index. LC 75-92912.
Concise history of art and architecture from pre-Constantinian times (circa 200 A.D.) through the art and architecture of Russia during the fifteenth and

sixteenth centuries. Well-chosen illustrations and useful maps, but no plans for architectural examples. Provides a balanced bibliography (pp. 257-59) that lists books in all languages. For the general reader and the beginning student.

544   *Volbach, Wolfgang F., and Jacqueline LaFontaine-Dosgne. **Byzanz und der christliche Osten.** Berlin, Propyläen, 1968. 366p. (text); 432p. (illus.). index. (Propyläen Kunstgeschichte, Band 3).

Comprehensive illustrated handbook of the art and architecture of Byzantium and the Christian art and architecture of Syria, Egypt, Nubia, Ethiopia, Armenia, Georgia, Russia, Rumania, Bulgaria, Yugoslavia, and Greece from the sixth through the fifteenth century. Introductory essay is followed by a corpus of excellent illustrations, essays on the development of the various arts and national subdivisions, extensive and informative notes to the plates, and plans and elevations. A chronological table comparing the artistic developments with political and religious developments is provided, and there is an excellent classified bibliography (pp. 380-98). Specialized literature is noted in the notes to the plates. A standard and basic illustrated handbook for the advanced student and the scholar.

COPTIC

545   *Du Bourguet, Pierre. **The Art of the Copts.** New York, Crown, 1971. 234p. illus. index. LC 78-147350.

Concise history of the art and architecture of the Copts from pre-Coptic times through the twelfth century. Provides maps, a chronological table, a good classified bibliography (pp. 224-27), and bibliographical footnotes to the text. Excellent history of Coptic art and architecture for the beginning and advanced student.

546   Gayet, Albert J. **L'art copte: École d'Alexandrie—architecture monastique—sculpture—peinture—art somptuaire** . . . Paris, Leroux, 1902. 334p. illus.

Comprehensive history of Coptic art and architecture. Illustrated with line drawings. Bibliographical footnotes. An old, standard history of Coptic art; should be known by the advanced student.

547   Grüneisen, Wladimir de. **Les caractéristiques de l'art copte.** Florence, Alinari, 1922. 193p. illus.

Illustrated survey of Coptic art and architecture. Good selection of plates. Provides a brief bibliography (pp. 27-29), with reference to more specialized literature in the footnotes. An older survey, still useful to the advanced student because of the plates.

548   Wessel, Klaus. **Coptic Art.** New York, McGraw-Hill, 1965. 247p. illus. index. LC 65-19075.

Survey of the art of early Christian Egypt. Does not include architecture. Maps, good selection of plates, and brief unclassified bibliography (pp. 238-47). A useful but controversial history of Coptic art for beginning and advanced students.

EARLY MEDIEVAL

General Works

549   Backes, Magnus, and Regine Dölling. **Art of the Dark Ages**. New York, Abrams, 1971. 263p. illus. index. LC 70-90886.
Concise survey of the art and architecture of the early Middle Ages from the period of the migrations through the Ottonian period. A short introduction is followed by explanations of the plates. Brief bibliography (pp. 258-59). For the general reader and the beginning student.

550   Bréhier, Louis. **L'art en France des invasions barbares à l'époque romane** . . . Paris, La Renaissance du Livre, 1930. 210p. illus.
Concise history of the art and architecture of France in the Merovingian, Carolingian, and pre-Romanesque periods. Illustrated with facsimiles and rather weak plates. Bibliography (pp. 207-208) lists major works. An old but still valuable study of a neglected period in French medieval art history. For the advanced student.

551   Busch, Harald, and Bernd Lohse. **Pre-Romanesque Art**. New York, Macmillan, 1966. 217p. illus. LC 66-16924.
Pictorial survey of art and architecture of Western Europe from the fourth through the middle of the eleventh century. Introduction by Louis Grodecki; informative notes to the plates by Eva Wagner. No bibliography. Good pictorial survey for the general reader and beginning student.

552   *Fillitz, Hermann. **Das Mittelalter, I**. Berlin, Propyläen, 1969. 350p. (text); 420p. (illus.). index. (Propyläen Kunstgeschichte, Band 5). LC 71-484515.
Comprehensive illustrated handbook of the art and architecture of the early Middle Ages. Covers the period from the late eighth century through the Romanesque period (circa middle of the twelfth century). Introductory essay is followed by a corpus of excellent illustrations with extensive and highly informative notes and separate essays on the development of the various arts. There is a chronological table comparing the developments in the arts with those in political and religious history, and an excellent classified bibliography (pp. 292-327). Specialized literature is mentioned in the notes to the illustrations. A standard and basic illustrated handbook for advanced students and scholars.

553   Henderson, George. **Early Medieval**. Harmondsworth, Penguin, 1972. 272p. illus. index. LC 72-171390.

Concise history of art and architecture in Western Europe from the eighth century through the middle of the eleventh century. Emphasis is placed on the relationship between the fine arts and the general culture of the early Middle Ages. Well-chosen illustrations with informative notes and some with bibliographical references. Bibliography (pp. 265-68) is a helpful annotated list of major literature in all languages. A good survey history for beginning and advanced students.

554   Hubert, Jean. **L'art pré-roman** . . . Paris, Éditions d'Art et d'Histoire, 1938. 202p. illus. index.
Concise history of the art and architecture of France from the fifth to the tenth century. Bibliographical references in the footnotes. Illustrated with plates, plans, and diagrams. A standard history for advanced students.

555   Kayser, Felix. **Kreuz und Rune; langobardisch-romanische Kunst in Italien.** Stuttgart, Urachhaus, 1964. 2v. illus. index. LC 67-85057.
History of the art and architecture of the Lombards in Italy from the sixth century through the twelfth century. Good plates and plans. General bibliography (pp. 138-40) and further reference to more specialized literature in the footnotes. A standard history of Lombardic art and architecture for the advanced student.

556   *Lasko, Peter. **Ars Sacra: 800-1200.** Baltimore, Penguin, 1972. 338p. illus. index. (Pelican History of Art, Z36).
Comprehensive history of ivory carving, metalwork, enamels, and bronze sculpture from the Carolingian through the Romanesque periods. Good selection of plates. Bibliography (pp. 315-17) is a selected list of major works in all languages. Further reference to more specialized literature in the notes. A good history of medieval minor arts for the advanced student.

557   Lautier, Raymond, and Jean Hubert. **Les origines de l'art français.** Paris, Le Prat, 1947. 180p. illus.
Concise history of art and architecture in France from prehistory through Carolingian era. Brief bibliography (p. 180). For the advanced student. The good selection of plates makes this work valuable for this neglected period of French art and architecture.

558   Mahr, Adolf. **Christian Art in Ancient Ireland.** Dublin, Stationery Office, 1932-41. 2v. illus. index.
Concise history of art and architecture in Ireland from the seventh century to the time of the Anglo-Norman conquest. Bibliography (pp. 169-76) of books and periodical articles. An older, general history of Irish medieval art and architecture for the beginning student.

559   Palol Salellas, Pedro de. **Early Medieval Art in Spain.** New York, Abrams, 1967. 500p. illus. index. LC 66-26609.
Illustrated handbook of art and architecture in Spain from the Visigothic through the Romanesque periods. Genealogical tables, maps, and excellent plates.

Bibliography in the notes to the plates. A good illustrated survey for the beginning and advanced student.

560 Picton, Harold W. **Early German Art and Its Origins from the Beginnings to About 1050**. London, Batsford, 1939. 148p. illus. index.
A survey of the development of the art and architecture of the Germanic peoples from neolithic times through the Ottonian period. A Pan-Germanic survey that treats Germanic art of the migrations epoch and the early Middle Ages in Eastern Europe, Italy, Spain, France, and the British Isles, as well as Central Europe. This provocative work is out of date in many of its conclusions, but it is still valuable for the advanced student.

561 Strzygowski, Josef. **Die altslavische Kunst**. Augsburg, Filser, 1929. 296p. illus. index.
Scholarly history of the art and architecture of the Slavic peoples during the early Middle Ages. Excellent plans and diagrams, good illustrations of rarely reproduced works, and thorough reference to specialized literature in the footnotes. Like all works by Strzygowski, this one is still controversial; but it remains one of the standard histories of early Slavic art and architecture. For the advanced student.

Pre-Carolingian

562 Henry, Françoise. **Irish Art in the Early Christian Period to 800 A.D.** 3rd rev. enl. ed. Ithaca, New York, Cornell University Press, 1965. 256p. illus. index. LC 65-22854 rev.
Concise history of art and architecture in Ireland from the fifth century to 800 A.D. Good bibliographical footnotes in the text. A standard history of early medieval art and architecture in Ireland for the beginning and advanced student.

563 *Hubert, Jean, Jean Porcher, and W. F. Volbach. **Europe of the Invasions**. New York, Braziller, 1969. 387p. illus. (The Arts of Mankind, 12). LC 75-81858.
Illustrated history of art and architecture of Western Europe from the fifth through the eighth centuries. Covers the art of the migrating Germanic tribes, the last manifestations of early Christian art in Italy, and the art and architecture of the established Germanic kingdoms in Western Europe and the British Isles. The arrangement by types of works of art does not give clarity to the complex history of art in this transitional time. Provides numerous plans, elevations, reconstructions, maps, notes to the plates, and a good but unclassified bibliography (pp. 331-35). One of the few books in English on this crucial period. For the beginning and advanced student.

564 Kendrick, Thomas D. **Anglo-Saxon Art to A.D. 900**. London, Methuen, 1938. 227p. illus. index.
Concise history of art and architecture in England from the Roman period to 900 A.D. Bibliographical references in the footnotes. A standard history for the beginning and advanced student.

565   Kendrick, Thomas D. **Late Saxon and Viking Art**. London, Methuen, 1949. 152p. illus. index.
Concise history of the art and architecture of England in the tenth century and Scandinavian art of the ninth and tenth centuries. Bibliographical references in the footnotes. This is a sequel to (564); together they form a standard history of the arts of the early Middle Ages in England with reference to contemporary Scandinavian art. For the beginning and advanced student.

566   Klindt Jensen, Ole, and David Wilson. **Viking Art**. Ithaca, Cornell University Press, 1966. 173p. illus. index. LC 66-13813 rev.
Concise history of Scandinavian art of the Viking period, 800-1100. The chapter on Scandinavian art before the Vikings adds to the usefulness of this survey. A standard work in English for the beginning and advanced student.

567   Palol Salellas, Pedro de. **Arte hispanico de la epoca Visigoda**. Barcelona, Ediciones Poligrafia, 1968. 237p. illus. LC 72-620.
Pictorial survey of Visigothic art and architecture in Spain. Text in Spanish, English, and French. Brief bibliography (p. 221). Useful pictorial survey for the general reader and beginning student.

568   *Puig Y Cadafalch, José. **L'art wisigothique et ses survivances**. Paris, de Nobelle, 1961. 204p. illus. index.
History of art and architecture of the Visigoths in Spain with chapters on the survival and influence of Visigothic art and architecture in Carolingian art, Mozarabic art, and the early Romanesque in Spain. Excellent bibliography (pp. 189-98). Standard history of Visigothic art for the advanced student.

569   Schaffran, Emerich. **Die Kunst der Langobarden in Italien**. Jena, Diederich, 1941. 196p. illus. index.
History of the art and architecture of the Lombards in Italy during the seventh and eighth centuries. Access to further literature through the numerous footnotes in the text. A standard history of Lombardic art for the advanced student.

570   Verzone, Paolo. **The Art of Europe: The Dark Ages from Theodoric to Charlemagne**. New York, Crown, 1968. 276p. illus. index. LC 68-9069.
Concise history of art and architecture in Western Europe from circa 425 to 800 A.D. Emphasis on Italian developments. Provides glossary of terms, chronological table, and brief bibliography (pp. 259-60). A useful, if somewhat complicated, history of a period on which little has been written for the beginning student.

Carolingian and Ottonian

571   *Beckwith, John. **Early Medieval Art**. New York, Praeger, 1964. 270p. illus. index. LC 64-19953.
Concise history of the art and architecture of Western Europe from the early ninth through the middle of the twelfth centuries. Excellent critical bibliographical

references in the notes to the text. Well-chosen illustrations. An excellent survey for the beginning student.

572   Braunfels, Wolfgang. **Die Welt der Karolinger und ihre Kunst**. Munich, Callwey, 1968. 402p. illus. index. LC 70-364845.
History of art and architecture of the Carolingian period. Well illustrated; the descriptive notes to the plates contain bibliographical references to specialized literature. General bibliography (pp. 392-95). Good survey for the advanced student.

573   *Grodecki, Louis, and Florentine Mütherich. **Die Zeit der Ottonen und Salier**. Munich, Beck, 1973. 470p. illus. index. (Universum der Kunst, Band 20).
History of art and architecture in Europe during the Ottonian and early Romanesque period (tenth through middle of the eleventh century). Provides good selection of plates, plans, diagrams, a glossary-index, and a good comprehensive bibliography of books and periodical articles. German edition in the series "The Arts of Mankind." For the beginning and advanced student.

574   Henry, Françoise. **Irish Art During the Viking Invasions, 800-1020**. Ithaca, Cornell University Press, 1967. 236p. illus. index. LC 67-15300.
Concise history of the art and architecture in Ireland, 800-1020. Good selection of plates and maps. Bibliographical references in the footnotes to the text. Sequel to (562); together with (590), it is a standard history of Irish medieval art. For the beginning and advanced student.

575   Hinks, Roger P. **Carolingian Art**. Ann Arbor, Mich., University of Michigan Press, 1962. 226p. illus. index.
First published in 1935 (London, Sidgwick and Jackson). Survey of Carolingian art, excluding architecture. Adequate bibliographical references in the footnotes in the text, plus a general bibliography (pp. 215-18). Although it is very much out of date, the beginning student will find the section on form and structure of Carolingian art to be informative reading.

576   *Hubert, Jean, Jean Porcher, and W. F. Volbach. **The Carolingian Renaissance**. New York, Braziller, 1970. 381p. illus. (The Arts of Mankind, 13). LC 72-99513.
Illustrated handbook of Carolingian art and architecture. Provides chronological table, glossary-index, and good comprehensive bibliography (pp. 321-35) with its own index by subject. Collection of plans, elevations, reconstructions, and maps. Basic illustrated handbook for the beginning student.

577   Jantzen, Hans. **Ottonische Kunst**. Reinbek bei Hamburg, Rowohlt, 1959. 175p. illus. index.
First published in 1947 (Munich, Münchner Verlag). History of the art and architecture in the Ottonian period covering the development within and outside Germanic lands. Separate chapters on the various arts. Unclassified bibliography of major works (pp. 166-67). A standard history of Ottonian art for the advanced student.

578   *Kubach, Hans Erich, and Victor Elbern. **Das frühmittelalterliche Imperium.** Baden-Baden, Holle, 1968. 308p. illus. index. LC 79-378251.
Concise history of the art and architecture of the Carolingian and Ottonian periods. Treats the arts separately by type. Provides a chronological table, a map, and a good classified bibliography (pp. 280-93). An excellent history for the advanced student.

ROMANESQUE

579   *Aubert, Marcel. **L'art français à l'époque romane, architecture et sculpture.** Paris, Morancé, 1929-1951. 4v. illus. index.
Pictorial survey of Romanesque architecture and architectural sculpture in France. Volume one: Ile-de-France, Champagne, Alsace, Normandie, Vallée de la Loire; Volume two: Poitou, Saintonge, Angoumois, Périgord, Nivernais, Auvergne, Velay; Volume three: Bourgogne; and Volume four: Provence, Languedoc. A collection of plates with short introductions but with useful bibliographies at the end of each volume. Basic compendium of illustrations for the advanced student.

580   Aubert, Marcel, ed. **L'art roman en France** . . . Paris, Flammarion, 1961. 464p. illus. index. LC 62-32085.
History of art and architecture of the Romanesque period in France. Consists of essays by specialists on the various regional styles. Well illustrated, but no bibliography. A good survey of French Romanesque for the advanced student.

581   Baldass, Ludwig, Bruno Buchowiecki, and Wilhelm Mrazek. **Romanische Kunst in Österreich.** Vienna and Hanover, Forum, 1962. 119p. (text); 96p. (illus.).
History of Romanesque art and architecture in Austria from the early eleventh century through the twelfth century. Well illustrated and provided with a good bibliography (pp. 115-16) that lists books and periodical articles. For the beginning and advanced student.

582   Bonet, Blas. **El movimento románico en España. The Romanesque Movement in Spain** . . . Barcelona, Poligrafia, 1967. 307p. illus. LC 68-74678.
Survey history of art and architecture in Spain from the fifth through the twelfth centuries. Text in Spanish, French, English, and German. No bibliography. For the general reader and the beginning student.

583   Busch, Harald. **Germania Romanica; die hohe Kunst der romanischen Epoche in mittleren Europa.** Vienna, Schroll, 1963. 316p. illus. LC 65-66409.
Pictorial survey of art and architecture of the Romanesque period in the German-speaking countries, with emphasis on architecture. A brief introductory essay is followed by a selection of black and white plates, with notes to those plates. No bibliography. Selections from this work are found in (592).

584   Courtens, André. **Romanesque Art in Belgium: Architecture, Monumental Art.** Brussels, M. Vokaer, 1969. 111p. (text); 125p. (illus.). index. LC 75-572505.

Pictorial survey of architecture and monumental sculpture in Belgium of the Romanesque period. The short introductory essay is followed by a collection of black and white plates (chiefly of architecture), notes to the plates, and a classified bibliography of general works (pp. 104-106). For the general reader and the beginning student.

585   Crozet, René. **L'art roman.** Paris, Presses Universitaires de France, 1962. 186p. illus. index. LC 63-38107.

Survey history of art and architecture of the Romanesque period, with an emphasis on France. A brief chapter called "Universalité de l'art Roman," sketches the history of Romanesque art and architecture outside France. Bibliography (pp. 185-86) lists chiefly books in French. For the beginning student.

586   Decker, Hans. **Romanesque Art in Italy.** New York, Abrams, 1959. 82p. (text); 240p. (illus.). LC 59-5999.

Pictorial survey of the Romanesque art and architecture in Italy. Emphasis is on architecture and its decoration. Text discusses the material by region. Bibliography (p. 82) lists a few major works in all languages. Good collection of plates. Text is for the general reader and the beginning student; plates are useful to the advanced student as well.

587   Durliat, Marcel. **L'art roman en Espagne.** Paris, Braun, 1962. 86p. (text); 248p. (illus.). LC 64-46252.

Pictorial survey of the art and architecture of Romanesque Spain, with the emphasis on architecture. The short introductory essay is followed by a good selection of black and white plates (also with emphasis on architecture), notes to the plates, and a brief, unclassified bibliography (pp. 88-89). For the general reader and the beginning student.

588   *Franz, Heinrich G. **Spätromanik und Frühgotik.** Baden-Baden, Holle, 1969. 283p. illus. index. LC 75-452952.

Concise history of late Romanesque and early Gothic art and architecture. Good color plates with a modest supplement of black and white plates, plans, and diagrams, plus a good classified bibliography (pp. 245-68) of major books and periodical articles in all languages. For the beginning and advanced student. German edition in the series "The Art of the World."

589   Gantner, Joseph, and Marcel Pobé. **Romanesque Art in France.** London, Thames & Hudson, 1956. 80p. (text); 271p. (illus.). index.

Pictorial survey of Romanesque art and architecture in France. Chief emphasis is on architecture, with less on monumental sculpture and little on painting. Introductory essay, notes on the plates, and general bibliography (p. 78). For the general reader and the beginning student.

590   Henry, Françoise. **Irish Art in the Romanesque Period, 1020-1170**. 3rd rev.
        enl. ed. Ithaca, New York, Cornell University Press, 1970. 240p. illus.
        index. LC 76-82117.
Concise history of art and architecture in Ireland, 1020-1170. Good selection of
plates and maps. Bibliographical references in the footnotes to the text. Sequel to
(562 and 574); together they form a standard history of Irish medieval art. For
beginning and advanced students.

591   *Kubach, Hans E., and Peter Bloch. **L'art roman, de ses débuts à son
        apogée**. Paris, Michel, 1966. 297p. illus. index. LC 67-42768.
History of Romanesque art and architecture from the middle of the eleventh to the
middle of the twelfth century. Good selection of color plates, modest but well-
chosen supplement of black and white plates; liberally provided with plans and
diagrams. Also provides map and chronological table and an excellent classified
bibliography (pp. 245-68), which lists books and periodical articles in all languages.
French edition of the series "The Art of the World." An excellent history of
Romanesque art and architecture for the beginning and advanced student.

592   Künstler, Gustav, comp. **Romanesque Art in Europe**. Greenwich, Conn.,
        New York Graphic Society, 1969. 327p. illus. index. LC 69-18001.
Pictorial survey of the art and architecture of Romanesque Europe, consisting of a
selection of text and illustrations from a six-volume series published between 1955
and 1968 by Schroll Verlag of Vienna. These volumes, three of which have been
translated into English, are annotated separately in this bibliography (514, 583, 584,
586, 589, and 598). Short introductory essays, selection of black and white plates
(with emphasis on architecture), notes on the plates, and maps and plans; no
bibliography. For the general reader and the beginning student.

593   Lefrançois, Louis Pillon. **L'art roman en France: architecture, sculpture,
        peinture, arts mineurs**. Paris, Le Prat, 1943. 118p. illus.
Concise history of art and architecture in France during the Romanesque period.
No bibliography. For the beginning student.

594   Rey, Raymond. **L'art roman et ses origines**. Paris, Didier, 1945. 511p.
        illus. index.
History of Romanesque art and architecture in France. Traces its origin back to
Gallo-Roman and Germanic art. Bibliographical footnotes. A good survey of
Romanesque art and architecture in France for the advanced student.

595   Souchal, François. **Art of the Early Middle Ages**. New York, Abrams,
        1968. 263p. illus. index. LC 68-27428.
Brief survey of the art and architecture of the Romanesque period. A short introductory essay is followed by explanations of the plates. Provides chronological
tables and a brief bibliography (pp. 258-59). For the general reader and the
beginning student.

596   *Swarzenski, Hanns. **Monuments of Romanesque Art: The Art of Church Treasures in North-Western Europe.** 2nd ed. Chicago, University of Chicago Press, 1967. 102p. (text); 238p. (illus.). index.
Comprehensive illustrated handbook of manuscript painting, metalwork, bronze sculpture, ivory carving, and enamels from France, Germany, the Low Countries, and England dating from the ninth century through the middle of the thirteenth century. The introduction, which traces the history of these arts, is followed by detailed notes on the plates with thorough reference to specialized literature. The excellent plates form an invaluable corpus of early medieval minor arts. A standard handbook for the advanced student.

597   Timmers, J. J. M. **A Handbook of Romanesque Art.** London, Nelson, 1969. 240p. illus. index. LC 79-80800.
Concise handbook of Romanesque art and architecture in Italy, France, Germany, Spain, British Isles, Scandinavia, the Low Countries, and Eastern Europe. After an introduction that traces its origins, Romanesque art is divided into national groupings. Excellent maps, good selection of plates, and general, unclassified bibliography (pp. 234-35). A good handbook for beginning and advanced students.

598   Tuulse, Armin. **Scandinavia Romanica: Die hohe Kunst der romanischen Epoche in Dänemark, Norwegen, und Schweden.** Vienna, Schroll, 1968. 35p. (text); 96p. (illus.). LC 73-281685.
Pictorial survey of Romanesque sculpture and architecture in Denmark, Norway, and Sweden. Short introductory essay is followed by a collection of black and white plates, with notes; emphasis is on architecture. There are a few ground plans and elevations. Selections from this work are contained in (592). For the general reader and beginning student.

599   Zarnecki, George. **Romanesque Art.** New York, Universe, 1971. 196p. illus. index. LC 75-122322.
Concise history of the art and architecture of the Romanesque period. Well-chosen illustrations with informative captions. Bibliography of general works (pp. 190-92). A good history for beginning and advanced students.

GOTHIC

600   *Aubert, Marcel. **The Art of the High Gothic Era.** New York, Crown, 1965. 227p. illus. index. LC 64-24750.
"With the collaboration of J. A. Schmoll-gen. Eisenwerth and contributions by Hans H. Hofstätter." Concise history of art and architecture in Western Europe, 1220-1350. Provides maps, glossary, chronological tables, and good classified bibliography (pp. 196-207). A good survey history of the climax of Gothic art in France and its spread to the rest of Europe. For beginning and advanced students.

601   *Bialostocki, Jan. **Spätmittelalter und beginnende Neuzeit**. Berlin, Propyläen Verlag, 1972. 474p. (text); 468p. (illus.). index. (Propyläen Kunstgeschichte, Band 7). LC 72-373268.

Comprehensive illustrated handbook of Western European art and architecture of the fifteenth century. The introductory essay is followed by a body of excellent plates, essays by specialists on the development of the various arts, informative notes on the plates with additional plans and reconstructions, and valuable bibliographical references. Excellent, classified bibliography (pp. 430-52). A standard handbook for advanced students and scholars.

602   Busch, Harald. **Deutsche Gotik**. Vienna and Munich, Schroll, 1969. 124p. illus. LC 76-487048.

Pictorial survey of Gothic art and architecture in Germany. Emphasis is on architecture and its sculptural and painted decoration. Consists of brief introductory sketch followed by a good selection of plates with informative notes. No bibliography. Useful collection of plates for the beginning student.

603   Decker, Heinrich. **Gotik in Italien**. Vienna, Schroll, 1964. 308p. illus. LC 65-66821.

Illustrated survey of Gothic art and architecture in Italy. Introductory essay discusses the development of Gothic in the various regions of Italy, followed by a good collection of plates with emphasis on architecture and its decoration. No bibliography. Useful collection of plates for beginning and advanced students.

604   Deuchler, Florens. **Gothic Art**. New York, Universe, 1973. 184p. illus. index. LC 72-85081.

Concise history of Gothic art and architecture from the mid-twelfth century through the fifteenth century in Northern Europe. The treatment of the Italian development ends with the thirteenth century. Well-chosen illustrations, many plans and elevations, and a balanced bibliography of general works (pp. 178-80). A good survey history for beginning and advanced students.

605   *Fischer, Friedhelm W., and J. J. M. Timmers. **Spätgotik; zwischen Mystik und Reformation**. Baden-Baden, Holle, 1971. 283p. illus. index. LC 74-570646.

Concise and well-balanced history of the art and architecture of Germany, France, the Low Countries, and England during the fourteenth and fifteenth centuries. Provides a good selection of color plates, plans, and diagrams, a glossary of terms, and a classified bibliography of books in all languages (pp. 264-71). This work is part of the German edition of the series "The Art of the World," and may be translated in the near future. A good history of late Gothic art for the advanced student.

606   Harvey, John H. **The Gothic World, 1100-1600: A Survey of Architecture and Art**. New York, Harper & Row, 1969. 160p. illus. index. LC 69-12465.

Concise survey of art and architecture in Western Europe during the Gothic period. Sets the history of art within the general context of cultural history, with good chapters on the methods and techniques of the Gothic artists and architects. Chief attention is given to architecture. Brief classified bibliography (pp. 133-36) and further bibliography in the footnotes. Rather poor illustrations, but useful maps and plans. For the general reader and the beginning student.

607   Henderson, George D. S. **Gothic**. Harmondsworth, Penguin, 1967. 223p. illus. index. (Style and Civilization). LC 67-9741.
An exploration of the factors that brought about the Gothic style in Europe, with chapters on the Gothic artists, the relation of theology to form, the development of Gothic style, and art and mysticism. Short but helpfully annotated bibliography (pp. 217-19). For beginning and advanced students.

608   Hofstätter, Hans H. **Art of the Late Middle Ages**. New York, Abrams, 1968. 264p. illus. index. LC 68-18131.
Brief survey of the art and architecture of the thirteenth through the mid-sixteenth centuries. Provides chronological tables of painting, sculpture, and architecture and a brief general bibliography (p. 253). For the general reader and the beginning student.

609   Lambert, Elie. **L'art gothique en Espagne**. Paris, Laurens, 1931. 314p. illus. index.
Concise history of art and architecture in Spain during the twelfth and thirteenth centuries. Good selection of plates, plans, and diagrams. Annotated bibliography (pp. 291-98). Standard history of Spanish Gothic art for beginning and advanced students.

610   Martindale, Andrew. **Gothic Art**. New York, Praeger, 1967. 287p. illus. index. LC 67-28194.
Concise history of Gothic art and architecture from the twelfth to the fifteenth century. Includes Italian art and architecture of the fourteenth century. Provides a chronological table, a glossary of terms, and a select bibliography (pp. 272-73). For the general reader and the beginning student.

611   Réau, Louis. **L'art gothique en France: architecture, sculpture, peinture, arts appliqués**. Rev. and exp. ed. Paris, Le Prat, 1968. 170p. illus. LC 79-373657.
Concise history of art and architecture in France during the Gothic period. Provides a one-page glossary of terms and brief bibliography (p. 170). For the beginning student.

612   Salet, François. **L'art gothique**. Paris, Presses Universitaires de France, 1963. 186p. illus. LC 66-46706.
Concise history of gothic art and architecture, chiefly in France, from 1125 to 1540. Bibliography (pp. 185-86) chiefly lists works in French. For the beginning student.

613   *Simson, Otto von. **Das Mittelalter II: Das Hohe Mittelalter.** Berlin,
       Propyläen, 1972. 475p. (text); 472p. (illus.). index. (Propyläen
       Kunstgeschichte, Band 6).
Comprehensive illustrated handbook of art and architecture in Western Europe from
the mid-twelfth century through the fourteenth century. Introductory essay by
von Simson is followed by a corpus of excellent plates, essays by specialists on the
development of the various arts in France, Germany, England, and Italy, informative
notes on the plates with valuable bibliographical references, and an excellent comprehensive and classified bibliography (pp. 437-56). A standard handbook for the
advanced student and scholar.

614   Van de Walle, A. J. L. **Gothic Art in Belgium.** Brussels, M. Vokaer, n.d.
       239p. illus. index.
Pictorial survey of architecture and monumental sculpture from the Gothic period
in Belgium. Includes examples from the thirteenth through the fifteenth centuries.
Introductory essay is concerned chiefly with the history of architecture in Belgium
during the Gothic period. Plates that follow include works of sculpture as well as
architecture. Brief, unclassified bibliography (pp. 77-78). For the general reader
and the beginning student; however, the introductory essay is sufficiently detailed
to be of value to the advanced student of medieval architecture.

III. RENAISSANCE (INCLUDING MANNERISM)

GENERAL WORKS

615   Batterberry, Michael, adapter. **Art of the Early Renaissance.** New York,
       McGraw-Hill, [c.1968]. 191p. illus. index. LC 79-115138.
Pictorial survey of the art and architecture of Northern and Southern Europe from
Giotto to Botticelli and Van Eyck to Bosch. No bibliography. For the general
reader.

616   Battisti, Eugenio. **Rinascimento e Baròcco.** Turin, Einaudi, 1960. 328p.
       illus. LC 62-42100.
History of European art and architecture from the early fourteenth century through
the middle of the eighteenth century. Emphasis is on Italian developments. Extensive bibliographical footnotes. A standard Italian history of Renaissance and baroque
art and architecture. For the advanced student.

617   *Baumgart, Fritz-Erwin. **Renaissance und Kunst des Manierismus.**
       Cologne, DuMont Schauberg, 1963. 232p. illus. index. LC 64-43125.
History and investigation of the meaning of the High Renaissance and Mannerism
in Western Europe. Provides a most useful collection of excerpts (translated into

German) from documents relating to the Renaissance and Mannerism from Serlio
to Erwin Panofsky. Bibliography (pp. 217-22) lists major works on the period in
chronological order. A scholarly definition and history of the High Renaissance
and Mannerism for the advanced student.

618   Gilbert, Creighton. **History of Renaissance Art: Painting, Sculpture,
       Architecture throughout Europe**. New York, Abrams, 1973. 460p. illus.
       index. LC 72-4791.
Concise history of art and architecture of the Renaissance in Western Europe.
Emphasis is on painting, beginning with Cimabue and ending with the late sixteenth
century. Chronological chart of artists and classified bibliography of works in
English (pp. 423-36). Survey history for the beginning and advanced student.

619   Huyghe, René, ed. **Larousse Encyclopedia of Renaissance and Baroque
       Art**. New York, Prometheus, 1964. 444p. illus. index. LC 64-13787.
Concise history composed of brief essays by specialists on the art and architecture
of Western Europe from the end of the Middle Ages through the baroque (actually
nineteenth century). No bibliography. For the general reader and the beginning
student.

620   *Kaufmann, Georg. **Die Kunst des 16. Jahrhunderts**. Berlin, Propyläen,
       1970. 468p. (text); 408p. (illus.). index. (Propyläen Kunstgeschichte,
       Band 8). LC 75-551182.
Comprehensive illustrated handbook of the art and architecture of Europe in the
sixteenth century. The introductory essay by Kauffmann is followed by a body of
excellent plates, essays by a number of specialists on the development of the
various arts, informative notes to the plates (with plans and diagrams), and valuable
references to specialized literature. Excellent classified bibliography of books and
periodical articles (pp. 405-441). Chronological table provides synopsis of events
in political history, the various arts, philosophy, literature, and cultural history. A
standard handbook for the advanced student and scholar.

621   Martindale, Andrew. **Man and the Renaissance**. New York, McGraw-Hill,
       1966. 186p. illus. index. LC 66-15837.
Art historical survey of the Renaissance in Italy and Northern Europe in a cultural
context. Treats architecture, sculpture, and painting. Enhanced by maps, a chronological table, brief biographical glossary and a general reading list (p. 167). For the
general reader and beginning student.

622   Ruskin, Ariane. **Art of the High Renaissance**. New York, McGraw-Hill,
       1968. 189p. illus. index. LC 76-110961.
Pictorial survey of art and architecture from Leonardo to El Greco. Covers both
Northern and Southern Europe. No bibliography. For the general reader.

623   Wolf, Robert E., and Ronald Millen. **Renaissance and Mannerist Art**. New
       York, Abrams, 1968. 263p. illus. index. LC 68-18132.

Concise survey of the art and architecture in Italy, Spain, Portugal, France, the Low Countries, Germany, and England during the fifteenth and sixteenth centuries. Well illustrated and with a brief, classified bibliography of books in English and foreign languages (pp. 258-60). For the general reader and the beginning student.

624   Wundram, Manfred. **Art of the Renaissance.** New York, Universe, 1972. 196p. illus. LC 73-175861.

Concise history of art and architecture in all of Western Europe during the fifteenth and sixteenth centuries. Very good selection of plates with informative captions, liberally provided with plans and diagrams. Bibliography (pp. 190-92) lists major books in all languages. Concise but balanced and factual text with emphasis on the development of style in Renaissance art and architecture. A very good survey for the general reader and the beginning student.

MANNERISM

625   Hauser, Arnold. **Mannerism: The Crisis of the Renaissance and the Origin of Modern Art.** New York, Knopf, 1965. 2v. illus. index.

Volume one, text; Volume two, plates. This scholarly study of the art and architecture of mannerism provides a good historical survey of the style and an investigation of the concept of mannerism and its relationship to contemporary culture. No separate bibliography, but the extensive footnotes provide thorough reference to literature on mannerism. For the advanced student and the scholar.

626   Shearman, John K. G. **Mannerism.** Harmondsworth, Penguin, 1967. 216p. illus. index. LC 67-98470.

Handbook of the art and architecture of mannerism in both Northern and Southern Europe. Not a history of mannerist art but an investigation of the meaning of the style in relationship to other arts and cultural developments. Chapter five gives an excellent account of the term mannerism in art history. A brief but useful bibliography of books and periodical articles in all languages (pp. 207-208). Further literature is noted in the catalog of illustrations. For beginning and advanced students; this is one of the best analyses of the mannerist style in English.

627   *Würtenberger, Franzsepp. **Mannerism, the European Style of the Sixteenth Century.** New York, Holt, Rinehart and Winston, 1963. 246p. illus. index. LC 63-18066.

Comprehensive history of the art and architecture of mannerism in Western Europe. Treats art, architecture, and the minor arts. Excellent illustrations and a good classified bibliography (pp. 230-38), which lists books and periodical articles in all languages. A standard history and study of mannerism for beginning and advanced students.

ITALIAN RENAISSANCE

628   *Battisti, Eugenio. **Hochrenaissance und Manierismus**. Baden-Baden, Holle, 1970. 255p. illus. index. LC 79-508918.
Concise history of Italian art and architecture of the High Renaissance and mannerism. Good selection of color plates, modest supplement of black and white illustrations. Bibliography (pp. 214-44) provides a good classified list of books and periodical articles in all languages. German edition of the series "Art of the World." A good survey of High Renaissance and mannerist art and architecture for the beginning and advanced student.

629   *Chastel, André. **The Flowering of the Italian Renaissance**. New York, Odyssey Press, 1965. 384p. illus. index. (The Arts of Mankind, 7). LC 65-27309.
History of art and architecture in Italy from circa 1460 to 1530 with a section on the spread of Italian Renaissance style to the rest of Europe. Provides maps and chronological tables; the bibliography of books in all languages (pp. 359-67) has its own subject index. With its companion volume (630), it forms a useful pictorial handbook to Italian Renaissance art and architecture for the advanced student. The somewhat confused arrangement by schools, types, etc., will frustrate the beginning student, who would otherwise benefit most from the text.

630   *Chastel, André. **Studios and Styles of the Italian Renaissance**. New York, Odyssey Press, 1966. 417p. illus. index. (The Arts of Mankind, 8). LC 66-18997.
Survey history of the art and architecture of the fifteenth century in Italy arranged by type, with an emphasis on workshops and local schools. Provides a glossary-index that treats artists, terms, and places; there are also maps and a good bibliography of books in all languages (pp. 387-98). See (629).

631   Decker, Heinrich. **The Renaissance in Italy**. New York, Viking, 1969. 338p. illus. index. LC 68-23210.
Pictorial survey of the art and architecture of Italy in the fifteenth and sixteenth centuries. After a short introductory essay the plates are arranged by geographical region, with informative notes. No bibliography. For the general reader and the beginning student.

632   Dvořák, Max. **Geschichte der italienischen Kunst im Zeitalter der Renaissance** . . . Munich, Piper, 1927-28. 2v. illus. index.
Comprehensive and scholarly history of art and architecture in Italy during the fourteenth, fifteenth, and sixteenth centuries. Well illustrated with plates and plans. Volume one covers the fourteenth and fifteenth centuries, Volume two the sixteenth century. Bibliography in the footnotes. An old but classic history of Italian Renaissance art by one of the greatest specialists. For the advanced student.

633   Eglinski, Edmund. **The Art of the Italian Renaissance**. Dubuque, Iowa,
       W. C. Brown, 1968. 104p. illus. index. LC 68-14576.
Brief survey of the art and architecture of Italy during the fifteenth and sixteenth
centuries. Short bibliography of books in English (pp. 100-102). For the
beginning student.

634   *Hartt, Frederick. **History of Italian Renaissance Art: Painting, Sculpture
       and Architecture**. New York, Abrams, 1969. 636p. illus. index. LC
       74-95193.
Comprehensive history of art and architecture in Italy from the late twelfth to the
late sixteenth century. Excellent choice of illustrations, plans, and diagrams, very
useful glossary of terms and subjects, chronological chart of artists and monuments, and classified bibliography of works in English (pp. 608-613). A standard
history of Italian Renaissance art and architecture for beginning and advanced
students.

635   *Heydenreich, Ludwig H. **Italie, 1400-1460: Éclosion de la Renaissance**.
       Paris, Gallimard, 1972. 452p. illus. index.
History of art and architecture in Italy from 1400 to 1460. Provides a good selection of plates, plans, and diagrams, a glossary-index, and a good comprehensive
bibliography of books and periodical articles. French edition in the series "The
Arts of Mankind." A good survey history of early quattrocento art and architecture for beginning and advanced students.

636   Keller, Harald. **The Renaissance in Italy: Painting, Sculpture, Architecture**.
       New York, Abrams, 1969. 394p. illus. index. LC 69-12485.
History of art and architecture in Italy from the early fourteenth century through
mannerism. Good selection of black and white and color plates, plans, and diagrams,
and a balanced, classified bibliography (pp. 375-79). An excellent history for
beginning and advanced students.

637   Levey, Michael. **Early Renaissance**. Harmondsworth, Penguin, 1967. 224p.
       illus. index. LC 68-88043.
History and analytical study of Italian art and architecture of the fifteenth century.
Emphasis is on the idea of the Renaissance and the relationship of the fine arts to
the general culture. Provides a good annotated bibliography (pp. 217-19) of books
in English. For beginning and advanced students.

638   Murray, Linda. **The High Renaissance**. New York, Praeger, 1967. 213p.
       illus. index. LC 67-18404.
Concise survey of the art and architecture of Italy in the first three decades of the
sixteenth century. Selected bibliography of books in English (pp. 195-97). For
the general reader and the beginning student.

639   Murray, Linda. **The Late Renaissance and Mannerism**. New York,
       Praeger, 1967. 215p. illus. index. LC 67-25566.

Concise survey of the art and architecture of Western Europe from circa 1530 to 1580. Short bibliography (pp. 200-202) of books in English. For the general reader and the beginning student.

640   Murray, Peter, and Linda Murray. **The Art of the Renaissance.** New York, Praeger, 1963. 286p. illus. index. LC 63-18834.
Survey history of the art and architecture of Western Europe of the fifteenth century. Good selection of illustrations and readable text, but no bibliography. For the general reader and the beginning student.

641   Paatz, Walter. **Die Kunst der Renaissance in Italien.** 3rd ed. Stuttgart, Urban, 1961. 240p. illus.
Concise history-handbook of art and architecture in Italy from the beginning of the fifteenth century until 1530. Treats the various arts separately. Excellent introductory chapters on the concept and definition of the Renaissance. Thorough bibliographical references in the footnotes of the text. A good survey handbook for the advanced student.

642   Smart, Alastair. **The Renaissance and Mannerism in Italy.** New York, Harcourt Brace Jovanovich, 1971. 252p. illus. index. LC 76-113711.
Survey of the art and architecture of Italy from the early fifteenth to the late sixteenth century. Emphasis is on painting and sculpture, although architecture is treated. Bibliography (pp. 245-46) lists only books in English. For the general reader and the beginning student.

643   *White, John. **Art and Architecture in Italy: 1250 to 1400.** Baltimore, Penguin, 1966. 449p. illus. index. (Pelican History of Art, Z28). LC 67-5664.
Comprehensive history of art and architecture in Italy from 1250 to 1400. Good selection of plates, plans, and diagrams; a good, classified bibliography (pp. 419-27) of books in English and foreign languages, with additional references to specialized literature in the notes to the text. A standard history for advanced students and scholars.

644   Wölfflin, Heinrich. **Classic Art, an Introduction to the Italian Renaissance.** 2nd ed. New York, Phaidon, 1953. 297p. illus. index.
History of painting and sculpture in Italy during the period of the High Renaissance. A preliminary survey outlines the development of Italian art during the fifteenth century; this is followed by a detailed analysis of the artistic development of Leonardo, Michelangelo, Raphael, Fra Bartolommeo and Andrea del Sarto. The work concludes with a formalistic investigation of the style of Italian Renaissance art. Bibliographical footnotes. A classic of art historical analysis, more important for its highly influential methodology than for its history of Italian Renaissance art. For the general reader, the beginning student, and the advanced student.

NORTHERN RENAISSANCE

General Works

645   *Benesch, Otto. **The Art of the Renaissance in Northern Europe**. 2nd ed. New York and London, Phaidon, 1965. 195p. illus. index.
History of art (exclusive of architecture) of Germany, France, and the Low Countries during the sixteenth century, with an emphasis on the interrelationship between the visual arts and the general intellectual climate of the times. Treats mannerist styles as well as Renaissance. Thorough bibliography of books and periodical articles in the notes to the text (pp. 169-85). A basic study for the advanced student.

646   *Osten, Gert von der, and Horst Vey. **Painting and Sculpture in Germany and the Netherlands: 1500 to 1600**. Baltimore, Penguin, 1969. 403p. illus. index. (Pelican History of Art, Z31). LC 73-8246.
Comprehensive history of painting and sculpture in Germany and the Netherlands in the sixteenth century. Good selection of plates; an unclassified bibliography in the form of a list of abbreviations (pp. 375-78) is supplemented by reference to specific literature in the notes to the text. A standard history for the advanced student and the scholar.

647   Smart, Alastair. **The Renaissance and Mannerism outside Italy**. New York, Harcourt Brace Jovanovich, 1972. 224p. illus. index. LC 70-165326.
Survey of art and architecture in France, Spain, the Low Countries, Portugal, and Germany from the early fifteenth century to the end of the sixteenth century. Emphasis is on painting and sculpture. Bibliography (pp. 218-20) is restricted to books in English. For the general reader and the beginning student.

648   Stokstad, Marilyn J. **Renaissance Art outside Italy**. Dubuque, Iowa, W. C. Brown, 1968. 113p. illus. index. LC 68-14577.
Survey of art and architecture in Spain, France, Germany, and the Low Countries during the Renaissance. Brief bibliography (pp. 107-108) lists major books in English. Designed as an inexpensive text for beginning students.

France

649   *Blunt, Anthony. **Art and Architecture in France: 1500-1700**. 3rd ed. Baltimore, Penguin, 1970. 315p. illus. index. (Pelican History of Art, Z4).
Comprehensive history of art and architecture in France during the sixteenth and seventeenth centuries. Good selection of plates, plans, and diagrams. Bibliography (pp. 289-94), with further, more specialized literature mentioned in the extensive footnotes. A standard history for beginning and advanced students.

650   Du Columbier, Pierre. **L'art de la renaissance en France.** 2nd ed. Paris,
       Le Prat, 1950. 133p. illus.
Brief survey of the art and architecture in France during the late fifteenth and
sixteenth centuries. Text arranged by media. No bibliography. For the general
reader and the beginning student.

651   Gébelin, François. **Le style renaissance en France.** Paris, Larousse, 1942.
       129p. illus.
Brief history of art and architecture in France during the sixteenth century. Brief
bibliography (pp. 126-29) and an appendix of short biographies of artists. For
beginning and advanced students.

652   Weese, Arthur. **Skulptur und Malerei in Frankreich vom 15. bis 17.**
       Jahrhundert. Berlin, Athenaion, 1927. 220p. illus. index.
Comprehensive history of sculpture and painting in France from the early fifteenth
through the seventeenth centuries. Some bibliographical references in the footnotes. For the advanced student.

Germany and Austria

653   Baldass, Peter von, Rudolf Feuchtmüller, and Wilhelm Mrazek.
       Renaissance in Österreich. Vienna and Hanover, Forum, 1966. 11p. (text);
       96p. (illus.). index. LC 67-77758.
History of art and architecture in Austria during the sixteenth century. Chapters
treat the major media of architecture, painting, and sculpture, as well as the minor
arts. Well illustrated. Provides a good bibliography (pp. 107-109) that lists books
and periodical articles. For beginning and advanced students.

654   Jahn, Johannes. **Deutsche Renaissance: Architektur, Plastik, Malerei,**
       Graphik, Kunsthandwerk. Vienna and Munich, Schroll, 1969. 50p. (text);
       158p. (illus.). LC 70-471461.
Pictorial survey of the art and architecture of the Renaissance in Germany, Austria,
and Switzerland. Short essays on the development of the various arts are followed
by a collection of good plates and descriptive notes. No bibliography. For the
general reader and the beginning student.

IV. BAROQUE AND ROCOCO

GENERAL WORKS

655   Andersen, Liselotte. **Baroque and Rococo Art.** New York, Abrams,
       1969. 264p. illus. index. LC 79-75041.

A survey history of painting, sculpture, architecture, and the decorative and minor arts of the baroque and rococo in Northern and Southern Europe. Includes chronological tables and a general bibliography (pp. 258-59). A good history for the general reader and the beginning student.

656   Bazin, Germain. **Baroque and Rococo.**New York, Praeger, 1964. 288p. illus. index. LC 64-22488.

Survey history of the art and architecture of the seventeenth and eighteenth centuries in Italy, Spain, Portugal, France, the Low Countries, Germany, Austria, Scandinavia, Great Britain, and Eastern Europe. Brief but annotated bibliography of books in all languages (pp. 273-75). A good survey for the general reader and the beginning student.

657   Held, Julius S., and Donald Posner. **17th and 18th Century Art: Baroque Painting, Sculpture, Architecture.** New York, Abrams, 1971. 439p. illus. index. LC 79-127417.

History of art and architecture in Italy, France, Spain, Portugal, the Low Countries, Germany, Austria, and England during the seventeenth and eighteenth centuries. Provides a chronological chart of artists and a brief selected bibliography of books chiefly in English (pp. 424-27). Reference to specialized literature is made in the notes to the text. An excellent history for beginning and advanced students.

658   *Hubala, Erich. **Die Kunst des 17. Jahrhunderts.** Berlin, Propyläen, 1970. 387p. (text); 408p. (illus.). (Propyläen Kunstgeschichte, Band 9). LC 79-518135.

Comprehensive illustrated handbook of the art and architecture of Europe in the seventeenth century. Introductory essay is followed by an excellent corpus of illustrations, specialists' commentaries on the development of the various arts, very informative notes to the plates (with plans, diagrams, and excellent bibliographies of specialized literature). Provides a very good, classified bibliography (pp. 347-58) of books and periodical articles in all languages. A standard handbook for the advanced student and the scholar.

659   *Keller, Harald. **Die Kunst des 18. Jahrhunderts.** Berlin, Propyläen, 1971. 479p. (text); 436p. (illus.). index. (Propyläen Kunstgeschichte, Band 10).

Comprehensive, illustrated handbook of the art and architecture of Europe and the New World in the eighteenth century. Introductory essay by Keller is followed by an excellent corpus of plates, short commentaries on the evolution of the arts in various countries, informative notes to the plates (with plans, diagrams, and very valuable bibliographies of specialized literature). An excellent, comprehensive, classified bibliography of books and periodical articles in all languages (pp. 446-56). A standard handbook for the advanced student and the scholar.

660   Kimball, S. Fiske. **The Creation of the Rococo.** New York, Norton, 1964. 242p. illus. index. Reprint of 1943 edition.

Scholarly history of rococo architecture and architectural decoration. Bibliographical references in the extensive footnotes; the numerous illustrations are poorly reproduced in this reprint. A standard work on rococo architectural decoration for the advanced student.

661   Kitson, Michael. **The Age of the Baroque.** New York and Toronto, McGraw-Hill, 1966. 175p. illus. index. LC 65-21591.
Pictorial survey of the architecture, painting, sculpture, and decorative and minor arts in all of Europe in the seventeenth and eighteenth centuries. Includes maps, chronological tables, and short biographical notes on baroque artists and architects. For the general reader.

662   Pignatti, Terisio. **The Age of Rococo.** London, Hamlyn, 1969. 157p. illus.
Pictorial survey of art and architecture in Western Europe during the eighteenth century. Emphasis on the Italian scene. All illustrations in color. No bibliography. For the general reader.

663   Ruskin, Ariane. **17th and 18th Century Art.** New York, McGraw-Hill, 1969. 191p. illus. index. LC 69-17190.
Pictorial survey of the art and architecture in Italy, Spain, France, the Netherlands, and Germany during the seventeenth and eighteenth centuries. All illustrations are in color. No plans for the architectural examples. No bibliography. For the general reader.

664   Soehner, Halldor, and Arno Schönberger. **The Rococo Age, Art and Civilization of the Eighteenth Century.** New York, McGraw-Hill, 1960. 394p. illus. index. LC 60-11310.
Survey of the art of Europe (exclusive of architecture) during the eighteenth century, with emphasis on the general cultural context. Informative notes to the plates, but no bibliography. For the general reader and the beginning student.

665   Stinson, Robert E. **Seventeenth and Eighteenth Century Art: An Introduction to Baroque and Rococo Art in Europe from A.D. 1600 to A.D. 1800.** Dubuque, Iowa, W. C. Brown, 1969. 149p. illus. LC 68-14580.
Brief survey of the art and architecture of Western Europe from 1600 to 1800. Brief bibliography of books in English (pp. 143-44). For the beginning student.

666   Tapie, Victor Lucien. **The Age of Grandeur: Baroque Art and Architecture** . . . New York, Praeger, 1961. 305p. illus. index. LC 61-17028.
Survey of the art and architecture of the seventeenth century in Italy, Spain, Portugal, France, Germany and Austria, the Low Countries, Eastern Europe, and the New World colonies. Classified bibliography (pp. 285-97) of books in all languages; further literature is referred to in the notes to the text. For the general reader and the beginning student.

FRANCE

667   Hildebrandt, Edmund. **Malerei und Plastik des 18. Jahrhunderts in Frankreich.** Berlin, Athenaion, 1924. 212p. illus. index.
Comprehensive history of painting and sculpture in France during the eighteenth century. Extensive bibliographies of books and periodical articles given at the end of the sections. An old but standard treatment of the subject for the advanced student.

668   *Kalnein, Wend Graf, and Michael Levey. **Art and Architecture of the Eighteenth Century in France.** Harmondsworth, Penguin, 1972. 443p. illus. index. (Pelican History of Art).
Comprehensive history of art and architecture in France during the eighteenth century. Part one, dealing with painting and sculpture, is by Levey; Part two, on architecture, is by Graf Kalnein. Does not cover the minor arts. Good selection of plates. Bibliography (pp. 405-417) lists books in all languages. Further reference to more specialized literature is made in the extensive footnotes. A standard history of French eighteenth century art and architecture for the advanced student.

669   Mauricheau-Beaupré, Charles. **L'art au XVIIe siècle en France.** Paris, Le Prat, 1946-47. 2v. illus.
Illustrated survey history of art and architecture in France during the seventeenth century. No bibliography. For the beginning and advanced student.

GERMANY AND AUSTRIA

670   Grimschitz, Bruno, Wilhelm Mrazek, and Ruppert Feuchtmüller. **Barock in Österreich.** Vienna and Hanover, Forum, 1960. 95p. (text); 92p. (plates). index.
History of art and architecture in Austria during the seventeenth and eighteenth centuries. Consists of essays on developments in the major media. No bibliography. Well illustrated. A good history of Austrian baroque for the beginning and advanced student.

671   *Hempel, Eberhard. **Baroque Art and Architecture in Central Europe.** Baltimore, Penguin, 1965. 370p. illus. index. (Pelican History of Art, Z22).
Comprehensive and scholarly history of art and architecture in Germany, Austria, Switzerland, Hungary, Czechoslovakia, and Poland. Painting and sculpture are treated from the early seventeenth through the eighteenth century, architecture from the beginning of the sixteenth century through the eighteenth century. Excellent selection of plates, maps, plans, and diagrams. Good, well-classified bibliography of books and periodical articles in all languages (pp. 335-43). Further reference to specialized literature in the notes to the text. A standard history for the advanced student and the scholar.

ITALY

672   Golzio, Vincenzo. **Seicento e Settecento**. 3rd ed. Turin, Unione Torinese, 1968. 2v. illus. index. (Storia dell'Arte Classica e Italiana, 4). LC 75-522328.
Comprehensive history of art and architecture in Italy during the seventeenth and eighteenth centuries. Well illustrated with good, selected bibliography of books (pp. 919-26). A standard and scholarly history for the advanced student.

673   Griseri, Andreina. **Le metamorfosi del barocco**. Turin, Einaudi, 1967. 383p. illus. index.
History of baroque art and architecture in Italy from its background in late mannerism to the mid-eighteenth century. Extensive bibliography in the footnotes. Good selection of plates. A standard history of the Italian baroque for the advanced student.

674   Lees-Milne, James. **Baroque in Italy**. London, Batsford, 1959. 216p. illus. LC 60-20309.
Concise history of art and architecture in Italy from mannerism through the late baroque (circa 1775). Emphasis is on architecture and its decoration. Bibliography (pp. 205-209) lists books and periodical articles in all languages. For the general reader and the beginning student.

675   *Wittkower, Rudolf. **Art and Architecture in Italy: 1600 to 1750**. 3rd rev. ed. Harmondsworth, Penguin, 1973. 485p. illus. index. (Pelican History of Art, Z16).
Comprehensive history of art and architecture in Italy, 1600 to 1750. Good selection of plates, plans, and diagrams, good classified bibliography (pp. 415-52), and further reference to specialized literature in extensive footnotes. A standard work for the advanced student and the scholar.

SPAIN AND PORTUGAL

676   Lees-Milne, James. **Baroque in Spain and Portugal, and Its Antecedents**. London, Batsford, 1960. 224p. illus. index. LC 61-1109.
Pictorial survey of architecture and art of the baroque in Spain and Portugal, with emphasis on architecture and its decoration. For the general reader and the beginning student.

677   Weisbach, Werner. **Spanish Baroque Art**. Cambridge, England, Cambridge University Press, 1941. 65p. illus.
Series of three lectures on Spanish baroque architecture, painting, and sculpture. Concentrates on the chief artistic personalities. No bibliography. A survey for the general reader and the beginning student.

EASTERN EUROPE

678 Angyal, Endre. **Die slawische Barokwelt**. Leipzig, Seemann, 1961. 321p. illus. LC 61-37650.
Concise history of art and architecture of the baroque in the Slavic countries. Good chapter treating the research on Slavic baroque. Bibliographical footnotes. For beginning and advanced students.

V. MODERN (19th AND 20th CENTURIES)

GENERAL WORKS

679 *Arnason, H. H. **History of Modern Art: Painting, Sculpture, Architecture**. Englewood Cliffs, N.J., Prentice-Hall; New York, Abrams, 1968. 663p. illus. index. LC 68-26863.
Comprehensive history of art and architecture in Europe and America from the impressionists through the many movements of the 1960s. Arranged according to movements, the text centers on important artists, using their lives and art as distillations of the movements and periods covered. Copiously illustrated with black and white and color illustrations. Good classified bibliography of books (pp. 631-43). A standard history for beginning and advanced students.

680 Bowness, Alan. **Modern European Art**. New York, Harcourt Brace Jovanovich, 1972. 224p. illus. index. LC 77-183243.
Concise history of art in Europe from Manet to the inheritors of abstract expressionism. Emphasis is on painting; arrangement is by movements. Separate chapters are devoted to modern European sculpture and architecture. Illustrated in black and white, with some color plates. Classified bibliography of books (pp. 217-20). A good survey for the general reader and the beginning student.

681 *Brizio, Anna M. **Ottocento; Novecento**. Turin, Unione Torinese, 1939. 571p. illus. index. (Storia Universale dell'Arte, vol. 6).
Comprehensive history of art and architecture in the West from Neoclassicism to circa 1930. Bibliography (pp. 549-58) lists books and periodical articles in all languages. A standard Italian history of nineteenth century art and architecture. Useful to the advanced student.

682 Canaday, John. **Mainstreams of Modern Art**. New York, Holt, Rinehart and Winston, 1959. 576p. illus. index. LC 59-8693.
Comprehensive history of Western painting, graphics, and sculpture from David

to surrealism. An appendix gives a short history of modern architecture. No bibliography. A good survey history for the general reader and the beginning student.

683　Evers, Hans Gerhard. **The Art of the Modern Age**. New York, Crown, 1970. 270p. illus. index. LC 72-125038. British title: **The Modern Age: Historicism and Functionalism** (1970).
Concise history of painting, sculpture, and architecture in Europe and America from the late nineteenth century to the mid-twentieth century. Chronological table of political history, art, literature, and science and technology, but no bibliography. A good balanced survey for beginning and advanced students.

684　Galloway, John C. **Modern Art: The Nineteenth and Twentieth Centuries**. Dubuque, Iowa, W. C. Brown, 1967. 149p. illus. index. LC 67-22713.
Survey of painting and sculpture in Europe and America during the nineteenth and twentieth centuries (only twentieth century American art is covered). Bibliography (pp. 131-39) lists major books and periodical articles chiefly in English. For the beginning student.

685　Hamilton, George H. **19th and 20th Century Art: Painting, Sculpture, Architecture**. New York, Abrams, 1970. 583p. illus. index. LC 70-100401.
Comprehensive history of art and architecture in Europe and America during the nineteenth and twentieth centuries. Good selection of plates, diagrams, and plans. Bibliography (pp. 459-64) lists books in English. A good survey history for the beginning student.

686　*Hamilton, George H. **Painting and Sculpture in Europe, 1880 to 1940**. Baltimore, Penguin, 1967. 443p. illus. index. (Pelican History of Art, Z29).
Comprehensive and scholarly history of painting and sculpture in Europe from 1880 to 1940. Excellent choice of illustrations. Provides a good, classified bibliography (pp. 391-419) that lists books in all languages. Further bibliographical references are to be found in the extensive footnotes. A standard history for the advanced student.

687　Hildebrandt, Hans. **Die Kunst des 19. und 20. Jahrhunderts**. Berlin, Athenaion, 1924. 460p. illus. index.
Comprehensive history of art and architecture in Europe from 1800 to 1920. The scholarly text is amplified by a large selection of plates and plans, but there is no bibliography. A volume in the series "Handbuch der Kunstwissenschaft." An older but classic history of nineteenth century and early twentieth century art and architecture. For the advanced student.

688　Huyghe, René, ed. **Larousse Encyclopedia of Modern Art, from 1800 to the Present Day**. New York, Prometheus, 1965. 444p. illus. index. LC 65-19759.
Not a true encyclopedia, but a general survey of modern painting, sculpture, and architecture amplified by summary discussions of parallel developments in history,

literature, and music. Written by a variety of specialists, the sections cover a range of subjects from classicism and romanticism to action painting and abstract expressionism. Includes a large section of "Later Eastern Arts" (oriental art from 1200 onward), which treats periods that are judged to have been influential on modern art. For the general reader.

689   Huyghe, René, and Jean Rudel, eds. **L'art et le monde moderne.** Paris, Larousse, 1969-70. 2v. illus. index.

Comprehensive history of modern art and architecture from 1880 to the present. Includes the minor arts and the cinema. Consists of a group of essays by French specialists. Well illustrated and provided with a useful chronological table, but no bibliography. A useful illustrated survey for the beginning and advanced student.

690   Lynton, Norbert. **The Modern World.** New York, McGraw-Hill, 1965. 175p. illus. index. LC 65-21593.

The text of this pictorial survey covers painting, sculpture, and architecture from the first half of the nineteenth century to just after 1940. Includes a glossary of terms, a chronological table (inside the covers), and a general bibliography (pp. 170-71). For the general reader.

691   Meier-Graefe, Julius. **Entwicklungsgeschichte der modernen Kunst.** 3rd ed. Munich, Piper, 1966. 2v. illus. index.

Comprehensive history of modern European art, chiefly painting, from neo-classicism through Les Fauves and German expressionists. No bibliography. A recent edition of an old but classic study of the development of modern art. For the advanced student.

692   Zervos, Christian. **Histoire de l'art contemporain.** Paris, Cahiers d'Art, 1938. 498p. illus.

Comprehensive history of modern European painting and sculpture from Les Fauves to the Dadaists. Numerous but poorly reproduced illustrations and no bibliography. An older history of European post-impressionist art. For beginning and advanced students.

AUSTRIA

693   Feuchtmüller, Ruppert, and Wilhelm Mrazek. **Kunst in Österreich, 1860-1918.** Vienna and Hanover, Forum, 1964. 130p. (text); 100p. (plates). index.

History of art and architecture in Austria from 1860 to 1918. Consists of essays on the development of various media. Well illustrated, with a good bibliography (pp. 123-26) that lists general studies, artist monographs, and periodicals. A standard history of Austrian art and architecture of the late nineteenth century. For the advanced student.

694   Sotriffer, Kristian. **Modern Austrian Art: A Concise History**. New York, Praeger, 1965. 140p. illus. index. LC 65-25389.
Concise history of Austrian painting, sculpture, and graphic art from the late nineteenth century to the 1960s. Includes two biographical dictionaries: the first is of 60 artists mentioned in the text, with literature citations, and the second is of 50 artists not mentioned. Includes a short, selective bibliography (pp. 136-37). For beginning and advanced students of modern art.

FRANCE

695   Fontainas, André, *et al.* **Histoire générale de l'art français de la révolution à nos jours**. Paris, Librarie de France, 1922. 3v. illus.
Concise history of French art and architecture from the Revolution to the early twentieth century. Volume 1 covers painting and graphic arts; Volume 2, architecture and sculpture; Volume 3, decorative arts. No bibliography. For the beginning student.

ITALY

696   Argan, Giulio Carlo. **L'arte moderna, 1770/1970**. Florence, Sansoni, 1970. 774p. illus. index. LC 79-564092.
Comprehensive history of art and architecture in Italy from 1770 to 1970. Well illustrated; has some bibliographical footnotes. For beginning and advanced students.

697   Carrieri, Raffaele. **Avant-Garde Painting and Sculpture (1890-1955) in Italy**. Milan, Domus, 1955. 318p. illus. index.
History of Italian painting and sculpture from 1890 to 1955. Consists of chapters on movements and major artists. No bibliography. A good survey of modern Italian art for the general reader and the beginning student.

698   *Lavagnino, Emilio. **L'arte moderna dai neoclassici ai contemporaei**. Turin, Edit. Torinese, 1956. 2v. illus. index. (Storia dell'Arte Classica e Italiana, 5).
Comprehensive history of art and architecture in Italy from the nineteenth century to the middle of the twentieth century. Well illustrated with plates, plans, and diagrams. Bibliography (pp. 1263-78) is a balanced list of books and periodical articles. The standard history of Italian nineteenth and twentieth century art. For the advanced student.

MEXICO

699   *Fernandez, Justino. **El arte moderno y contemporaneo en Mexico.**
Mexico City, Imprenta Universitaria, 1952. 522p. illus. index.
Comprehensive history of art and architecture in Mexico from the early nineteenth
century to the middle of the twentieth century. Numerous but poor illustrations;
good but unclassified bibliography (pp. 505-512). A standard history of modern
Mexican art and architecture for beginning and advanced students.

RUSSIA

700   Gray, Camilla. **The Russian Experiment in Art, 1863-1922.** New York,
Abrams, c. 1962; reissued in new format, 1970. 296p. illus. index. LC
76-106290.
Concise history of painting and sculpture in Russia from the 1860s to 1922.
Bibliography (pp. 280-82). For beginning and advanced students.

UNITED STATES

701   Cahill, Holger, and Alfred H. Barr, Jr. **Art in America in Modern Times.**
Freeport, N.Y., Books for Libraries, 1969. 110p. illus. LC 69-17569.
Reprint of 1934 edition.
Survey history of art and architecture in America from 1865 to 1934. Covers
photography, film, and stage design as well as architecture, painting, and
sculpture. Brief bibliographies (pp. 107-110) list major books. For the general
reader and the beginning student.

702   Myron, Robert, and Abner Sundell. **Modern Art in America.** New York,
Crowell-Collier, 1971. 218p. illus. index. LC 76-153760.
Survey of art and architecture in America from circa 1870 to 1970. Modest
selection of black and white plates and brief bibliography of popular books
(p. 214). For the general reader.

19TH CENTURY

General Works

703   Hansen, Hans Jürgen. **Late Nineteenth Century Art: Architecture and
Applied Art of the "Pompous Age."** New York, McGraw-Hill, 1972.
264p. illus. index. LC 72-148989.

Pictorial survey of art and architecture in Europe and the United States during the second half of the nineteenth century. Emphasis is on Victorian art and architecture and its equivalents in Germany and France. Consists of essays on the various arts, written by specialists. Provides a bibliography (pp. 257-60) that lists major books in all languages. For the general reader and the beginning student.

704   Hofmann, Werner. **Art in the Nineteenth Century.** London, Faber & Faber, 1960. 435p. illus. index.
History of art and architecture in Europe and America, with an emphasis on the relationship between the fine arts and the general culture. Bibliographical references in the footnotes. An important study of nineteenth century art for beginning and advanced students.

705   Lankheit, Klaus. **Révolution et Restauration.** Paris, Michel, 1966. 286p. illus. index.
Concise history of art and architecture in Europe and America from neo-classicism through realism. Good selection of color plates, modest supplement of black and white illustrations, plans, and diagrams. Provides a good bibliography (pp. 253-63) that lists books and periodical articles in all languages. French edition of the series "Art of the World." A good survey of early nineteenth century art and architecture for beginning and advanced students.

706   *Novotny, Fritz. **Painting and Sculpture in Europe: 1780 to 1880.** Baltimore, Penguin, 1960. 288p. illus. index. (Pelican History of Art, Z20).
Comprehensive history of painting and sculpture in Europe from neo-classicism through impressionism. Good selection of plates and good classified bibliography (pp. 253-69), which lists books and periodical articles in all languages. Further reference to specialized literature can be found in the extensive footnotes. A standard history of nineteenth century painting and sculpture for the advanced student and the scholar.

707   Schultze, Jürgen. **Art of Nineteenth Century Europe.** New York, Abrams, 1972. 264p. illus. index. LC 79-92913.
Concise history of art and architecture in Europe during the nineteenth century. Begins with neo-classicism and hence reaches back into the mid-eighteenth century. Good selection of illustrations, mostly in color. No plans are given for the architecture. Provides a useful chronological table that coordinates events in the fine arts with events in literature, music, politics, and science and technology. Good bibliography (pp. 253-55) lists books in all languages. A good survey of nineteenth century art and architecture for the general reader.

708   Vogt, Adolf M. **Art of the Nineteenth Century.** New York, Universe, 1973. 189p. illus. index. LC 72-85082.
Concise history of art and architecture in Europe during the nineteenth century. A concluding chapter treats the influence of foreign cultures on nineteenth century Western art. Good selection of plates, informative captions, and a good,

balanced bibliography (pp. 184-86) of books and periodical articles in all languages. A good survey history of the art and architecture of the nineteenth century for the general reader and the beginning student.

709   *Zeitler, Rudolf W. **Die Kunst des 19. Jahrhunderts.** Berlin, Propyläen, 1967. 411p. (text); 440p. (illus.). index. (Propyläen Kunstgeschichte, Band 11). LC 67-104178.
Comprehensive illustrated handbook of the art and architecture of the nineteenth century in Europe and America. The introductory essay by Zeitler is followed by essays on various styles and media by different specialists, an excellent corpus of plates, very informative notes to the plates with reference to specialized literature, and a very good, comprehensive, and classified bibliography (pp. 373-83) of books and periodical articles in all languages. A standard handbook of nineteenth century art and architecture for the advanced student and the scholar.

Belgium

710   Hymans, Henri S. **Belgische Kunst des 19. Jahrhunderts.** Leipzig, Seemann, 1906. 253p. illus. index.
General history of art and architecture in Belgium during the nineteenth century. No bibliography. Still valuable for illustrations. For the advanced student.

Denmark

711   Hannover, Emil. **Dänische Kunst des 19. Jahrhunderts.** Leipzig, Seemann, 1907. 168p. illus. index.
General history of art and architecture in Denmark during the nineteenth century. No bibliography. Still valuable for illustrations. For the advanced student.

Germany

712   Beenken, Hermann T. **Das neunzehnte Jahrhundert in der deutschen Kunst.** Munich, Bruckmann, 1944. 563p. illus. index. LC 46-12460.
A comprehensive history of art and architecture in Germany during the nineteenth century. Bibliographical references in the footnotes. A standard history for the advanced student.

Sweden

713   Nordensvan, Georg G. **Schwedische Kunst des 19. Jahrhunderts.** Leipzig, Seemann, 1904. 140p. illus.
General survey of art and architecture in Sweden in the nineteenth century. No bibliography. Still valuable for illustrations. For the advanced student.

United States

714   Garrett, Wendell D., *et al.* **The Arts in America: The Nineteenth Century.**
New York, Scribner's, 1969. 412p. illus. index. LC 78-852.
History of art and architecture in the United States during the nineteenth century.
Good coverage of the minor and decorative arts. Bibliography (pp. 385-90) lists
major books. A good survey of nineteenth century American art and architecture
for the general reader and the beginning student.

Romanticism

715   Brion, Marcel. **Art of the Romantic Era: Romanticism, Classicism, Realism.** New York, Praeger, 1966. 285p. illus. index. LC 65-20070.
Concise history of art and architecture in Europe and the United States during the
period 1750-1850 (American art and architecture to circa 1900). Good selection
of illustrations. Bibliography (pp. 267-68) lists major books in all languages. For
the general reader and the beginning student.

716   Brion, Marcel. **Romantic Art.** New York, McGraw-Hill, 1960. 239p.
illus. index. LC 60-12761.
Pictorial history of romantic art and architecture in Western Europe and the
United States. Architecture and sculpture are treated in a brief chapter; the rest of
the book consists of essays and notes with plates of romantic painting in the
various countries. No bibliography. For the general reader and the beginning
student.

Realism

717   *Nochlin, Linda. **Realism.** Baltimore, Penguin, 1971. 283p. illus. index.
Study of realist art and architecture of the nineteenth century. Emphasis is on the
relationship of realism to contemporary culture and the nature of realist style
rather than its historical development. Provides a good annotated bibliography
(pp. 271-74) that lists books and periodical articles in all languages. For the
advanced student.

Impressionism, Post-Impressionism, and
Neo-Impressionism

718   Abbate, Francesco, ed. **Impressionism, Its Forerunners and Influences.**
London and New York, Octopus, 1972. 158p. illus. LC 73-151617.
Pictorial survey of impressionistic painting in Europe and America. Inadequate one-
page bibliography. For the general reader.

719   Bowness, Alan, ed. **Impressionists and Post-Impressionists.** New York, Franklin Watts, 1965. 296p. illus. index. LC 65-10269.
Pictorial history of painting and sculpture in Europe and America in the second half of the nineteenth century, with an emphasis on the impressionist and post-impressionist phases. The brief introduction, which sketches the chief characteristics of the period, is followed by a substantial section devoted to artists' biographies. The work concludes with a succinct historical sketch of the development of late nineteenth century art. Well illustrated, with portraits of most of the artists discussed. Brief and inadequate bibliographies at the end of the introduction and in some of the biographies. Although it is awkwardly arranged, its numerous illustrations and its responsible (if too brief) text make it a useful survey for the general reader and the beginning student.

720   Hamann, Richard, and Jost Hermand. **Impressionismus.** Berlin, Akademie-Verlag, 1960. 414p. illus. index. (Deutsche Kunst und Kultur von der Gründerzeit bis zum Expressionism, Band III). LC 61-40068.
Comprehensive history of German art and architecture during the last decade of the nineteenth and first decade of the twentieth century, with emphasis on the general cultural context. Brief bibliographical note (p. 406). Together with other volumes in the series, it forms a good history of German art for the period 1870 to 1930. For the advanced student.

721   Hamann, Richard, and Jost Hermand. **Naturalismus.** Berlin, Akademie-Verlag, 1959. 336p. illus. index. (Deutsche Kunst und Kultur von der Gründerzeit bis zum Expressionismus,Band II). LC 60-2589.
Comprehensive history and analysis of German art and architecture in the 1880s with an emphasis on the general cultural context. Excellent chapter on naturalism as a stylistic principle in nineteenth century art history. Brief bibliographical note (p. 330). Together with other volumes in the series, it forms a good history of German art for the period 1870 to 1930. For the advanced student.

722   Leymarie, Jean. **Impressionism.** Cleveland, World; Geneva, Switzerland, Skira, 1955. 2v. illus. index. LC 55-7701.
Survey history of French impressionist painting. Handsomely illustrated. The bibliography in Volume 1 (pp. 127-29) lists books and periodical articles in all languages. For the general reader and the beginning student.

723   Lucie-Smith, Edward. **Symbolist Art.** New York, Praeger, 1972. 216p. illus. index. LC 72-77068.
Concise history of symbolist art since its origin in the symbolist movement of the late nineteenth century through its heirs in the twentieth century. Illustrated in black and white, with some color plates. Brief bibliography (p. 209). For the general reader and the beginning student, a good survey of the subject.

724   Mathey, François. **The Impressionists.** New York, Praeger, 1961. 289p. illus. index. LC 61-5759.

Pictorial survey of French impressionist painting. Good selection of illustrations. For the general reader.

725   Pool, Phoebe. **Impressionism.** New York, Praeger, 1967. 282p. illus. index. LC 67-25263.
Concise history of impressionistic painting in Europe and America. Good selection of plates. Bibliography (pp. 270-72) lists major books in all languages. For the general reader.

726   *Rewald, John. **The History of Impressionism.** 4th ed. Greenwich, Conn., New York Graphic Society, 1973. 672p. illus. index. LC 68-17468.
Comprehensive history of French impressionistic painting. Thoroughly illustrated and provided with a useful chronological table of events and an excellent annotated bibliography (pp. 608-652) of books and periodical articles in all languages. A standard history of impressionism. For beginning and advanced students.

727   Rewald, John. **Post-Impressionism, from Van Gogh to Gauguin.** New York, Museum of Modern Art, 1956. 614p. illus. index.
History of French post-impressionist painting from 1886 to 1893. Well illustrated; the good bibliography (pp. 551-95) lists books and periodical articles in all languages. A standard history of the early phase of post-impressionism in France. For beginning and advanced students.

20TH CENTURY

General Works

728   Batterberry, Michael. **Twentieth Century Art.** New York, McGraw-Hill, 1969. 191p. illus. index. LC 70-76821.
A pictorial survey of modern painting and sculpture beginning with Matisse and Les Fauves and ending with the New York School of the 1950s. No bibliography. For the general reader.

729   Delevoy, Robert L. **Dimensions of the 20th Century: 1900-1945.** Geneva, Switzerland, Skira, 1965. 223p. illus. index. LC 65-24417.
A conceptually treated survey of modern art, demonstrated by examples of painting, sculpture, and architecture. Exceptionally good tipped-in color plates. Indexed by names of artists. Includes a general bibliography (pp. 215-16). For the beginning student.

730   Einstein, Carl. **Die Kunst des 20. Jahrhunderts.** 3rd ed. Berlin, Propyläen, 1951. 575p. illus. index.

Illustrated handbook of painting and sculpture during the first half of the twentieth century. Excellent collection of plates, brief text, and informative notes to the plates. No bibliography. Until the appearance of the new "Propyläen Kunst-geschichte" volume covering the twentieth century, this is still a useful handbook for beginning and advanced students.

731   *Grohmann, Will. **Bildende Kunst und Architektur.** Berlin, Suhrkamp,
       1953. 551p. illus. index. (Zwischen den Beiden Kriegen, Dritter Band).
Comprehensive history of European and American art and architecture between the two world wars. Provides a useful chronological table of events from 1890 to 1950 and a good classified bibliography (pp. 521-26) of books and periodical articles. A good history of art and architecture of the 1920s and 1930s for the advanced student.

732   Haack, Friedrich. **Die Kunst des XX. Jahrhunderts und der Gegenwart.**
       6th ed. Esslingen, Neff, 1922-25. 2v. illus.
Comprehensive history of European art and architecture of the nineteenth and early twentieth centuries. First published in 1905, it was one of the first attempts to trace systematically the stylistic development of nineteenth century art and architecture. Despite its age, it should be known by the advanced student.

733   Langui, Emile. **50 Years of Modern Art.** New York, Praeger, 1959. 335p.
       illus. LC 59-7300.
Illustrated survey of painting and sculpture from fauvism to non-representational art. Good collection of illustrations and useful section of artists' biographies. No bibliography. For the general reader and the beginning student.

734   *Richardson, Tony, and Nikos Stangos, eds. **Concepts of Modern Art.**
       New York and Evanston, Harper & Row, 1974. 281p. illus. index.
Concise history of modern art, exclusive of architecture, from 1900 to the present. Consists of essays by specialists on the various "isms" of modern art, beginning with fauvism and ending with minimal art. Provides a good classified bibliography of major literature in all languages. A good survey history of twentieth century art for the general reader and the beginning student.

735   Schug, Albert. **Art of the Twentieth Century.** New York, Abrams, 1972.
       264p. illus. index.
Concise history of twentieth century European and American painting, sculpture, architecture, and graphic arts arranged according to movements. Illustrated with black and white and color plates. Includes a chronological table of the arts, political history, and science and technology; there is a general bibliography (pp. 258-60), which is heavily European in the citations. A good survey for the general reader and the beginning student.

736   Sylvester, David, ed. **Modern Art, from Fauvism to Abstract Expressionism.**
       New York, Franklin Watts, 1965. 296p. illus. index. LC 65-10270.

Survey history of modern painting, drawing, graphic art, and sculpture from Matisse to the abstract expressionists. Following a succinct introduction, a biographical section treats the lives and works of important modern artists, with brief literature citations. Illustrated with color and black and white plates. For the general reader and the beginning student.

Africa

737   Beier, Ulli. **Contemporary Art in Africa**. New York, Praeger, 1968. 173p. illus. index. LC 68-19432.
Survey of mid-century painting and sculpture in Black Africa, with an emphasis on West African artists. Well illustrated. No bibliography. For the general reader and the beginning student.

Austria

738   Feuerstein, Günther, *et al.* **Moderne Kunst in Österreich**. Vienna and Hanover, Forum, 1965. 119p. (text); 114p. (illus.). index.
History of art and architecture in Austria from 1918 to 1964. Consists of essays on the development of the various media. Well illustrated. The good bibliography (pp. 120-23) lists books and periodical articles. A good survey for beginning and advanced students.

China

739   Sullivan, Michael. **Chinese Art in the Twentieth Century**. Berkeley and Los Angeles, University of California Press, 1959. 110p. illus. index.
History of Chinese art, exclusive of architecture, from 1912 to 1950. Provides a good selection of plates, a biographical index of modern Chinese artists, and a bibliography (p. 98), which lists books and periodicals in Chinese and Western languages. A good survey of modern Chinese art for the beginning student and general reader.

Germany

740   Roh, Franz. **German Art in the 20th Century**. Greenwich, Conn., New York Graphic Society, 1968. 516p. illus. index. LC 68-12367.
Comprehensive history of art and architecture in Germany from Jugendstil to the present. Additional chapters on developments since 1955 have been written by

Juliane Roh. Good selection of plates. No bibliography. A good survey of modern German art and architecture for the beginning student and the general reader.

741   Thoene, Peter. **Modern German Art**. Harmondsworth, Penguin, 1938. 108p. illus.
Survey history of German painting and sculpture from impressionism through the abstract styles of the 1930s. No bibliography. An older survey, still valuable for the advanced student because of its comments on the state of German modern art at the time of the Nazi campaign on "degenerate" art.

Great Britain

742   Rothenstein, John K. M. **British Art Since 1900, an Anthology**. London, Phaidon, 1962. 181p. illus. LC 62-51567.
Pictorial survey of painting and sculpture in Britain from 1900 to 1955. Brief introductory essay and biographical notes to the plates. No bibliography. For the general reader.

Japan

743   Kung, D. **The Contemporary Artist in Japan**. Honolulu, East-West Center Press, 1966. 187p. illus. LC 66-31499.
Survey of Japanese painting and sculpture since the last war. Introduction on the development of modern Japanese art is followed by biographies of leading artists. No bibliography. For the general reader and the beginning student.

Mexico

744   Schmeckebier, Laurence E. **Modern Mexican Art**. Westport, Conn., Greenwood, 1971. 191p. illus. index. LC 70-141418.
Reprint of 1939 edition. Survey history of painting and sculpture in Mexico during the first three decades of the twentieth century. Poor illustrations. Provides a section of artists' biographies and a brief selected bibliography (pp. 181-83). For the beginning student.

Netherlands

745   Kersten, Wim. **Moderne Kunst in Nederland.** Amsterdam, de Bussy, 1969.
       140p. illus. index. LC 76-485611.
Survey of modern art and architecture in the Netherlands from the early twentieth
century to the present. No bibliography. For the general reader and the beginning
student.

746   Loosjes-Terpstra, Aleide B. **Moderne Kunst in Nederland, 1900-1914.**
       Utrecht, Dekker & Gambert, 1959. 352p. illus. index. (Orbis Artium,
       Utrechtse Kunsthistorische Studiën, 3). LC 61-34142.
Comprehensive study of art and architecture in the Netherlands from 1900 to
1914. Bibliographical footnotes. A good study for the advanced student.

United States

747   Baur, John I. H. **Revolution and Tradition in Modern American Art.**
       Cambridge, Mass., Harvard University Press, 1958. 170p. illus. index.
Survey of painting and sculpture in the United States during the first half of the
twentieth century. The introductory chapter, which traces the main outlines of the
development of modern American art, is followed by chapters investigating the
various movements. Concluding chapters discuss the position of the artist in modern
society and attempt to characterize what is American in contemporary art.
Bibliographical references in the footnotes. A standard study of modern American
art. For beginning and advanced students.

748   Goodrich, Lloyd, and John I. H. Baur. **American Art of Our Century.**
       New York, Praeger, 1961. 309p. illus. index.
Concise history of painting and sculpture in the United States from 1900 to 1960.
Consists of short essays on the major phases. Designed as a guide to the collections in the Whitney Museum of American Art; thus, all examples illustrated are
from that collection. Provides a catalog of the Whitney Collection and a list of the
exhibitions and books published by the Museum. For the general reader and the
beginning student.

749   *Hunter, Sam. **American Art of the 20th Century.** New York, Abrams,
       1972. 487p. illus. index. LC 72-3634.
Comprehensive history of American painting and sculpture of the twentieth
century. Copiously illustrated with black and white and color illustrations. The
excellent classified bibliography (pp. 437-70) is in two sections: literature to
1959 by Bernard Karpel; and literature since 1959, by Roberta Smith and Nicole
Metzner. A standard history suitable for all levels.

750   Rose, Barbara. **American Art Since 1900: A Critical History**. New York,
       Praeger, 1967. 320p. illus. index. LC 67-20743.
This concise history of modern American art centers on painting but includes a
chapter each for sculpture and architecture. Illustrated in black and white, with
some color plates. General bibliography (pp. 298-300) is supplemented by the
notes to the text. Of interest to all levels.

Art Nouveau

751   Abbate, Francesco, ed. **Art Nouveau: The Style of the 1890's**. London
       and New York, Octopus, 1972. 158p. illus.
Pictorial survey of the art and architecture of art nouveau. All illustrations are in
color; brief popular text. Inadequate one-page bibliography. For the general
reader.

752   Amaya, Mario. **Art Nouveau**. New York, Dutton, 1966. 168p. illus. index.
Brief history of art nouveau art and architecture in Britain, America, Spain, Belgium,
Holland, France, Germany, and Austria. No bibliography. For the general reader.

753   Barilli, Renato. **Art Nouveau**. London, Hamlyn, 1969. 157p. illus.
Pictorial survey of art nouveau art and architecture. All illustrations are in color.
Popular text. No bibliography. For the general reader.

754   Champigneulle, B. **L'art nouveau**. Paris, Somogy, 1972. 288p. illus. index.
Survey of art nouveau art and architecture in all countries. Poor illustrations. No
bibliography. For the beginning student.

755   Cremona, Italo. **Il tempo dell'art nouveau**. Florence, Vallecchi, 1964.
       230p. illus. index.
Survey of art nouveau art and architecture throughout Europe. Provides a biographical dictionary of major art nouveau artists and architects, but no bibliography. For
the beginning student.

756   Madsen, S. Tschudi. **Art Nouveau**. New York, McGraw-Hill, 1967. 256p.
       illus. index. LC 66-24159.
Concise history of art nouveau art and architecture in Europe and America.
Brief bibliography (pp. 247-48), and further reference to specialized literature in
the footnotes. For the general reader and the beginning student.

757   *Schmutzler, Robert. **Art Nouveau**. New York, Abrams, 1964. 322p.
       illus. index. LC 64-10765.
Comprehensive history of art nouveau art and architecture. Traces the origin of the
style to proto-art nouveau art of the earlier nineteenth century and its development
to late art nouveau of the 1920s. Good selection of plates, and excellent bibliography (pp. 299-307), which lists books and periodical articles in all languages. There

are special sections on literary sources. A standard history of art nouveau. For the advanced student.

758   *Seling, Helmut. **Jugendstil: Der Weg ins 20. Jahrhundert.** Heidelberg
        and Munich, Keyser, 1959. 459p. illus. index.
Comprehensive history of art nouveau art and architecture consisting of essays by German specialists on the development of the various arts. Good coverage of the minor arts. Good bibliographies at the end of each chapter. Also provides a useful dictionary of artists' biographies. A standard work for the advanced student.

759   *Selz, Peter. **Art Nouveau: Art and Design at the Turn of the Century.**
        New York, Doubleday, 1960. 192p. illus. index. LC 60-11987.
Survey of art nouveau art and architecture consisting of a group of essays by various specialists. Designed to accompany an exhibition formed by the Museum of Modern Art in New York. Provides an excellent bibliography (pp. 152-61), compiled by James Grady. A good survey for beginning and advanced students.

Fauvism

760   Crespelle, Jean-Paul. **The Fauves.** Greenwich, Conn., New York Graphic
        Society, 1962. 351p. illus. index.
Illustrated survey of the painting and graphics of the Fauves. Well illustrated and provided with a bibliography (pp. 349-51) that lists books and periodical articles. For the general reader and the beginning student.

761   Leymarie, Jean. **Fauvism, Biographical and Critical Study.** Paris and New
        York, Skira, 1959. 163p. illus. index. LC 59-7255.
Survey of painting of the Fauves with emphasis on the major personalities. Bibliography (pp. 149-52) lists major books and periodical articles in English and French. For the general reader and the beginning student.

762   Muller, Joseph E. **Fauvism.** New York, Praeger, 1967. 260p. illus. index.
History of French Fauves, with emphasis on the movement's influence on such major painters as Matisse and Dufy. Well illustrated. A good survey for the general reader and the beginning student.

763   Rewald, John. **Les Fauves.** New York, Museum of Modern Art, 1952.
        illus. index.
Survey of fauvism designed to accompany an exhibition at the Museum of Modern Art in New York. Good selection of illustrations, and good bibliography. For the general reader and the beginning student.

Cubism

764   Barr, Alfred H. **Cubism and Abstract Art**. New York, Museum of Modern
       Art, 1936. 250p. illus. index.
Survey of the history of cubist painting and sculpture in Europe and America.
Good selection of illustrations and good bibliography (pp. 234-49) of books and
periodical articles, compiled by B. Newhall. A good survey for beginning and
advanced students.

765   Fry, Edward. **Cubism**. New York, McGraw-Hill, 1966. 200p. illus. index.
This study of cubism consists of a history of cubism and an extensive collection of
documentary texts related to cubism. Provides an excellent bibliography (pp. 176-
83), which lists books and periodical articles in all languages, and a useful listing
of cubist exhibitions. A standard work on cubism for the advanced student.

766   Habasque, Guy. **Cubism: Biographical and Critical Study**. Paris and New
       York, Skira, 1959. 170p. illus. index.
Survey of cubist painting in Europe. Color illustrations. Provides a good bibliog-
raphy (pp. 154-57), which lists books on and sources for cubism in all languages.
For the beginning student and the general reader.

767   Kozloff, Max. **Cubism/Futurism**. New York, Charterhouse, 1973. 243p.
       illus. LC 72-84221.
Study and concise history of cubism and futurism. Bibliography (pp. 221-22) provides a selected list of books in English. For the beginning student.

768   Pierre, José. **Cubism**. London, Heron, 1970. 207p. illus. LC 70-598812.
Survey of cubism with emphasis on French cubist painting. Bibliography (p. 204)
lists major books in French and English. For the general reader and the beginning
student.

769   *Rosenblum, Robert. **Cubism and Twentieth Century Art**. New York,
       Abrams, 1961. illus. index. LC 61-7155.
History and analysis of cubism from Picasso and Braque to circa 1939. Emphasis
is on painting. Provides a chronological table and a good critical bibliography
(pp. 312-17). A good scholarly study of cubism for beginning and advanced
students.

770   Schwartz, Paul W. **Cubism**. New York, Praeger, 1971. 216p. illus. index.
       LC 70-100034.
Survey of cubist painting and sculpture, along with literature and the theatre.
Brief, selected bibliography (pp. 203-204) of books in all languages. For the
general reader and the beginning student.

Expressionism

771   Cheney, Sheldon. **Expressionism in Art**. Rev. ed. New York, Boni, 1958.
        415p. illus. index.
Survey of expressionistic elements in European and American art of the nineteenth
and twentieth centuries. Bibliographical footnotes. For the general reader and the
beginning student.

772   Dube, Wolf D. **Expressionism**. New York, Praeger, 1973. 215p. illus. index.
        LC 72-79505.
Concise history of German expressionistic painting and graphic arts from its origins
to the late 1920s. Provides a section (pp. 208-213) of artists' biographies with
bibliographies of major monographs. A good survey of expressionism for the
general reader and the beginning student.

773   Kuhn, Charles L. **German Expressionism and Abstract Art: The Harvard
        Collections**. Cambridge, Mass., Harvard University Press, 1957. illus.
        index.
History of German expressionistic painting and sculpture, with emphasis on the
pieces in the Harvard University Collections. A good survey for the general reader
and the beginning student.

774   Myers, Bernard S. **The German Expressionists: A Generation in Revolt**.
        New York, Praeger, 1957.
Survey history of German expressionistic painting and graphic arts. Good selection
of illustrations. Bibliography provides a good list of major books in all languages.
For the general reader and the beginning student.

775   Willett, John. **Expressionism**. New York, McGraw-Hill, 1970. 256p. illus.
        index. LC 70-96434.
Survey history of expressionistic art and literature from its beginnings to 1945.
Good selection of illustrations and a useful, annotated bibliography (pp. 248-52),
which lists books in all languages. For the general reader and the beginning student.

Constructivism and Abstraction

776   Brion, Marcel. **Art abstrait**. Paris, Albin Michel, 1956. 315p. illus.
Survey of twentieth century abstract art in Europe and America. Bibliographical
footnotes. For beginning and advanced students.

777   Poensgen, Georg, and Leopold Zahn. **Abstrakte Kunst: Eine Weltsprache**.
        Baden-Baden, Woldemar, 1958. 224p. illus.
Survey of painting and sculpture in the abstract style throughout the world.
Introductory essay on the nature and development of abstract art is followed by a

series of artists' biographies, which are accompanied by excellent illustrations and short bibliographies. The bibliography on page 125 deals with the documentary sources of abstract art in the twentieth century. For beginning and advanced students.

778   *Rickey, George. **Constructivism: Origins and Evolution.** New York, Braziller, 1967. 305p. illus. index. LC 67-24210.
Concise history of the constructivist movement from its origins in the early twentieth century to movements and persons still working under constructivist influence. Black and white illustrations. Includes a chronology of constructivist events, a table of museum holdings of major artists, and a good classified and annotated bibliography (pp. 247-301). A good survey for beginning and advanced students.

779   *Vallier, Dora. **Abstract Art.** New York, Orion, 1970. 342p. illus. index. LC 75-86121.
Translated from the French *L'art abstrait* (1967). Concise history of abstract sculpture and painting, beginning with Kandinsky and including abstract art after 1945. The idea of abstraction is discussed at length in the introduction. In addition to a chronology of events, there is a good general bibliography (pp. 322-30). A straightforward and responsible work for beginning students and general readers.

Futurism

780   *Baumgarth, Christa. **Geschichte des Futurismus.** Reinbek bei Hamburg, Rowohlt, 1966. 313p. illus. index.
Comprehensive history of futurism, covering the period from 1905 to the influence of futuristic art in the mid-twentieth century. Covers art and architecture. Provides a collection of documents (translated into German), a section of further source material, and a good bibliography (pp. 299-306) of books and periodical articles in all languages. A good history of futurism for the advanced student.

781   *Carrieri, Raffaele. **Futurism.** Milan, Milione, 1963. 183p. (text); 163p. (illus.).
Concise history of futurism in Italian art and literature. Provides a good bibliography (pp. 171-77), which lists books and periodical articles on futurism; there is also a list of writings, manifestoes, and exhibitions of futurism. A definitive work on futurism. For the advanced student.

782   Rye, Jane. **Futurism.** London, Studio Vista, 1972. 159p. illus. index.
Survey of futuristic literature, art, and architecture in and outside Italy. Brief bibliography (p. 156). For the general reader.

783   Taylor, Joshua. **Futurism.** New York, Museum of Modern Art, 1961. 153p. illus.

Survey of futurist painting and graphics. Provides a collection of excerpts from futurist writings and a useful chronology of events in the futurist movement. Good bibliography (pp. 148-51).

De Stijl

784   Jaffe, Hans. **De Stijl, 1917-1931**. Amsterdam, Meulenhoff, 1956. 293p. illus.
Comprehensive history of Dutch art and architecture from 1917 to 1931. Discusses the origin, character, and influence of De Stijl. Good selection of plates and excellent bibliography (pp. 269-91). For the advanced student. A standard work on De Stijl.

785   Overy, Paul. **De Stijl**. New York, Dutton, 1969. 167p. illus. index.
Brief history of modern Dutch art and architecture from 1895 to 1930. Provides a short bibliography (p. 164) of books in all languages. For the general reader.

Dada and Surrealism

786   Barr, Alfred H. **Fantastic Art: Dada, Surrealism**. 2nd ed. New York, Museum of Modern Art, 1937. 271p. illus. index.
Collection of essays on fantastic art, Dada, and surrealism designed to accompany an exhibition at the Museum of Modern Art. Well illustrated and provided with a good bibliography (pp. 263-67) of books and periodical articles. For beginning and advanced students.

787   Gascoyne, David. **A Short Survey of Surrealism**. London, Cass, 1970. 162p. illus. index. LC 77-571396.
Brief survey of surrealism, with a section containing translations of major works of surrealist poetry. Poor illustrations and no bibliography. For the beginning student.

788   Gaunt, William. **The Surrealists**. London, Thames and Hudson, 1972. illus. index.
Survey of surrealist painting in Europe. Well illustrated and provided with a bibliography listing major books and periodical articles in all languages. For the general reader and the beginning student.

789   Read, Herbert. **Surrealism** . . . New York, Harcourt, Brace, 1936. 251p. illus.
Survey history and conceptual study of surrealist art. Contents: introduction, by Herbert Read; "Limits Not Frontiers of Surrealism," by André Breton; "Surrealism at This Time and Place," by Hugh S. Davies; "Poetic Evidence," by Paul Éluard; "1870-1936," by George Hugnet. A standard collection of essays on surrealism for beginning and advanced students.

790   *Richter, Hans. **Dada: Art and Anti-Art**. New York, McGraw-Hill, 1965. 246p. illus. index. LC 65-19077.

History of Dada in Europe and America. Divided into "schools" of Dada (Zurich Dada, New York Dada, etc.), with a chapter on Dada's influence on art since 1923. Appendix provides a translation of the Zurich Dada *Chronicle*. Good bibliography (pp. 229-37) lists works on Dada as well as literary works by major Dada figures. A standard history of Dada. For beginning and advanced students.

791   *Rubin, William S. **Dada and Surrealist Art**. New York, Abrams, [1968]. 525p. illus. index. LC 68-13064.

Comprehensive history of Dada and surrealist art in Europe and America. Excellent selection of plates, thorough and scholarly text. Provides a comprehensive chronology (pp. 453-72) by Irene Gordon and an excellent bibliography (pp. 492-512) listing books, periodical articles, and editions of writings by Dada and surrealist artists and writers. A standard study of Dada and surrealism for the advanced student.

792   Verkauf, Willy, ed. **Dada: Monograph of a Movement**. New York, Wittenborn, 1957. 188p. illus. index.

Collection of essays on various aspects, phases, and media of Dada. Provides a useful bibliography (pp. 176-83) arranged by artists. A standard work on Dada for beginning and advanced students.

793   Waldberg, Patrick. **Surrealism**. Cleveland, Skira-World, 1962. 140p. illus. index. LC 62-10989.

Brief history of surrealism. Good color plates. Select bibliography (p. 135) lists major works in all languages. Also has a useful chronological survey of events in surrealism and a list of the major writings by surrealist authors. For the beginning student.

Art in Mid-Century

794   Brion, Marcel, *et al.* **Art Since 1945**. New York, Washington Square Press, 1962. 336p. illus.

This survey history of modern art since 1945 is comprised of essays by ten specialists on painting and sculpture in the following countries: France, Spain, Italy, Yugoslavia, Poland, Germany, Austria, Switzerland, Great Britain, Holland, Scandinavia, and the United States. No bibliography and no index. A regional approach for the beginning student.

795   Hunter, Sam, *et al.* **New Art around the World: Painting and Sculpture**. New York, Abrams, 1966. 509p. illus. index. LC 66-29665.

History of painting and sculpture in the major art-generating countries around the world between 1945 and 1965. Consists of essays by various specialists on the art of United States, Paris, Great Britain, Italy, Spain, The Netherlands, Scandinavia, Belgium, Japan, South America, Greece, Israel, Poland, Czechoslovakia, Yugoslavia, Germany, Austria, and Switzerland. No bibliography. A good survey of art at mid-century for the general reader and the beginning student.

796   Lucie-Smith, Edward. **Late Modern: The Visual Arts since 1945.** New
          York, Praeger, 1969. 288p. illus. index. LC 74-92585.
Survey history of painting and sculpture since 1945 with sections on abstract expressionism, the European scene, Pop Art, Op Art, kinetic art, sculpture, and environments. General reading list (p. 275). For beginning students and general readers.

CHAPTER NINE

NATIONAL HISTORIES AND HANDBOOKS
OF EUROPEAN ART

I. WESTERN EUROPE

FRANCE

Topographic Handbooks

797 **Dictionnaire des églises de France.** Paris, Laffont, 1966-1971. 5v. illus. index.
Topographical guide to the art and architecture of the churches of France, Belgium, Luxembourg, and French Switzerland. Volume one is a history of church art and architecture in the above countries with bibliographies at the end of sections and a glossary of terms at the end of the volume. Volumes two through five treat the churches (by region and place), giving attention to the art contents along with the architecture of the major buildings. Contents: Vol. 2, Centre et Sud-Est; Vol. 3, Sud-Ouest; Vol. 4, Ouest et Ile-de-France; Vol. 5, Nord et Est, Belgique, Luxembourg, Suisse. The entry for each church has a brief bibliography. Although not the in-depth coverage of an official inventory, this is still a valuable reference work for beginning and advanced students.

798 **Inventaire général des monuments et des richesses artistiques de la France.** Paris, Imprimerie Nationale, 1969– .
Published by the Ministère des Affaires Culturelles. Official inventory of the art and architecture in France, arranged by region. To date, the following have appeared:
> *Finistère: Canton Carhaix-Plouguer* (1969; 2v.)
> *Haut-Rhin: Canton Guebwiller* (1972; 2v.)
> *Landes: Canton Peyrehorade* (1973; 2v.)
> *Gard: Canton Aigues-Mortes* (1973; 2v.)
Each section is introduced with a chapter on the pertinent archival sources and a sketch of the local history and art history. The inventory of the monuments and their contents is arranged by place. For each section there is a volume of plates to

accompany the inventory text. Two sub-series are attached to the *Inventaire*: the first is "Répertoire des inventaires," 1970– , which is a series of bibliographies on the art and architecture of the major regions of France. To date, the following volumes have appeared: *Région Nord* (1970); *Limousin* (1970); *Languedoc-Roussillon* (1970). The other sub-series is "Principes d'analyse scientifique," 1971– , which consists of illustrated glossaries of the terminology used in the description of the various arts. Volumes that have appeared to date are: *Tapisserie* (1971); *Architecture* (1972; 2v.). The *Inventaire* and its sub-series are intended, when complete, to replace the old and incomplete inventory. They will fill a long-standing gap in the information on art and architecture *in situ* in France. The volumes of the sub-series deserve to be better known as reference tools in their own right. The *Répertoire* has the potential of becoming the long-needed retrospective bibliography on French art and architecture. The volumes of the "Principes d'analyse scientifique" are excellent dictionaries of art terminology.

799   Olivier-Michel, Françoise, *et al.* **A Guide to the Art Treasures of France.**
        London, Methuen, 1966. 555p. illus. index. LC 66-74412.
Topographical guide to the art and architecture of France. Arrangement is by region, then by place. Includes art in museums as well as *in situ*. Text consists of brief descriptions accompanied by numerous small illustrations. No bibliography. Too large to be used in the field, but it can be used for quick reference to illustrations of the major works. For the general reader and the beginning student.

800   Keller, Harald. **Die Kunstlandschaften Frankreichs.** Wiesbaden, F.
        Steiner, 1963. 100p. illus. index. LC 64-44002.
Handbook of the regional styles of French art and architecture on the model of the same author's work on Italian art (870). Modest selection of plates, good maps, and extensive bibliographical footnotes. For the advanced student.

801   **Reclams Kunstführer Frankreich.** Herausgegeben von Manfred Wundram.
        Stuttgart, Reclam, 1967– . 2v. to date. illus. index.
Topographical guide to the art and architecture of France, including all major works from prehistoric times to the present. The two volumes that have appeared to date are: *Band I, Paris und Versailles* (1970); *Band II, Provence; Côte d'Azur; Dauphiné; Rhône-Tal* (1967). Within the volumes arrangement is by place and, in the case of Paris, by city quartier. Each place is introduced by an historical sketch, followed by a thorough description of the major buildings, their art contents and decoration, sites and monuments. Major museums and their buildings and collections are also included. Modestly illustrated with plates; liberally provided with plans and diagrams. No bibliography. Designed as pocket guides for the serious art tourist, the thoroughness of the Reclam guides makes them valuable reference tools for the advanced student.

Histories

802   **Art Treasures in France: Monuments, Masterpieces, Commissions, and Collections.** General eds., Bernard S. Myers and Trewin Copplestone. New York and Toronto, McGraw-Hill, 1969. 176p. illus. index. LC 69-13326.
Pictorial survey of the architecture, painting, sculpture, and decorative and minor arts in France from prehistory to the present. Written by a variety of period specialists. Contains maps and a glossary-index of museums and monuments in France, but no bibliography. For the general reader.

803   Laclotte, Michel. **French Art from 1350 to 1850.** New York, Franklin Watts, 1965. 249p. illus. index. LC 65-10267.
Pictorial survey of art and architecture in France from 1350 to 1850, with an emphasis on painting and sculpture. The introduction, which outlines the chief characteristics, schools, and artists of France, is followed by a substantial section devoted to artists' biographies. The work concludes with a brief historical sketch of the development of art and architecture in France. Well illustrated. Brief and inadequate bibliographies are found at the end of the introduction and in some of the biographies. It is awkwardly arranged, but its numerous illustrations and responsible (if too brief) text make it a useful survey for the general reader.

804   Réau, Louis. **Histoire de l'expansion de l'art français** . . . Paris, Laurens, 1924-33. 3v. illus. index.
History of French art and architecture in other countries and the influence of French art and architecture in other countries. Contents: Vol. 1, *Le monde latin—Italie, Espagne, Portugal, Roumanie, Amérique du Sud*; Vol. 2, pt. 1, *Belgique et Hollande, Suisse, Allemagne et Autriche, Bohème et Hongrie*; Vol. 2, pt. 2, *Pays scandinaves, Angleterre, Amérique du Nord*; Vol. 3, *Le monde slave et l'Orient*. Each volume provides a list of documents and bibliography. A useful study for the advanced student.

805   Schneider, René. **L'art français** . . . Paris, Laurens, 1925-30. 6v. illus. index.
General history of art and architecture in France from the early Middle Ages to the early twentieth century. Popular text, but there are good bibliographies at the end of each volume. For the general reader and the beginning student.

GERMAN-SPEAKING COUNTRIES

General Works

806   **Deutsche Kunstgeschichte.** Munich, Bruckmann, 1942-1956. 6v. illus. index.
Comprehensive history of art and architecture in the German-speaking countries from Carolingian times through the twentieth century. Band I, *Baukunst*, by

Eberhard Hempel; Band II, *Plastik*, by Adolf Feulner and Theodor Müller; Band III, *Malerei*, by Otto Fischer; Band IV, *Zeichnung und Graphik*, by Otto Fischer; Band V, *Kunstgewerbe*, by Heinrich Kohlhaussen; Band VI, *Die Kunst des 20. Jahrhunderts*, by Franz Roh. Good, classified bibliographies at the end of each volume. Excellent illustrations. A standard history of German art and architecture for beginning and advanced students.

Austria

Topographic Handbooks

807   **Dehio-Handbuch: Die Kunstdenkmäler Österreichs.** Vienna, Schroll, 1953– . 6v. to date. illus. index.
Edited by the Bundesdenkmalamt and Institut für österreichische Kunstforschung. This is the fourth and fifth editions of the original work by Georg Dehio, *Handbuch der deutschen Kunstdenkmäler . . . 2. Abteilung: Österreich . . .* (Berlin, 1933-35) expanded, rearranged, and rewritten by a team of specialists. List of volumes to date: *Wien*, by Justus Schmidt and Hans Tietze; *Niederösterreich*, by Richard Kurt Donin; *Oberösterreich*, by Erwin Hainisch; *Salzburg*, by Franz Martin; *Steiermark*, by Eberhard Hempel and Eduard Andorfer; *Tirol*, by Heinrich Hammer *et al.* Additional volumes covering the remaining provinces are planned. Topographical handbook of the art and architecture of Austria, divided by province and arranged by place. A short history of the place with reference to documents is followed by a thorough description and discussion of the major architectural monuments of Austria. Does not include works in museums. Intended as a field guide, it is also a major reference tool for the advanced student.

808   Hootz, Reinhardt. **Kunstdenkmäler in Österreich: Ein Bildhandbuch.** Munich, Berlin, Deutscher Kunstverlag, 1965-1968. 4v. illus. index. LC 67-96968.
Illustrated handbook of the art and architecture of Austria. Volume one covers the provinces of Salzburg, Tirol and Vorarlberg; Volume two, Carinthia and Styria; Volume three, Upper and Lower Austria and Burgenland; Volume four, the city and county of Vienna. Each volume has an introductory essay on the history of art and architecture in the particular regions, followed by an excellent collection of plates arranged by place. Informative notes to the plates give dates, attribution, plans, etc. There is a chronological listing of the works illustrated. A standard handbook for beginning and advanced students.

809   **Österreichische Kunsttopographie.** Band I– . Vienna, Schroll, 1907– . illus. index.
Official inventory of art and architecture in Austria. After 1918 it was published by Deutschösterreiches Staatsdenkmalamt, and after 1924 by Bundesdenkmalamt. Between 1937 and 1945 the name changed to *Ostmärkische Kunsttopographie*. In progress. To date the following volumes have appeared:

Band I, *Bezirk Krems* (1907)
Band II, *Stadt-Wien (XI-XXI Bezirk)* (1908)
Band III, *Bezirk Melk* (1909)
Band IV, *Pöggstall* (1910)
Band V, *Bezirk Horn* (1911)
Band VI, *Bezirk Waidhofen a.d. Thaya* (1911)
Band VII, *Benediktiner-Frauen-Stift Nonnberg in Salzburg* (1911)
Band VIII, *Bezirk Zwettl (ohne Stift Zwettl)* (1911)
Band IX, *Stadt Salzburg-Kirchliche Denkmale der Stadt Salzburg* (1912)
Band X, *Bezirk Salzburg* (1913)
Band XI, *Bezirk Salzburg* (1916)
Band XII, *Stift St. Peter in Salzburg* (1913)
Band XIII, *Profanen Denkmale der Stadt Salzburg* (1914)
Band XIV, *Hofburg in Wien* (1914)
Band XV, *Kunsthistorischer Atlas Wien* (1916)
Band XVI, *Die Kunstsammlungen der Stadt Salzburg* (1919)
Band XVII, *Urgeschichte des Kronlandes Salzburg* (1918)
Band XVIII, *Bezirk Baden* (1924)
Band XIX, *Stift Heiligenkreuz* (1926)
Band XX, *Bezirk Hallein* (1927)
Band XXI, *Bezirk Schärding* (1927)
Band XXII, *Bezirk Tamsweg* (1929)
Band XXIII, *St. Stephansdom in Wien* (1931)
Band XXIV, *Bezirk und Städte Eisenstadt und Rust* (1932)
Band XXV, *Bezirk Zell am See* (1933)
Band XXVI, *Volkskunde des Burgenlandes* (1935)
Band XXVII, *Vorgeschichtlichen Vorarlbergs* (1937)
Band XXVIII, *Landkreise Bischofshofen* (1940)
Band XXIX, *Zisterzienserkloster Zwettl* (1940)
Band XXX, *Bezirk Braunau* (1947)
Band XXXI, *Benediktinerstift St. Lambert* (1971)
Band XXXII, *Bezirk Feldkirch* (1949)
Band XXXIV, *Bezirk Lambach* (1959)
Band XXXV, *Bezirk Murau* (1964)
Band XXXVI, *Die Linzer Kirchen* (1964)
Band XXXVII, *Benediktinerstift St. Paul im Lavnattal* (1969)
Band XXXVIII, *Die Profanen Kunstdenkmäler der Stadt Innsbruck* (1972)
Band XXXIX, *Gerichtsbezirk Oberwölz* (1973)

Each volume devoted to a region is introduced by an historical sketch of the area followed by a description of major buildings (including their art contents and decoration), monuments, archaeological sites, and other *in situ* remains. The history of major places and monuments is discussed in detail with thorough reference to documentary sources and to specialized literature in the footnotes. Well and extensively illustrated with plates, plans, and diagrams. A standard reference work for the advanced student.

810   Oettinger, Karl, ed. **Reclams Kunstführer Österreich**. Stuttgart, Reclam,
       1961. 2v. illus. index.
Topographical guide to the art and architecture of Austria. Divided into regions
and arranged by place. Band I, *Wien, Niederösterreich, Oberösterreich, Burgenland*
(3rd ed., 1961; 703p.); Band II, *Salzburg, Tirol, Vorarlberg Kärnten, Steiermark*
(2nd ed., 1961; 895p.). Each place is introduced with an historical sketch followed
by a description and discussion of the major buildings. Although emphasis is on
architecture, the art contents of the buildings are briefly discussed. Illustrated with
plates and plans of the major buildings. Volume one has a useful glossary of terms;
each volume has an index by place and by artist-architect. Designed as a comprehensive, pocket-sized field guide, this work is remarkably thorough, but not as
detailed as the Dehio-Handbuch (807) or as definitive as the official inventories
(809). For the advanced student and art tourist.

Histories

811   Feuchtmüller, Rupert. **Kunst in Österreich vom frühen Mittelalters bis
       zur Gegenwart**. v. 1– . Vienna, Hanover, and Basel, Forum, 1972– .
       illus. index. LC 75-315996.
Comprehensive history of art and architecture in Austria from the early Middle
Ages to the present. Volume one covers the Middle Ages. Bibliographical references
are given at the end of each section. Well illustrated with plates, plans, and diagrams. Promises to be a standard history of Austrian art and architecture. For
beginning and advanced students.

812   Grimschitz, Bruno. **Ars Austriae**. Vienna, Wolfrum. 1960. 60p. (text);
       244p. (illus.). index. LC A61-5108.
Pictorial survey of the art and architecture of Austria from the seventh century
B.C. through the twentieth century. Introductory essay provides a brief historical
survey supplemented by more detailed information in the notes to the plates. No
bibliography. Popular survey in English for the general reader and the beginning
student.

Germany

Topographic Handbooks

813   Dehio, Georg. **Handbuch der deutschen Kunstdenkmäler**. New edition by
       the Vereinigung zur Herausgabe des Dehio-Handbuches. Munich,
       Deutscher Kunstverlag, 1964– . 8v. to date. illus. index.
New, expanded, and rewritten edition of the original five-volume work published
from 1900 to 1906. Comprehensive topographical handbook of the art and architecture of Germany from prehistoric times to the present. To date the following
volumes have appeared: *Baden-Württemberg*, by Friedrich Piel (1964); *Hamburg;
Schleswig-Holstein*, by Johannes Habich (1971); *Hessen*, by Magnus Backes (1966);

Nordrhein-Westfalen. Erster Band: Rheinland, by Ruth Schmitz-Ehmke (1967); *Nordrhein-Westfalen. Zweiter Band: Westfalen*, by Dorothea Kluge and Wilfried Hansmann (1969); *Rheinland-Pfalz, Saarland*, by Hans Caspary, Ekkart Klinge, and Wolfgang Götz (1972); *Die Bezirke Dresden, Karl-Marx-Stadt, Leipzig* (1965); *Die Bezirke Neubrandenburg, Rostock, Schwerin* (1968).

Additional volumes completing the coverage of both East and West Germany are in progress. Arranged by place, each volume provides a historical sketch of the place and a detailed description of the important buildings and their contents. Illustrated only with ground plans. No bibliography. A standard topographical handbook of German art and architecture. Indispensable for serious field study and a basic reference tool for the advanced student and scholar.

814   Hootz, Reinhardt. **Deutsche Kunstdenkmäler: Ein Bildhandbuch.**
Munich, Deutscher Kunstverlag, 1966-1974. 14v. illus. index.
Illustrated handbook of the art and architecture of Germany consisting of separate volumes for each of the present states of both East and West Germany. Consists of the following volumes:

> *Baden-Württemberg* (2nd ed., 1970)
> *Bayern nördlich der Donau* (2nd ed., 1967)
> *Bayern südlich der Donau* (2nd ed., 1967)
> *Bremen; Niedersachsen* (2nd ed., 1974)
> *Hamburg; Schleswig-Holstein* (2nd ed., 1968)
> *Hessen* (2nd ed., 1974)
> *Niederrhein* (2nd ed., 1966)
> *Rheinland-Pfalz und Saar* (2nd ed., 1969)
> *Westfalen* (2nd ed., 1972)
> *Thüringen (Bezirke Erfurt, Suhl, Gera)* (1968)
> *Provinz Sachsen und Land Anhalt (Bezirke Halle, Magdeburg)* (1968)
> *Sachsen (Bezirke Leipzig, Dresden, Karl-Marx-Stadt)* (1968)
> *Mecklenburg (Bezirke Schwerin, Rostock, Neu-Brandenburg)* (1971)
> *Mark Brandenburg und Berlin (Bezirke Potsdam, Frankfurt an der Oder, Cottbus, Berlin)* (1971).

Each volume has an introductory essay that surveys the art history of the region, followed by an excellent collection of plates arranged by place, notes to the plates with plans and basic historical data, a chronological list of the works of art illustrated, and maps indicating the locations of the places. No bibliography. Although they do not substitute for the more intensive and extensive treatment of art and architectural monuments in the numerous official inventories (809), these volumes are handy and competent reference tools to the major works of art and architecture *in situ* in Germany. Their small size permits their use as field guides for intensive art travel. For the advanced student.

Inventories of Art and Architecture

German art and architecture inventories present a complex bibliographical problem. Territorial changes after the two wars have broken the continuity of earlier series, changing their titles and scope, and have brought new series into being. To facilitate the use of these extremely valuable reference works for advanced study in German art history, they are arranged here under headings corresponding to major regions of Germany. The present-day territorial equivalents are given in parenthesis.

All of the inventories are thoroughly illustrated with plates, diagrams, and plans. Many provide old views of places and buildings. All follow a geographical arrangement by place within counties (*Kreise*). And all provide invaluable bibliographical references either in the form of footnotes or as separate bibliographies at the end of sections or volumes.

Bavaria (Land Bayern)

815   **Die Kunstdenkmäler Bayerns**. Munich, Oldenbourg, 1895– . 95v. illus. index.
Official inventory of art and architecture in Bavaria. The series is divided by the eight *Regierungsbezirke* and then by *Kreise*. To date the following have appeared:
    I, *Oberbayern*
        1) *Ingolstadt, Pfaffenhofen, Schrobenhausen, Aichach, Friedberg, Dachau, Freising, Bruck, Landsberg, Schongau, Garmisch, Tölz, Weilheim, München I und II* (1895); 2) *München Stadt, Erding, Ebersberg, Miesbach, Rosenheim, Traunstein, Wasserburg* (1895); 3) *Mühldorf, Alt-Ötting, Laufen, Berchtesgaden, Register zu Teil 1* [Index to section I] (1908)

    II, *Oberpfalz und Regensburg*
        1) *Roding* (1905); 2) *Neuburg v. W.* (1906); 3) *Waldmünchen* (1906); 4) *Parsberg* (1906); 5) *Burglengenfeld* (1906); 6) *Cham* (1906); 7) *Oberviechtach* (1906); 8) *Vohenstrauss* (1907); 9) *Neustadt a. W.* (1907); 10) *Kemnath* (1907); 11) *Eschenbach* (1909); 12) *AG. Beilngries* (1908); 13) *AG. Riedenburg* (1908); 14) *Tirschenreuth* (1908); 15) *BA. Amberg* (1909); 16) *Stadt Amberg* (1909); 17) *Neumarkt* (1909); 18) *Nabburg* (1910); 19) *Sulzbach* (1910); 20) *Stadtamhof* (1914); 21) *BA. Regensburg* (1910); 22) *Stadt Regensburg* (3v.; 1933)

    III, *Unterfranken und Aschaffenburg*
        1) *Ochsenfurt* (1911); 2) *Kitzingen* (1911); 3) *BA. Würzburg* (1911); 4) *Hassfurt* (1912); 5) *Hofheim* (1912); 6) *Karlstadt* (1912); 7) *Marktheidenfeld* (1913); 8) *Gerolzhofen* (1913); 9) *Lohr* (1914); 10) *Kissingen* (1914); 11) *Brückenau* (1914); 12) *Stadt Würzburg* (1915); 13) *Königshofen* (1915); 14) *Hammelburg* (1915); 15) *Ebern* (1916); 16) *Alzenau* (1916); 17) *BA. Schweinfurt* (1917);

18) *Miltenberg* (1917); 19) *Stadt Aschaffenburg* (1918); 20)
Gemünden (1920); 21) *Mellrichstadt* (1921); 22) *Neustadt a. S.*
(1922); 23) *Obernburg* (1925); 24) *BA. Aschaffenburg* (1927)

IV, *Niederbayern*
1) *Dingolfing* (1912); 2) *BA. Landshut* (1914); 3) *Stadt Passau* (1919);
4) *BA. Passau* (1920); 5) *Vilsbiburg* (1921); 6) *Stadt Straubing* (1921);
7) *Kelheim* (1922); 8) *Eggenfelden* (1923); 9) *Kötzting* (1922);
10) *Pfarrkirchen* (1923); 11) *Wegscheid* (1924); 12) *BA. Straubing*
(1925); 13) *Landau a.I.* (1926); 14) *Vilshofen* (1926); 15) *Viechtach*
(1926); 16) *Stadt Landshut* (1927); 17) *Deggendorf* (1928); 18)
Mainburg (1928); 19) *Regen* (1928); 20) *Bogen* (1929); 21) *Griesbach*
(1929); 22) *Rottenburg* (1930); 23) *Wolfstein* (1931); 24) *Grafenau*
(1933); 25) *Mallersdorf* (1936)

V, *Mittelfranken*
1) *Stadt Eichstätt* (1924); 2) *BA. Eichstätt* (1928); 3) *BA. Hilpoltstein*
(1929); 4) *Stadt Dinkelsbühl* (1931); 5) *Weissenburg* (1932); 6)
Gunzenhausen (1937); 7) *Schwabach* (1939); 8) *Rothenburg o. T.*
kirchl. Bauten (1959); 10) *Hersbruck* (1959); 11) *Landkreis Lauf an*
der Pegnitz (1966)

VII, *Schwaben und Neuburg*
1) *BA. Nördlingen* (1938); 2) *Stadt Nördlingen* (1940); 3) *LK.*
Donauwörth (1951); 4) *Lindau* (1954); 5) *Neuburg/Donau* (1958);
6) *Stadt Dillingen* (1964); 8) *LK. Sonthofen* (1964)

VIII, *Oberfranken*
1) *Wundsiedel und Stadt Marktredwitz* (1954); 2) *Pegnitz* (1961).

Baden-Württemberg (Land Baden-Württemberg)

816   **Die Kunstdenkmäler Badens.** Various places and publishers. Presently:
Munich, Deutscher Kunstverlag. 1887– . 22v. illus. index. LC 53-23592.
Official inventory of the art and architecture in Baden. Until 1933 it was titled
Die Kunstdenkmäler des Grossherzogthums Baden. To date the following volumes
have appeared:
Band 1: *Kreis Konstanz*; Band 2: *Kreis Villingen*; Band 3: *Kreis Waldshut*;
Band 4,1: *Kreis Mosbach. Amtsbezirk Wertheim*; Band 4,2: *Kreis*
Mosbach. Amtsbezirk Tauberbischofsheim; Band 4,3: *Kreis Mosbach.*
Amtsbezirke Buchen und Adelsheim; Band 4,4: *Kreis Mosbach. Amtsbezirke*
Mosbach und Eberbach; Band 5: *Kreis Lörrach*; Band 6,1: *Kreis Freiburg.*
Amtsbezirke Breisach, Emmendingen, Ettenheim, Freiburg Land,
Neustadt, Staufen und Waldkirch; Band 7: *Kreis Offenburg*; Band 8,1:
Kreis Heidelberg. Amtsbezirke Sinsheim, Eppingen und Weisloch; Band
8,2: *Kreis Heidelberg. Amtsbezirk Heidelberg*; Band 9,1: *Kreis Karlsruhe.*
Amsbezirk Bretten; Band 9,2: *Kreis Karlsruhe. Amtsbezirk Bruchsal*;
Band 9,3: *Kreis Karlsruhe. Amtsbezirk Ettlingen*; Band 9,5: *Kreis*
Karlsruhe. Amtsbezirk Karlsruhe Land; Band 9,6: *Kreis Karlsruhe.*

Amtsbezirk Pforzheim Stadt; Band 9,7: *Kreis Karlsruhe. Amtsbezirk Pforzheim Land*; Band 10,2: *Kreis Mannheim. Stadt Schwetzingen*; Band 10,3: *Kreis Mannheim. Landkreis Mannheim*; Band 11,1: *Kreis Baden-Baden. Stadt Baden-Baden*; Band 12,1: *Kreis Rastatt. Landkreis Rastatt.*

817   **Die Kunstdenkmäler Hohenzollerns.** Stuttgart, Spemann, 1939-1948.
         2v. illus. index.
Official inventory of the art and architecture in the former province of Hohenzollern.
Contents: Band 1, *Kreis Hechingen* (1939); Band 2, *Kreis Sigmaringen* (1948).

818   **Die Kunst- und Altertumsdenkmale im Königreich Württemberg.** Stutt-
         gart, Deutsche Verlags-Anstalt, 1897-1914. 4v. illus. index.
Official inventory of the art and architecture in the former kingdom of
Württemberg. Succeeded by *Die Kunst- und Altertumsdenkmale in Württemberg*
(819). Contents: Band 1, *Schwarzwaldkreis* (1897); Band 2, *Neckarkreis* (1889);
Band 3, *Jagstkreis* (2v.; 1907-1913); Band 4, *Donaukreis I* (1914).

819   **Die Kunst- und Altertumsdenkmale in Württemberg.** Stuttgart, Deutsche
         Verlags-Anstalt, 1924-1936. 4v. illus. index.
Official inventory of the art and architecture in Württemberg. Succeeds *Die Kunst-
und Altertumsdenkmale im Königreich Württemberg* (818) and is succeeded by
Die Kunstdenkmäler in Württemberg (820). Contents: Band 1, *Donaukreis II*
(1924); Band 2, *Oberamt Münsingen* (1926); Band 3, *Oberamt Ravensburg* (1931);
Band 4, *Kreis Riedlingen* (1936).

820   **Die Kunstdenkmäler in Württemberg.** Stuttgart, Deutsche Verlags-
         Anstalt, 1937– . 5v. to date. illus. index. LC 38-8276 rev. 2.
Official inventory of art and architecture in the German Federal State of
Württemberg. Succeeds *Die Kunst- und Altertumsdenkmale in Württemberg*
(819). To date the following volumes have appeared:
         Band 1, *Kreis Tettnang* (1937)
         Band 2, *Kreis Saulgau* (1938)
         Band 3, *Ehemaliger Kreis Waldsee* (1943)
         Band 4, *Ehemaliger Kreis Wangen* (1954)
         Band 5, *Ehemaliges Oberamt Künzelsau* (1962).

Hesse (Land Hessen)

821   **Die Kunstdenkmäler im Grossherzogtum Hesse.** Darmstadt, Bergsträsser,
         1885-1934. 9v. illus. index.
Official inventory of the art and architecture in the former grand duchy of Hesse.
In 1919 the title changed to *Die Kunstdenkmäler im Freistaat Hessen*; in 1933,
to *Die Kunstdenkmäler im Volkstaat Hessen*. Succeeded by *Bau- und
Kunstdenkmäler des Landes Hessen* (822). Contents:

Provinz Starkenburg: Kreis Bensheim (1914)
Provinz Starkenburg: Kreis Offenbach (1885)
Provinz Starkenburg: Kreis Wimpfen (1898)
Provinz Starkenburg: Kreis Erbach (1891)
Provinz Oberhessen: Kreis Friedberg (1895)
Provinz Oberhessen: Kreis Büdingen (1890)
Provinz Oberhessen: Kreis Giessen. Band II (1919)
Provinz Rheinhessen: Stadt und Kreis Mainz (1919)
Provinz Rheinhessen: Kreis Bingen (1934).

822   **Die Bau- und Kunstdenkmäler des Landes Hessen.** Munich, Berlin,
Deutscher Kunstverlag, 1958– . 4v. to date. illus. index.
Official inventory of the art and architecture in the German Federal State of
Hessen. Succeeds *Die Kunstdenkmäler im Grossherzogtums Hessen* (821). To date
the following volumes have appeared: Band 1, *Kreis Biedenkopf* (1958); Band 2,
Rheingau Kreis; Band 3, *Kreis Bergstrasse* (2v.; 1969).

823   **Die Bau- und Kunstdenkmäler im Regierungsbezirk Cassel.** Marburg,
1901-1939. 10v. illus. index.
Official inventory of the art and architecture in the former Prussian Regierungsbe-
zirk Cassel. Today the territory is part of the German Federal State of Hessen. In
1937 it began a new series (Neue Folge) with its own volume numbers. Contents:
Band 1, *Kreis Gelnhausen* (1901)
Band II, *Kreis Fritzlar* (1909)
Band III, *Kreis Grafschaft Schaumburg* (1907)
Band IV, *Kreis Cassel-Land* (1910)
Band VI, *Kreis Cassel-Stadt* (1923)
Band VII, *Kreis Hofgeismar* (1926)
Band VIII, *Kreis Marburg-Stadt* (1934)
Neue Folge (published in Kassel):
Band 1, *Kreis Wolfhagen* (1937)
Band 2, *Kreis der Twiste* (1938)
Band 3, *Kreis des Eisenberges* (1939).

824   **Die Bau- und Kunstdenkmäler des Regierungsbezirks Wiesbaden.**
Frankfurt am Main, 1907-1921. 6v. illus. index. Reprint: Walluf, Sandig,
1973. 5v.
Official inventory of the art and architecture in the former Prussian Regierungsbe-
zirk Wiesbaden. The territory is today part of the German Federal State of Hessen.
Contents:
Band I, *Rheingau* (1907)
Band II, *Ost-Taunus* (1905)
Band III, *Lahngebiets* (1908)
Band IV, *Oberwesterwald. Westerburg* (1910)
Band V, *Nassauischen Kreise* (1914)
Band VI, *Nachlese zu Band I bis V* (1921).

825   **Die Baudenkmäler in Frankfurt am Main.** Frankfurt/Main, 1896-1914.
3v. illus. index.
Official inventory of the art and architecture in the city of Frankfurt am Main.

Rhineland (Land Rheinland-Pfalz, Land Nordrhein)

826   **Die Kunstdenkmäler der Pfalz.** Munich, Oldenborg, 1926-1939. illus.
index. 8v.
Official inventory of the art and architecture in the former Bavarian province of the
Palatinate. Series consists of:
     Band 1, *Stadt und Bezirksamt Neustadt (Haardt)* (1926)
     Band 2, *Stadt und Bezirksamt Landau* (1928)
     Band 3, *Stadt und Bezirksamt Speyer* (1934)
     Band 4, *Bezirksamt Bergzabern* (1935)
     Band 5, *Bezirksamt Germersheim* (1927)
     Band 6, *Stadt und Bezirksamt Ludwigshafen* (1936)
     Band 7, *Bezirksamt Kircheimbolanden* (1938)
     Band 8, *Stadt und Landkreis Frankenthal* (1939).

827   **Die Kunstdenkmäler der Rheinprovinz.** Düsseldorf, Schwann, 1891-
1944. 19v. in 41. illus. index.
Official inventory of art and architecture in the former Prussian province of the
Rhineland, which is today divided between the German Federal States of Nordrhein-
Westfalen and Rheinland-Pfalz. For successor series see (828). The following volumes
appeared:
     Band 1, *Kreis Kempen, Geldern, Moers, Kleve*
     Band 2, *Kreis Rees, Duisburg, Mulheim, Ruhrort, Essen*
     Band 3, *Kreis Düsseldorf, Barmen, Elberfeld, Remscheid, Lennep, Mett-
          mann, Solingen, Neuss, M-Gladbach, Krefeld, Grevenbroich*
     Band 4, *Landkreis Köln, Kreis Rheinbach, Bergheim, Euskirchen*
     Band 5,1, *Kreis Gummersbach, Waldrael, Wipperfurth*
     Band 5,2, *Kreis Mülheim am Rhein*
     Band 5,3, *Stadtkreis Bonn*
     Band 6, *Stadt Köln* (4v.)
     Band 7, *Stadt Köln* (4v.)
     Band 8,1, *Kreis Jülich*
     Band 8,2, *Kreis Erkeleuz und Geilenkirchen*
     Band 8,3, *Kreis Heinsburg*
     Band 9,1, *Kreis Düren*
     Band 9,2, *Landkreis Aachen und Eupen*
     Band 10, *Stadt Aachen* (3v.)
     Band 11, *Monschau*
     Band 12,1, *Kreis Bitburg* (1927)
     Band 12,2, *Kreis Prüm* (1927)
     Band 12,3, *Kreis Daun* (1928)
     Band 12,4, *Kreis Wittlich* (1934)

Band 13, *Stadt Trier* (2v.; 1938)
Band 15,1, *Kreis Bernkastel* (1935)
Band 15,2, *Landkreis Trier* (1936)
Band 15,3, *Kreis Saarburg* (1939)
Band 16,1, *Kreis Altenkirchen* (1935)
Band 16,2, *Kreis Neuwied* (1940)
Band 16,3, *Landkreis Koblenz* (1944)
Band 17,1, *Kreis Ahrweiler* (1938)
Band 17,2, *Kreis Mayen* (1941)
Band 18,1, *Kreis Kreuznach* (1935)
Band 19,3, *Kreis Zell an der Mosel* (1938)
Band 20,1, *Die kirchlichen Denkmäler der Stadt Koblenz* (1937)

828   **Die Kunstdenkmäler von Rheinland-Pfalz.** Munich, Berlin, Deutscher
Kunstverlag, 1954— . 5v. illus. index.
Official inventory of art and architecture in the German Federal State of
Rheinland-Pfalz. In part successor to the series *Die Kunstdenkmäler der
Rheinprovinz* (827) and *Die Kunstdenkmäler der Pfalz* (826). To date the
following volumes have appeared:
Band I, *Stadt Koblenz* (1954)
Band II, *Stadt und Landkreis Pirmasens* (1957)
Band III, *Kreis Cochem* (1959)
Band IV, 1, *Stadt Mainz*
Band V, *Der Dom zu Speyer.* (3v., 1973)

Westphalia (Land Westfalen)

829   **Die Bau- und Kunstdenkmäler von Westfalen.** Münster, 1893— . 52v.
illus. index.
Official inventory of art and architecture in Westphalia. Contents:

Kreis Ahaus (1900)	*Gelsenkirchen-Stadt* (1908)
Kreis Altena (1911)	*Hagen-Stadt* (1910)
Kreis Arnsberg (1906)	*Kreis Hagen-Land* (1910)
Kreis Beckum (1897)	*Stadt Hamm* (1936)
Bielefeld-Stadt (1906)	*Kreis Halle* (1908)
Kreis Bielefeld-Land (1906)	*Kreis Hattingen* (1909)
Stadt Bocholt (1931)	*Kreis Herford* (1908)
Bochum-Stadt (1906)	*Kreis Hörde* (1895)
Kreis Bochum-Land (1907)	*Kreis Höxter* (1914)
Kreis Borken (1954)	*Kreis Iserlohn* (1900)
Kreis Brilon (1952)	*Kreis Lippstadt* (1911)
Kreis Büren (1926)	*Kreis Lübbecke* (1907)
Creis Coesfeld (1913)	*Kreis Lüdinghausen* (1893)
Dortmund-Stadt	*Kreis Meschede* (1908)
Kreis Dortmund-Land (1895)	*Kreis Minden* (1902)

Stadt Münster (7v.; 1932-62)
Kreis Münster-Land (1897)
Kreis Olpe (1903)
Kreis Paderborn (1899)
Kreis Recklinghausen (1929)
Kreis Schwelm (1910)
Kreis Siegen (1903)
Kreis Soest (1905)

Kreis Steinfurt (1904)
Kreis Tecklenburg (1907)
Kreis Unna (1959)
Kreis Warburg (1939)
Kreis Warendorf (1936)
Kreis Wiedenbrück (1901)
Witten-Stadt (1910)
Kreis Wittgenstein (1903)

Lower Saxony (Land Niedersachsen, Land Bremen)

830   **Die Kunstdenkmäler der Provinz Hannover.** Hanover, Provinzialverwaltung, 1899-1941. 25v. illus. index. LC 53-34984.
Official inventory of the art and architecture of the former province of Hanover. Territory now part of the German Federal State of Niedersachsen. Succeeded by *Die Kunstdenkmäler des Landes Niedersachsen* (832). Contents:
Band I,1, *Landkreise Hannover und Linden* (1899)
Band I,2, *Stadt Hannover* (in two parts; 1932)
Band I,3, *Kreis Springe* (1941)
Band II,1, *Stadt Goslar* (1901)
Band II,2, *Stadt Goslar* (1901)
Band II,3, *Kreis Marienburg* (1910)
Band II,4, *Stadt Hildesheim* (in two parts; 1912)
Band II,6, *Kreis Alfeld* (1929)
Band II,7, *Landkreis Goslar* (1937)
Band II,8, *Kreis Peine* (1938)
Band II,9, *Landkreis Hildesheim* (1938)
Band II,10, *Kreis Alfeld II* (1939)
Band III,1, *Kreise Burgdorf und Fallingbostel* (1902)
Band III,2, *Stadt Lüneburg*
Band III,4, *Kreis Gifhorn* (1931)
Band III,5, *Stadt Celle* (1937)
Band III,6, *Kreis Soltau* (1939)
Band IV,1, *Stadt Osnabrück* (1907)
Band IV,2, *Stadt Osnabrück* (1907)
Band IV,3, *Kreise Wittlage und Bersenbrück* (1915)
Band IV,4, *Kreise Lingen und Grafschaft Bentheim* (1919)
Band V,1, *Kreise Verden, Rotenburg und Zeven* (1908)
Band VI,1, *Stadt Emden* (1927)
Band VI,2, *Stadt Emden* (1927)
In 1939 two volumes not numbered with the above volumes appeared: *Die Kunstdenkmäler des Kreises Wesermünde. I: Die ehemalige Kreis Lehe*, and *II: Der frühere Kreis Geestemünde.*

831 **Die Bau- und Kunstdenkmäler des Herzogtums Braunschweig.**
Wölfenbüttel, various publishers, 1896-1922. 7v. illus. index.
Official inventory of art and architecture in the former duchy of Braunschweig, which is now part of the German Federal State of Niedersachsen. See (832) for successor series. Contents:
Band I, *Kreis Helmstedt* (1896)
Band II, *Kreis Braunschweig mit Ausschluss der Stadt Braunschweig* (1900)
Band III,1, *Stadt Wölfenbüttel* (1904)
Band III,2, *Die Ortschaften des Kreises Wölfenbüttel* (1906)
Band IV, *Kreis Holzminden* (1907)
Band V, *Kreis Gandersheim* (1910)
Band VI, *Kreis Blankenburg* (1922)

832 **Die Kunstdenkmäler des Landes Niedersachsens.** Berlin and Munich, Deutscher Kunstverlag, 1956– . 5v. to date. illus. index.
Official inventory of the art and architecture in the German Federal State of Niedersachsen. Successor to *Die Kunstdenkmäler der Provinz Hannover* (830). To date the following volumes have appeared:
Band I,1, *Land Hadeln und der Stadt Cuxhaven* (1956)
Band I,2, *Stadt Stade* (1960)
Band I,3, *Landkreis Stade* (2v.; 1965)
Band II,1, *Kreis Neustadt am Rübenberge* (1958)

Schleswig-Holstein (Land Schleswig-Holstein, Land Hamburg)

833 **Die Kunstdenkmäler der Provinz Schleswig-Holstein.** Berlin, Deutscher Kunstverlag, 1939. 4v. illus. index.
Official inventory of the art and architecture in the former province of Schleswig-Holstein. Succeeded by *Die Kunstdenkmäler des Landes Schleswig-Holstein* (834). Contents: Band 1, *Kreis Husum* (1939); Band 2, *Kreis Eiderstedt* (1939); Band 3, *Kreis Pinneberg* (1939); Band 4, *Kreis Südtondern* (1939).

834 **Die Kunstdenkmäler des Landes Schleswig-Holstein.** Munich, Berlin, Deutscher Kunstverlag, 1950– . 6v. to date. illus. index.
Official inventory of the art and architecture in the Federal German State of Schleswig-Holstein. Successor to *Die Kuntsdenkmäler der Provinz Schleswig-Holstein* (833), numbering its volumes together with the older series. To date the following volumes have appeared: Band 5, *Kreis Eckenförde* (1950); Band 6, *Landkreis Flensburg* (1952); Band 7, *Stadt Flensburg* (1955); Band 8, *Landkreis Schleswig* (1957); Band 9, *Kreis Pinneberg* (1961); Band 10,2, *Stadt Schleswig. Der Dom und ehemalige Dombezirk* (1966).

835 **Die Bau- und Kunstdenkmäler der Hansestadt Lübeck.** Lübeck, 1906-1939. 6v. illus. index.

Official inventory of the art and architecture in the city and county of Lübeck.
Contents:
Band I, *Profane Denkmäler* (1939)
Band II, *Petrikirche, Marienkirche, Heilig-Geist Kirche* (1906)
Band III,1, *Der Dom* (1919)
Band III,2, *Dom, Jakobikirche, Ägidienkirche* (1920)
Band IV,1, *Die Klöster* (1926)
Band IV,2, *Aussengebieten* (1928).

Mecklenburg (Bezirke Neubrandenburg, Rostock, Schwerin)

836   **Die Kunst- und Geschichtsdenkmäler des Grossherzogtums Mecklenburg-Schwerin.** Schwerin, 1896-1902. 5v. illus. index.
Official inventory of art and architecture in the former grand duchy of Mecklenburg-Schwerin. The following volumes appeared:
Band I, *Amtsgerichtsbezirke Rostock, Ribnitz, Sülze-Marlow, Tessin, Laage, Gnoien. Dargun. Neukalen* (1898)
Band II, *Amtsgerichtsbezirke Wismar, Grevesmühlen, Rehna, Gadebusch, Schwerin* (1899)
Band III, *Amtsgerichtsbezirke Hagenow, Wittenburg, Boizenburg, Lübtheen, Dömitz, Grabow, Ludwigslust, Neustadt, Crivitz, Brüel, Warin, Neubukow, Kröpelin, Doberan* (1900)
Band IV, *Amtsgerichtsbezirke Schwaan, Bützow, Sternberg, Güstrow, Krakow, Goldberg, Parchim, Lübz, Plau* (1901)
Band V, *Amtsgerichtsbezirke Teterow, Malchin, Stavenhagen, Penzlin, Waren, Malchow, Röbel* (1902).

837   **Kunst- und Geschichtsdenkmäler des Freistaates Mecklenburg-Strelitz.** Neubrandenburg, various publishers, 1921-1934. 4v. illus. index.
Official inventory of the art and architecture in the former state of Mecklenburg-Strelitz. Successor to *Die Kunst- und Geschichtsdenkmäler des Grossherzogtums Mecklenburg-Schwerin* (836). Contents:
Band I,1, *Amtsgerichtsbezirke Neustrelitz, Strelitz, Mirow* (1921)
Band I,2, *Amtsgerichtsbezirke Fürtenberg, Feldberg, Woldegk, Friedland (Des Land Stargard)* (1925)
Band I,3, *Amtsgerichtsbezirke Friedland, Stargard, Neubrandenburg* (1929)
Band II, *Das Land Ratzeburg* (1934).

838   **Die Kunstdenkmäler im Bezirk Rostock.** v. 1– . Leipzig, Seemann, 1963– . illus. index.
Official inventory of the art and architecture in the Bezirk Rostock of the German Democratic Republic (East Germany). To date one volume has appeared: Band 1, *Kreis Rügen* (1963).

Thuringia (Bezirke Erfurt, Gera, Suhl, Halle, Magdeburg)

839   **Die Bau- und Kunstdenkmäler der Provinz Sachsen.** Halle, Historische Commission der Provinz Sachsen. Halle, 1879-1911. 29v. illus. index.
Official inventory of the art and architecture in the former Prussian Province of Saxony. Succeeded by *Die Kunstdenkmäler der Provinz Sachsen* (840). Contents:
Band 1, *Kreis Zeitz* (1879)
Band 2, *Kreis Langensalza* (1879)
Band 3, *Kreis Weissenfels* (1880)
Band 4, *Kreis Mühlhausen* (1881)
Band 5, *Kreis Sangerhausen* (1881)
Band 6, *Kreis Weisensee* (1882)
Band 7, *Grafschaft Wernigerode* (1883)
Band 8, *Kreis Merseburg* (1883)
Band 9, *Kreis Eckartsberga* (1883)
Band 10, *Kreis Calbe* (1885)
Band 11, *Stadt Nordhausen* (1888)
Band 12, *Grafschaft Hohenstein* (1889)
Band 13, *Stadt Erfurt und des Erfurter Landkreis* (1890)
Band 14, *Kreis Oschersleben* (1891)
Band 15, *Kreis Schweinitz* (1891)
Band 16, *Kreis Delitzsch* (1892)
Band 17, *Kreis Bitterfeld* (1893)
Band 18, *Mansfelder Gebirgskreises* (1893)
Band 19, *Mansfelder Seekreis* (1895)
Band 20, *Kreis Gardelegen* (1897)
Band 21, *Kreis Jerichow* (1898)
Band 22, *Kreis Ziegenrück und Schleusingen* (1901)
Band 23, *Halberstadt Land und Stadt* (1902)
Band 24, *Stadt Naumburg* (1903)
Band 25, *Stadt Aschersleben* (1904)
Band 26, *Kreis Naumburg (Land)* (1905)
Band 27, *Kreis Querfurt* (1909)
Band 28, *Kreis Heiligenstadt* (1909)
Band 29, *Kreis Wolmirstadt* (1911)

840   **Die Kunstdenkmäler der Provinz Sachsen.** Burg, Hopfer, 1929-1938. 5v. illus. index. LC 50-47346.
Official inventory of the art and architecture in the former Province of Saxony (Provinz Sachsen). Succeeds *Die Bau- und Kunstdenkmäler der Provinz Sachsen* (839). Contents:
Band 1, *Die Stadt Erfurt* (1929)
Band 2, *Die Stadt Erfurt* (1931)
Band 2,2, *Die Stadt Erfurt* (1932)
Band 3, *Kreis Stendal Land* (1933)
Band 4, *Kreis Osterburg* (1938)

841   **Die Kunstdenkmäler im Bezirk Magdeburg.** Halle, Leipzig, Seemann,
       1961– . v.1– . illus. index.
Official inventory of the art and architecture in the Bezirk Magdeburg in the
German Democratic Republic (East Germany). Bezirk Magdeburg is part of the old
Freistaat and Königreich Sachsen. Successor to the series (839) and (840). To date
one volume has appeared: Band 1, *Kreis Haldensleben* (1961).

Saxony (Bezirke Dresden, Karl-Marx-Stadt, Leipzig)

842   **Beschreibende Darstellung der älteren Bau- und Kunstdenkmäler des
       Königreichs Sachsen.** Dresden, various publishers, 1882-1923. 42v.
       illus. index.
Official inventory of the art and architecture in the former kingdom of Saxony.
Succeeded in 1929 by the series *Die Kunstdenkmäler des Freistaates Sachsen*
(843). Contents:
   Heft 1, *Amtshauptmannschaft Pirna* (1882)
   Heft 2, *Amtshauptmannschaft Dippoldiswalde* (1883)
   Heft 3, *Amtshauptmannschaft Freiberg* (1884)
   Heft 4, *Amtshauptmannschaft Annaberg* (1885)
   Heft 5, *Amtshauptmannschaft Marienberg* (1886)
   Heft 6, *Amtshauptmannschaft Flöha* (1886)
   Heft 7, *Amtshauptmannschaft Chemnitz* (1886)
   Heft 8, *Amtshauptmannschaft Schwarzenberg* (1887)
   Heft 9, *Amtshauptmannschaft Auerbach* (1888)
   Heft 10, *Amtshauptmannschaft Oelnitz* (1888)
   Heft 11, *Amtshauptmannschaft Plauen* (1888)
   Heft 12, *Amtshauptmannschaft Zwickau* (1889)
   Heft 13, *Amtshauptmannschaft Glauchau* (1890)
   Heft 14, *Amtshauptmannschaft Rochlitz* (1890)
   Heft 15, *Amtshauptmannschaft Borna* (1891)
   Heft 16, *Amtshauptmannschaft Leipzig* (1894)
   Heft 17, *Amtshauptmannschaft Stadt Leipzig* (1895)
   Heft 18, *Amtshauptmannschaft Stadt Leipzig* (1896)
   Heft 19/20, *Amtshauptmannschaft Grimma* (1897)
   Heft 21, *Stadt Dresden* (1909)
   Heft 22, *Stadt Dresden* (1901)
   Heft 23, *Stadt Dresden* (1903)
   Heft 24, *Amtshauptmannschaft Dresden-Altstadt* (1904)
   Heft 25, *Amtshauptmannschaft Döbeln* (1903)
   Heft 26, *Amtshauptmannschaft Dresden-Neustadt* (1904)
   Heft 27/28, *Amtshauptmannschaft Oschatz* (1905)
   Heft 29, *Amtshauptmannschaft Zittau* (1906)
   Heft 30, *Stadt Zittau* (1907)
   Heft 31/32, *Amtshauptmannschaft Bautzen* (1908)
   Heft 33, *Stadt Bautzen* (1909)
   Heft 34, *Amtshauptmannschaft Löbau* (1910)

Heft 35, *Amtshauptmannschaft Kamenz* (1912)
Heft 36, *Städte Kamenz und Pulsnitz* (1912)
Heft 37, *Amtshauptmannschaft Grossenhain* (1914)
Heft 38, *Städte Grossenhain, Radeburg und Riesa* (1914)
Heft 39, *Meissen* (1917)
Heft 40, *Meissen (Burgberge)* (1919)
Heft 41, *Meissen-Land* (1923)
    Erganzungsheft- Altenzella (1922)

843   **Die Kunstdenkmäler des Freistaates Sachsen.** Dresden, 1929. illus. index.
Official inventory of the art and architecture in the former free state of Sachsen
(successor state to the kingdom of Saxony). Only one volume appeared: Band I,
Die Stadt Pirna (Dresden, 1929).

Brandenburg (Bezirke Potsdam, Frankfurt an der Oder, Cottbus)

844   **Die Kunstdenkmäler der Provinz Mark Brandenburg.** Berlin, Deutscher
       Kunstverlag, 1907-1960. 21v. illus. index. LC 50-49544.
Official inventory of art and architecture in the former province of Brandenburg.
Contents:
       Band I,1, *Kreis Westpriegnitz* (1909)
       Band I,2, *Kreis Ostpriegnitz* (1907)
       Band I,3, *Kreis Ruppin* (1914)
       Band II,1, *Kreis Westhavelland* (1913)
       Band II,3, *Stadt und Dom Brandenburg* (1912)
       Band III,1, *Kreis Prenzlau* (1921)
       Band III,2, *Kreis Templin* (1937)
       Band III,3, *Kreis Angermünde* (1934)
       Band III,4, *Kreis Niederbarnim* (1939)
       Band IV,1, *Kreis Teltow* (1941)
       Band V,1, *Kreis Luckau* (1917)
       Band VI,1, *Kreis Lebus* (1909)
       Band VI,2, *Stadt Frankfurt a. Oder* (1912)
       Band VI,3, *Kreis Weststernberg* (1913)
       Band VI,4, *Kreis Oststernberg* (1960)
       Band VI,6, *Kreis Crossen* (1921)
       Band VII,1, *Kreis Königsberg* (1928)
       Band VII,3, *Kreis Landsberg* (1937)

Silesia (now under Polish administration)

845   **Verzeichnis der Kunstdenkmäler der Provinz Schlesien.** Breslau, 1886-
       1903. 5v. illus. index.
Official inventory of art and architecture in the former German province of
Silesia. Contents:

Band I, *Die Stadt Breslau* (1886)
Band II, *Die Landkreis des Reg. Bezirks Breslau* (1889)
Band III, *Reg. Bezirk Liegnitz* (1891)
Band IV, *Reg. Bezirk Oppeln* (1894)
Band V, *Register* [Index] (1903).

846   **Die Bau- und Kunstdenkmäler Schlesiens.** Breslau, 1939-1943. 3v. illus.
       index.
Official inventory of the former German province of Silesia. Succeeded by *Bau-
und Kunstdenkmäler des deutschen Ostens* (847). Contents: Band II, *Kreis
Namslau* (1939); Band IV, *Stadtkreis Oppeln* (1939); Band V, *Kreis Tost-
Gleiwitz* (1943).

847   **Die Bau- und Kunstdenkmäler des deutschen Ostens.** Frankfurt am
       Main, Weidlich, 1965– . illus. index.
Inventory of the art and architecture in the former German territories in Eastern
Europe. To date one volume has appeared: *Die Bau- und Kunstdenkmäler des
Landkreises Breslau* (1965).

East and West Prussia (now under Polish administration)

848   **Die Bau- und Kunstdenkmäler der Provinz Westpreussen.** Danzig,
       Provinzial-Landtag, 1884-1919. 14v. illus. index.
Official inventory of art and architecture of the former German province of West
Prussia. Contents:
       Band I,1, *Kreis Carthaus, Berent und Neustadt* (1885)
       Band I,2, *Landkreis Danzig* (1885)
       Band I,3, *Kreis Pr. Stargard* (1885)
       Band I,4, *Kreis Marienwerder westl. der Weichsel, Schwetz, Konitz,
           Schlochau, Tuchel, Flatow, Deutsch Krone* (1887)
       Band II,5, *Kreis Kulm* (1887)
       Band II,6, *Kreis Thorn* (1889)
       Band II,7, *Stadt Thorn* (1889)
       Band II,8, *Kreis Strasburg* (1891)
       Band II,9, *Kreis Graudenz* (1894)
       Band II,10, *Kreis Löbau* (1895)
       Band III,11, *Kreis Marienwerder östl. der Weichsel* (1898)
       Band III,12, *Kreis Rosenberg* (1906)
       Band III,13, *Kreis Stuhm* (1909)
       Band IV,14, *Neuteich, Tiegenort und die ländlichen Ortschaften* (1919)

Histories

849   **Art Treasures in Germany: Monuments, Masterpieces, Commissions, and Collections.** General eds., Bernard S. Myers and Trewin Copplestone. New York and Toronto, McGraw-Hill, 1970. 196p. illus. index. LC 73-76759.
Pictorial survey of architecture, painting, sculpture, and the decorative and minor arts in Germany from the time of the Celts (550 B.C.) to the present. Periods are treated by a variety of specialists. Contains maps and a glossary-index of museums and monuments, but no bibliography. For the general reader.

850   Dehio, Georg. **Geschichte der deutschen Kunst** . . . 3rd ed. Berlin and Leipzig, de Gruyter, 1923-1934. 4v. and atlas of plates. illus. index.
Comprehensive history of art and architecture in Germany from time of the Germanic migrations through the early twentieth century. Volume four, covering nineteenth and twentieth century art and architecture, is written by Gustav Pauli. Separate volume of plates for each volume of text. No bibliography. An old but classic history of German art. For the advanced student.

851   Lindemann, Gottfried. **History of German Art: Painting, Sculpture, Architecture.** New York, Praeger, 1971. 228p. illus. index. LC 79-89605.
Survey history of art and architecture in Germany from the Carolingian period through the first half of the twentieth century. No bibliography. For the general reader and the beginning student.

852   Pinder, Wilhelm. **Von Wesen und Werden deutscher Formen** . . . Leipzig, Seemann, 1937-1951. 4v. in 5. illus. index.
A new edition, edited by Georg Scheja, was published in 1957 (Frankfurt am Main, Menck) with four volumes of text and three volumes of illustrations. Comprehensive history of art and architecture in Germany from the Carolingian period through the middle of the sixteenth century. No bibliography. A standard history of German medieval and Renaissance art and architecture for the advanced student.

853   Vey, Horst, and Xavier de Salas. **German and Spanish Art to 1900.** New York, Franklin Watts, 1965. 307p. illus. index. LC 64-23687.
Pictorial survey of art and architecture in Germany and Spain from Carolingian times to 1900. Emphasis is on painting and sculpture. The introduction, which outlines the chief characteristics, schools, and artists of Germany and Spain, is followed by a substantial section devoted to artists' biographies. The work concludes with a brief historical sketch of the development of art and architecture in Germany and Spain. Well illustrated. Brief and inadequate bibliographies of books in English are given at the end of the introduction and in some of the biographies. Awkwardly arranged, but the numerous illustrations and responsible (if too brief) text make it a useful survey for the general reader.

854   Weigert, Hans. **Geschichte der deutschen Kunst.** 2nd ed. Frankfurt am Main, Umschau, 1963. 2v. illus. index. LC 63-36375.

Concise history of art and architecture in Germany from paleolithic times through the early twentieth century. Selected bibliography (pp. 951-58). Reissue of an older, popular history of German art and architecture. Still useful to the beginning student and the general reader.

Switzerland

Topographic Handbooks

855   Deuchler, Florens. **Reclams Kunstführer: Schweiz und Liechtenstein.** Stuttgart, Reclam, 1966. 905p. illus. index.
Topographical guide to the art and architecture in Switzerland and Liechtenstein. Arranged alphabetically by place. Each city, town, or village is introduced with an historical sketch; for the major places, there are city plans, aerial views, and old views. Following the introduction, the various buildings and their artistic contents are thoroughly discussed. The major works of art and architecture are illustrated by interspersed plates. The entries for the major cities provide a brief description of the art museums. Excellent glossary of terms; indexed by place and artists. Designed as a pocket-sized field guide, this work is remarkably thorough. As a ready source for information on Swiss art and architecture, its coverage is exceeded only by the official inventories (857). For the advanced student and the art tourist.

856   Hootz, Reinhardt. **Kunstdenkmäler in der Schweiz: Ein Bildhandbuch.** Munich, Deutscher Kunstverlag, 1969-1970. 2v. illus. index.
Comprehensive illustrated handbook of the art and architecture in Switzerland arranged by canton then by location. Erster Band, *Mit den Kantonen Aargau, Appenzell, Graubünden, Glarus, Luzern, St. Gallen, Schaffhausen, Schwyz, Thurgau, Unterwalden, Uri, Zürich, Zug*; Zweiter Band, *Mit den Kantonen Basel, Bern, Freiburg, Genf, Neuenburg, Solothurn, Tessin, Waadt, Wallis.* Each volume provides an introductory essay that briefly sketches the history of art and architecture in the particular region. This is followed by a collection of excellent plates, concise and factual notes to the plates, with plans (but no bibliography), and a chronological list of the works illustrated at the end. Does not include works in museums. Although it is no substitute for the official inventory of art and architecture in Switzerland (857) these volumes comprise a handy and competent reference tool to works of art *in situ*; their small size permits their use as field guides for intensive art travel. For the advanced student.

857   **Die Kunstdenkmäler der Schweiz. Les monuments d'art et d'histoire de la Suisse.** Basel, Birkhäuser, 1927– . 57v. to date. illus. index.
Official topographical inventory of the art and architecture in Switzerland and Liechtenstein. To date the following have appeared:
Kanton Aargau (5v.; 1948-67)
Kanton Basel-Stadt (4v.; 1932-61)
Kanton Basel-Landschaft (1v.)
Kanton Bern (5v.; 1947-69)

Canton de Fribourg (3v.; 1956-57)
Kanton Graubünden (7v.; 1937-48)
Kanton Luzern (6v.; 1946-63)
Canton de Neuchâtel (3v.; 1955-68)
Kanton Schaffhausen (3v.; 1951-60)
Kanton Schwyz (2v.; 1927-30)
Kanton Solothurn (1v.; 1957)
Kanton St. Gallen (5v.; 1951-70)
Kanton Thurgau (3v.; 1950-62)
Canton de Vaud (1v.; 1944)
Kanton Zug (2v.; 1933-37)
Kanton Zürich (6v.; 1938-52)
Fürstentum Liechtenstein (1v.; 1950)

Within the volumes material is arranged by place. A thorough history of the place, with maps and old views, serves as an introduction. The important buildings and sites are thoroughly described and discussed, with footnotes referring to specialized literature. The art contents and decoration of the monuments are given extensive coverage. Well illustrated. The epitome of a comprehensive and scholarly inventory of art and architecture. A basic reference and research tool for the advanced student and scholar.

Histories

858   Gantner, Joseph, and Adolf Reinle. **Kunstgeschichte der Schweiz von den Anfängen bis zum Beginn des 20. Jahrhunderts.** Frauenfeld, Huber, 1936-1962. 4v. illus. index. LC 38-8266 rev.

A second edition of Volume I, completely rewritten by Adolf Reinle, appeared in 1968 (Huber). Comprehensive history of art and architecture in Switzerland from ancient Roman times to the end of the eighteenth century. Very well illustrated with plates, plans, and diagrams. Excellent bibliographies are given at the end of each chapter and throughout the text in footnotes. The standard history of Swiss art and architecture. For the advanced student.

859   Ganz, Paul. **Geschichte der Kunst in der Schweiz von den Anfängen bis zur Mitte des 17. Jahrhunderts.** Basel, B. Schwabe, 1960. 646p. illus. index. LC A61-1709.

History of art and architecture in Switzerland from prehistoric times through the Renaissance. The minor arts are given particularly good treatment. Excellent selection of plates and good, classified bibliography (pp. 613-16). A standard history of old Swiss art and architecture. For beginning and advanced students.

860   Meyer, Peter. **Schweizerische Stilkunde.** 6th ed. Zürich, Spiegel, 1969. 288p. illus. index. LC 79-593833.

Concise history of art and architecture in Switzerland from prehistoric times to the present, with emphasis on the development of style. Well illustrated and provided with a bibliography (pp. 267-69) that lists major books in German and French. For beginning and advanced students.

GREAT BRITAIN AND IRELAND

Topographic Handbooks

861   Royal Commission on the Ancient and Historical Monuments of England. **An Inventory of Ancient Monuments.** London, H. M. Stationery Office, 1910– . 34v. to date. illus. index.

Official inventory of art and architecture in England. Covers all major works from prehistory to the present. To date the following have appeared:

> *Buckinghamshire* (2v.; 1912)
> *City of Cambridge* (2v.; 1959)
> *County of Cambridgeshire* (2v.; 1968)
> *Dorset* (4v.; 1952-72)
> *Essex* (4v.; 1916-34)
> *Herefordshire* (3v.; 1931-34)
> *Hertfordshire* (1910)
> *Huntingdonshire* (1926)
> *London* (5v.; 1925-30)
> *Middlesex* (1937)
> *Oxford* (1939)
> *Wales and Monmouthshire* (5v.; 1911-64)
> *City of York* (3v.; 1962-72)

Within the volumes the material is arranged by place. Following a brief history of the place, the major buildings, sites, monuments, etc., are described and discussed. Thorough reference to specialized literature is provided in the footnotes. Well illustrated with plates, maps, plans, and diagrams. Standard reference tool for the advanced student and scholar.

862   Royal Commission on the Ancient and Historical Monuments in Scotland. **An Inventory of Ancient Monuments.** Edinburgh, H. M. Stationery Office, 1933– . 13v. to date. illus. index.

Official inventory of art and architecture in Scotland. To date the following have appeared:

> *Argyll* (v. 1– , 1971–)
> *City of Edinburgh* (1951)
> *Peeblesshire* (2v.; 1967)
> *Roxburghshire* (2v.; 1956)
> *Counties of Fife, Kinross, Clackmannan* (1933)
> *Orkney and Shetland* (3v.; 1946)
> *Selkirkshire* (1957)
> *Stirlingshire* (2v.; 1963)

Within the volumes the material is arranged by place. Following a history of the place are descriptions and discussions of the major buildings, their art contents, and their decoration. Archaeological sites are also covered. Specialized literature is referred to in the footnotes. Well illustrated with plates, maps, plans, and diagrams. Many volumes also provide a glossary of terms. Standard reference tool for advanced students and scholars.

Histories

863 Arnold, Bruce. **A Concise History of Irish Art.** New York, Praeger, 1968. 213p. illus. index. LC 68-54497.
Survey history of art and architecture in Ireland from the early Bronze Age through the twentieth century. Brief bibliography (pp. 206-207). A good survey history for the general reader.

864 **Art Treasures in the British Isles: Monuments, Masterpieces, Commissions, and Collections.** General eds., Bernard S. Myers and Trewin Copplestone. New York and Toronto, McGraw-Hill, 1969. 176p. illus. index. LC 76-76757.
Pictorial survey of English painting, sculpture, architecture, and minor arts from prehistory to the present. Period sections are written by variety of specialists. Contains maps and a glossary-index of museums and monuments, but no bibliography. For the general reader.

865 Boase, T. S. R. **The Oxford History of English Art.** Oxford, Clarendon, 1949– . 7v. to date. illus. index.
Comprehensive history of art and architecture in England from prehistoric times to the present. It is planned for 11 volumes, of which the following have appeared to date:
    Vol. II, *English Art 871-1110*, by D. Talbot Rice (1952)
    Vol. III, *English Art 1100-1216*, by T. S. R. Boase (1953)
    Vol. IV, *English Art 1216-1307*, by Peter Brieger (1957)
    Vol. V, *English Art 1307-1461*, by Joan Evans (1949)
    Vol. VII, *English Art 1553-1625*, by Eric Mercer (1962)
    Vol. VIII, *English Art 1625-1714*, by Margaret Whinney and Oliver Millar (1957)
    Vol. X, *English Art 1800-1870*, by T. S. R. Boase (1959)
Each volume is well illustrated with plates, plans, drawings and diagrams, and each has a thorough classified bibliography at the end. The standard history of English art and architecture. For beginning and advanced students.

866 Finley, Ian. **Art in Scotland.** London, Oxford University Press, 1948. 180p. illus. index.
Survey history of art and architecture in Scotland from Celtic times to the early twentieth century. For the general reader.

867   Garlick, Kenneth. **British and North American Art to 1900.** New York, Franklin Watts, 1965. 250p. illus. index. LC 65-10268 rev.
Survey history of the painting, drawing, and sculpture of Great Britain and North America from the sixteenth century to 1900. Following a succinct introduction, a biographical section treats the life and works of major British and American painters, with brief literature citations. Illustrated with color and black and white plates. For the general reader and the beginning student.

868   Osmond, Edward. **The Arts in Britain, from the Eighth to the Twentieth Centuries.** London, Studio, 1961. 207p. illus. index. LC 62-52391.
Survey history of art and architecture in the British Isles from early medieval times to the present. Good selection of illustrations. For the general reader.

ITALY

Topographic Handbooks

869   Hootz, Reinhardt, ed. **Kunstdenkmäler in Italien: Ein Bildhandbuch.** Munich, Deutscher Kunstverlag, 1973– .
A comprehensive series of illustrated handbooks on the art and architecture of Italy. To date one volume has appeared: *Südtirol und Trentino (Trentino-Alto Adige)*, by Reinhardt Hootz (1973; 441p. illus. index.). Volumes covering all the major regions of Italy are planned. When completed, it should provide a most needed topographical guide to art and architectural monuments *in situ* in Italy. Does not include works of art in museums. The introductory essay, which sketches the art history of the particular region, is followed by a collection of excellent plates, concise and factual notes on the plates (with plans), and a chronological list of the works illustrated at the end. No bibliography. This will be a valuable reference tool for the advanced student. The small size of the volumes permits their use as field guides for intensive art travel.

870   Keller, Harald. **Die Kunstlandschaften Italiens.** Munich, Prestel, 1960. 387p. illus. index. LC A61-3518.
Handbook of the regional styles of Italian art and architecture. The art, history, and geography of the various regions of Italy are discussed and coordinated by the use of maps. The pocket edition, published in 1965 by the same publisher, provides a collection of plates as well. Extensive bibliography in the notes. A standard work in the field of art geography. For the advanced student.

871   Ministero della Educazione Nazionale Direzione Generale delle Antichità e Belle Arti. **Inventario degli oggetti d'arte d'Italia.** Rome, La Libreria dello Stato, 1931-1938. 9v. illus. index.
Beginning of an official inventory of art objects in Italy. Does not include architecture. The series consists of:

Bergamo (1931)
Calabria (1932)
Parma (1934)
Aquila (1934)
Pola (1935)
Mantua (1935)
Padua (1936)
Ancona, Ascoli Piceno (1936)
Sondrio (1938).

Within the volumes the objects are arranged by location. Fairly well illustrated, the volumes have descriptive and historical text, with reference in the footnotes to specialized literature. Useful reference tool for the advanced student and the scholar.

872 **Reclams Kunstführer Italien.** Herausgegeben von Manfred Wundram. Stuttgart, Reclam, 1965– . 6v. to date. illus. index.

Topographical guide to the art and architecture in Italy from prehistoric times to the present. To date the following have appeared:

Band 2,1, *Venedig, Brenta- Villen, Chioggia, Murano, Torcello* (2nd ed., 1974)
Band 2,2, *Südtirol, Trentino, Venezia-Giulia, Friaul, Veneto* (2nd ed.,1972)
Band 3, *Florenz* (2nd ed., 1969)
Band 4, *Emilia-Romagna, Marken, Umbrien* (1971)
Band 5, *Rom und Latium* (2nd ed., n.d.)
Band 6, *Neapel und Umgebung* (1971).

Arranged by place or site. Each place is introduced by a brief historical sketch that precedes a thorough description of the major buildings and monuments, including their art contents and decoration. Modestly illustrated with plates, liberally provided with plans and diagrams, and well indexed; no bibliography. The Reclam guides are intended as pocket guides for the serious art tourist, but their thoroughness makes them valuable reference works for the advanced student as well. This is especially so for Italy, where official inventories are lacking or inadequate.

Histories

873 Alazard, Jean. **L'art italien.** Paris, H. Laurens, 1949-60. 4v. illus. index. LC A51-2809 rev.

Comprehensive history of art and architecture in Italy from earliest times through the nineteenth century. Contents: Vol. 1, *Des origines à la fin du XIVe siècle*; Vol. 2, *Au XVe siècle, le quattrocento*; Vol. 3, *Au XVIe siècle*; Vol. 4, *De l'ère baroque au XIXe siècle.* The volumes are well illustrated, and there are bibliographies of major books at the end of each volume. A standard history of Italian art for beginning and advanced students.

874   Ancona, Paolo d'. **Storia dell'arte italiana**. Florence, Marzocco, 1953-54. 3v. illus. index. LC 60-34627.
History of art and architecture in Italy from ancient Roman times to the present. Vol. 1, *Dall antichità classica al romanico*; Vol. 2, *L'arte gotica e il quattrocento*; Vol. 3, *Dal cinquecento all'arte contemporanea*. These well illustrated volumes have responsible, factual text, with a bibliography at the end of each volume. A good general history of Italian art and architecture for beginning and advanced students.

875   **Art Treasures in Italy: Monuments, Masterpieces, Commissions, and Collections**. General eds., Bernard S. Myers and Trewin Copplestone. New York and Toronto, McGraw-Hill, 1969. 176p. illus. index. LC 72-76756.
Pictorial survey of architecture, painting, sculpture, and the minor arts in Italy from prehistory to the present. Periods are treated by a variety of specialists. Contains maps and a glossary-index of museums and monuments, but no bibliography. For the general reader.

876   Bottari, Stefano. **Storia dell'arte italiana**. Milan, Principato, 1955-57. 3v. illus. index. LC A55-10697.
History of art and architecture in Italy from ancient Roman times to the present. Vol. 1, *Dall'antichità al trecento*; Vol. 2, *Il Rinascimento: L'arte del quattrocento*; Vol. 3, *Dal cinquecento ai nostri giorni*. The good classified bibliography (Volume 3, pp. 540-60) lists books in all languages. For the beginning student.

877   Chastel, André. **Italian Art**. New York, T. Yoseloff, 1963. 526p. illus. index. LC 63-6134.
Concise history of art and architecture in Italy from the fifth century through the mid-twentieth century. Provides a good annotated and classified bibliography (pp. 403-422); and further specialized literature is given in the biographical and geographical indexes. The best history of Italian art in English. For the general reader and the beginning student.

878   Maltese, Corrado. **Storia dell'arte in Italia, 1785-1943**. Turin, Einaudi, 1960. 471p. illus. index. LC A61-5671.
History of art and architecture in Italy during the nineteenth and twentieth centuries. Well illustrated. No bibliography. For the beginning student.

879   Mazzariol, Giuseppe, and Terisio Pignatti. **Storia dell'arte italiana**. Milan, Mondadori, 1960-1961. 3v. illus. index. LC 66-34913.
History of art and architecture in Italy from 2000 B.C. to the present. No bibliography. Popular survey history for the general reader and the beginning student.

880   Monteverdi, Mario. **Italian Art to 1850**. New York, Franklin Watts, 1965. 433p. illus. index. LC 64-23685.
Pictorial survey of the art and architecture of Italy from the middle of the thirteenth century to 1850. Emphasis is on painting and sculpture. The introduction, which outlines the chief characteristics, schools, and artists, is followed by a

substantial section devoted to artists' biographies. The work concludes with an historical sketch of the development of Italian art and architecture. Well illustrated. Brief and inadequate bibliographies at the end of the introduction and in some of the biographies. Awkwardly arranged, but the numerous illustrations and responsible (though somewhat too brief) text make it a useful survey for the general reader.

881   Toesca, Pietro. **Storia dell'arte italiana**. 2nd ed. Turin, Unione Torinese, 1965. 3v. illus. index. (Storia dell'Arte Classica e Italiana, v. 3). LC 67-117871.
Comprehensive history of art and architecture in Italy from the early Christian period through the fourteenth century. Well illustrated with extensive bibliographical references in the footnotes. A standard, scholarly history of Italian medieval art and architecture. For the advanced student.

882   Venturi, Adolfo. **Storia dell'arte italiana**. Milan, Hoepli, 1901-1940. 11v. illus. index. Repr.: New York, Kraus, 1967. 11v. in 25. LC 66-9698.
Comprehensive history of art and architecture in Italy from the early Christian period through the sixteenth century. Footnotes with bibliography. The standard history of Italian art. For the advanced student.

LOW COUNTRIES

General Works

883   Hammacher, A. M., and R. Hammacher Vandenbrande. **Flemish and Dutch Art**. New York, Franklin Watts, 1965. 316p. illus. index. LC 64-23686.
Pictorial survey of the art and architecture of the Low Countries from the thirteenth century through post-impressionism. Introduction outlines the major characteristics, schools, and artists. This is followed by a substantial section devoted to biographies of major artists. A concluding section, "Influences and Developments," ties the first two parts together in a brief history. Well illustrated. Brief and inadequate bibliographies are given at the end of the introduction and in some of the biographies. Awkwardly arranged, but the numerous illustrations and responsible, if brief, text make it a useful survey for the general reader and beginning student.

Belgium

Topographic Handbooks and Inventories

There is no official national inventory of art and architecture in Belgium. Instead, there are several regional inventories published by regional societies of art and archaeology. Although they vary somewhat in format, all are arranged by place and all give reference to specialized literature either in footnote form or in separate bibliographies that follow sections of volumes. Included here are the major series.

884   Dhannens, Elisabeth. **Inventaris van het Kunstpatrimonium van Oostvlaanderen.** Ghent, 1951– . 6v. illus. index.
Inventory of art and architecture in the Belgian province of Oostvlaanderen (East Flanders). Thorough reference to bibliography in the footnotes. Contents:
   Vol. 1, *Temse* (1951)
   Vol. 2, *Kanton Kaprijke* (1956)
   Vol. 3, *Sint-Niklaaskerk, Gent* (1960)
   Vol. 4, *Dendermonde* (1961)
   Vol. 5, *Sint-Baafskathedral, Gent* (1965)
   Vol. 6, *Het retabel van het Lam Gods in de Sint-Baafskathedral te Gent* (1965).

885   Donnet, Fernand, and G. Van Doorslaer. **Inventaris der Kunstvoorwerpen bewaard in de openbare gestichten der Provincie Antwerpen.** Antwerp, 1902-1940. 12v. illus. index.
Inventory of works of art in churches and other buildings open to the public in the Belgian province of Antwerp.

886   **Inventaire archéologique de Gand.** Ghent, 1897-1915. 57v. in 3 series. illus. index.
Inventory of art and architecture in Ghent.

887   **Inventaire des objets d'art et d'antiquité de la Province du Hainaut.** Mons, 1923-41. 10v. illus. index.
Inventory of art and architecture in the Belgian province of Hainaut.

888   **Inventaire des objets d'art et d'antiquité de la Province de Liège.** Liège, 1911-1930. 2v. illus. index.
Inventory of art and architecture in the Belgian province of Liège.

889   **Oudheidkundig Inventaris der Kunstvoorwerken in Kerken en openbare Gebouwen van de Provincie Limburg.** Hasselt, 1916-35. 9v. illus. index.
Inventory of art and architecture in the Belgian province of Limburg. Covers churches and other buildings open to the public. Includes only objects dating before 1830.

890   **Oudheidkundig Inventaris van Oost Vlaanderen.** Ghent, 1911-1915. 11v.
       illus. index.
Inventory of art and architecture in the Belgian province of East Flanders. In part
superseded by (884).

891   **Province de Brabant: Inventaire des objets d'art.** Brussels, 1904-1912. 3v.
       illus. index.
Inventory of art in the Belgian province of Brabant.

Histories

892   Clemen, Paul. **Belgische Kunstdenkmäler.** Munich, Bruckmann, 1923.
       2v. illus. index.
A collection of essays by various specialists (Clemen, Julius Baum, Greta Ring,
etc.) on various aspects of the history of art and architecture in Belgium. Arrangement is chronological; Volume one covers the ninth through fifteenth centuries,
Volume two covers the sixteenth through eighteenth centuries. Together they form
a valuable history of art and architecture in Belgium. For the advanced student.

893   Fierens, Paul. **L'art en Belgique du Moyen Âge à nos jours.** Brussels,
       Renaissance du Livre, 1947. 535p. illus. index.
This history of art and architecture in Belgium is composed of essays, written by
specialists, on the development of the various arts from the eleventh century
through the early twentieth century. There are occasional footnotes with bibliography. For the general reader and the beginning student.

894   Fierens, Paul. **L'art flamand.** Paris, Larousse, 1945. 164p. illus. index.
Concise history of art and architecture in Belgium from the eleventh to the mid-
twentieth century. A useful, classified bibliography is included (pp. 156-59). A
popular survey history for the general reader and the beginning student.

895   Gerson, Horst, and E. H. ter Kuile. **Art and Architecture in Belgium: 1600
       to 1800.** Baltimore, Penguin, 1960. 236p. illus. index. (Pelican History of
       Art, Z18). LC 60-3193.
Comprehensive history of art and architecture in Belgium from 1600 to 1800.
Excellent selection of plates, plans, diagrams, and maps. Provides a good,
classified bibliography of major works (pp. 197-217) and thorough reference to
specialized literature in the extensive footnotes. The standard history of Flemish
art in the baroque and rococo periods. For the advanced student.

896   Leurs, Stan, ed. **Geschiedenis van de Vlaamsche Kunst ...** Antwerp,
       de Sikkel, 1936-1940. 2v. illus. index.
A history of Flemish art and architecture from the early Middle Ages through the
early twentieth century. Sections were written by various specialists, with bibliographies at the end of chapters. Well illustrated with plates, plans, and diagrams.

A standard history of Flemish art and architecture for beginning and advanced students.

897   Rooses, Max. **Art in Flanders.** New York, AMS Press, 1970. 341p. illus. index. LC 79-100819.
Pictorial history of art and architecture in Belgium from the late Middle Ages to the early twentieth century. For the general reader.

Netherlands

Topographic Handbooks

898   Hootz, Reinhardt. **Kunstdenkmäler in den Niederlanden: Ein Bildhandbuch.** Munich, Deutscher Kunstverlag, 1971. 421p. illus. index.
Illustrated handbook of art and architecture in the Netherlands from the early Middle Ages through the present, arranged by place. An introductory essay sketching the art history of the Netherlands is followed by an excellent collection of plates, with informative notes to the plates (with plans). There is no bibliography. At the end of the volume is a useful chronological list of the works illustrated. Does not cover works of art in museums. Although it is not a substitute for the intensive and extensive coverage of art and architectural monuments in the official Dutch inventory (899), this work is a most handy and competent reference tool and field guide to the art and architecture *in situ* in the Netherlands. For the advanced student.

899   **De Nederlandsche Monumenten vom Geschiedenis en Kunst.** Utrecht, Oosthoek, 1912– . 16v. to date. illus. index.
Official inventory of art and architecture in the Netherlands. To date the following volumes have appeared:
> Deel 1, *De Provincie Noordbrabant. Part 1. Voormalige Baronie van Breda*
> Deel 2, *De Provincie Utrecht. Part 1. Gemeente Utrecht; Part 2. De Dom van Utrecht*
> Deel 3, *De Provincie Gelderland. Part 1. Het Kwartier van Nijmegen* (2v.); *Part 2. Het Kwartier van Zutphen*
> Deel 4, *De Provincie Overijsel. Part 1. Twente; Part 2. Zuid-Salland*
> Deel 5, *De Provincie Limburg. Part 1. Gemeente Masstricht; Part 2. Noord-Limburg; Part 3. Zuid-Limburg*
> Deel 6, *De Provincie Groningen. Part 1. Oost-Groningen*
> Deel 7, *De Provincie Zuidholland. Part 1. Leiden en westelijk Rijnland*
> Deel 8, *De Provincie Noordholland. Part 1. Waterland; Part 2. Westfriesland.*

Histories

900   Gelder, Hendrik E. van, and J. Duverger. **Kunstgeschiedenis der Neder-
landen van de Middeleeuwen tot onze Tijd** . . . 3rd ed. Utrecht, de Haan,
1954-1956. 3v. illus. index.
General history of art and architecture in the Netherlands and the Flemish part of
Belgium from the early Middle Ages to modern times. Sections were written by
various specialists. Bibliographical footnotes. Well illustrated. The standard history
of Netherlandish art and architecture. For the advanced student.

901   **Guide to Dutch Art.** 3rd rev. ed. The Hague, Government Printing and
Publishing Office, 1961. 355p. illus. LC 62-5438.
Produced by the Netherlands Department van Onderwijs, Kunsten en
Wetenschappen. Handbook to art and architecture in the Netherlands from the
Carolingian period through the twentieth century. An historical introduction is
followed by essays on the development of the various arts, a good collection of
plates, and a useful guide to the principal towns (with maps). Also included are a
brief bibliography (pp. 95-96) and a list and description of notable museums
(pp. 90-94). A useful handbook for the general reader, the tourist, and the
beginning student.

902   Rosenberg, Jakob, and Seymour Slive. **Dutch Art and Architecture:
1600 to 1800.** London, Penguin, 1966. 330p. illus. index. (Pelican History
of Art, Z27). Rev. paperback ed., Harmondsworth, Penguin, 1972.
Comprehensive history of art and architecture in the United Netherlands from
1600 to 1800. Contains an excellent selection of illustrations (though they are
poorly reproduced), useful plans, diagrams, and maps. A good, classified bibliography (pp. 279-308) lists reference to more specialized literature in the extensive
footnotes. The standard history of Dutch baroque and eighteenth century art and
architecture; for the advanced student.

903   Timmers, J. J. M. **A History of Dutch Life and Art.** Amsterdam, Elsevier,
1959. 201p. illus. index. LC 60-3972. British edition: London, Nelson,
1959. LC 60-427.
Concise survey of the art and architecture of the Netherlands from prehistory
through the twentieth century. Although it is chiefly a history of art and
architecture, each section is preceded by a brief cultural history of the period under
consideration. Well illustrated, it has informative notes to the plates, but no bibliography. A good survey history for the general reader and the beginning student.

SCANDINAVIA

General Works

904   Kusch, Eugen. **Ancient Art in Scandinavia.** Nuremberg, Carl, 1965. 83p. (text); 176p. (illus.). LC 71-8618.
Pictorial survey of the art and architecture in Denmark, Sweden, and Norway from the Viking period through the sixteenth century. Introductory essay provides a popular history of Scandinavian art, followed by more specific information in the notes to the plates. No bibliography. For the general reader.

905   Laurin, Carl, ed. **Scandinavian Art.** New York, American Scandinavian Foundation, 1922. 662p. illus. index. (Scandinavian Monographs, V).
Collection of essays by specialists on various aspects of the history of art and architecture in Denmark, Sweden, and Norway from the early Middle Ages through the early twentieth century. Contents: "A Survey of Swedish Art," by Laurin; "Danish Art in the 19th Century," by Emil Hannover; "Modern Norwegian Art," by J. Thiis. No bibliography. Still a useful introduction for the general reader.

Denmark

906   Nørlund, Poul. **Danish Art through the Ages.** Copenhagen, 1948. 90p. illus.
This history of Danish art and architecture consists of essays by specialists; coverage extends from the romanesque period through the twentieth century. No bibliography. For the general reader.

907   Poulsen, Vagn, ed. **Dansk Kunsthistorie: Billedkunst og Skulptur.** v. 1– . Copenhagen, Politiken, 1972– . illus. index. LC 73-327315.
History of painting and sculpture in Denmark from the Carolingian period to the middle of the nineteenth century. The fourth and final volume will cover the period 1850 to 1950. Well illustrated, but there is no bibliography and there are no footnotes. Text for the general reader and beginning student; plates useful to the advanced student.

908   Poulsen, Vagn. **Illustrated Art Guide to Denmark.** Copenhagen, Gyldendal, 1959. 84p. illus. index. LC 59-8958.
Pocket handbook of art and architecture in Denmark with a survey history of Danish art and architecture, a list of museums, and a collection of small illustrations. No bibliography. For the general reader and the tourist.

Iceland

909   Eldjárn, Kristján. **Icelandic Art.** New York, Abrams, 1961. 14p. (text); 70p. (illus.). LC 61-5785.
Pictorial survey of painting, sculpture, and the minor arts of Iceland from the twelfth century through the nineteenth century. Brief text sketches the main lines of artistic development in Iceland. No bibliography. For the general reader.

Norway

910   Aars, Harald, *et al.* **Norsk Kunsthistorie.** Oslo, Gyldendal, 1925. 2v. illus. index.
This history of Norwegian art and architecture consists of essays, written by specialists, on various periods from prehistoric times to the twentieth century. The classified bibliography is arranged by chapters (pp. 661-72). A standard history of Norwegian art and architecture for the advanced student.

911   Lexow, Einar Jacob. **Norges Kunst.** Oslo, Steenske, 1926. 342p. illus.
Concise history of art and architecture in Norway from prehistoric times to the twentieth century. Brief bibliography of major works (pp. 340-42). No index. A popular history for the general reader and the beginning student.

Sweden

Topographic Handbooks

912   **Sveriges Kyrkor. Konsthistoriskt Inventarium.** Stockholm, Generalstabers Litografiska Austalts Förlag, 1912– . 125v. illus. index.
Official inventory of art and architecture of the churches of Sweden. Summaries are given in English and German. Bibliographies in footnotes or at the ends of sections. In progress. Contents to date:

Blekinge
I,1, *Östra härad* (1926)
I,2, *Medelsta härad* (1932)
II, *Bräkne härad och Listers härad* (1941)
III,1, *Fredrikskyrkan i Karlskrona* (1946)
III,3, *Amiralitetskyrkan i Karlskrona* (1959)
IV,1, *Ronneby Kyrkor* (1959)
IV,2, *Karlshamns Kyrkor* (1960)
IV,3, *Sölvesborgs Kyrkor* (1962)
V,2, *Generalregister till Blekinge Band I-V* (1965)

Bohuslän
I,1, *Västra Hisings härad* (1944)
I,2, *Kyrkor i Bohuslän. Inlands Sodre härad* (1965)

I,3, *Ytterby, Kareby och Romelanda* (1967)
II,1, *Kyrkor i Inlands Nordre härad, sodra Delen* (1962)
III,1, *Hjärtums och Västerlanda Kyrkor* (1968)
IV,3, *Kungälvs Kyrkor, Inlands södre härad* (1969)

Dalarne
I,1, *Kyrkor i Leksands och Gagnefs tingslag* (1916)
I,2, *Kyrkor i Falu Domsagas norra tingslag* (1920)
I,3, *Kyrkor i Falu Domsagas södra tingslag* (1932)
II,1, *Falu stads Kyrkor* (1940)

Dalsland
I,1, *Sundals härad* (1931)
   Gastrikland (2v.; 1930-32)

Gotland
I,1, *Kyrkor i Lummelunda ting* (1914)
I,2, *Tingstäde Kyrka* (1925)
I,3, *Kyrkor i Bro ting* (1929)
I,4, *Kyrkor i Erdre ting* (1931)
I,5, *Kyrkor i Dede ting* (1931)
II, *Rute setting* (1933)
III, *Hejde setting* (1942)
IV,2, *Kyrkor i Halla ting* (1952)
IV,4, *Kyrkor i Kräklinge ting, nordvästra delen* (1959)
IV,5, *Kyrkor i Kräklinge ting, sydöstra delen* (1963)
IV,6, *Samt Register till Band IV*
V,1, *Kyrkor pa Gotland; Garde ting, södra delen* (1965)
V,2, *Alskogs Kyrka, Garde ting* (1908)
VI,1, *Burs Kyrka. Burs ting* (1967)
VI,2, *Stanga Kyrka. Burs ting* (1968)
VI,3, *Hems Kyrkor, Hemse ting* (1969)
VI,4, *Alva Kyrka, Hemse ting* (1970)

Härjedalen
I,1, *Kyrkor i Svegs tingslag, norvästra delen* (1961)
I,2, *Svegs tingslag södra delen* (1965)
I,3, *Svegs tingslag östra delen* (1966)

Medelpad
I, *Njurunda och Sköns tingslag samt Sundsvalls stadt* (1929)
II, *Kyrkor i Ljustorps, Indals samt Medelpads Västra Domsagas tingslag* (1939)

Närke
I,1, *Örebro stads kyrkor* (1939)
I,3, *Kyrkor i Glanshammars härad, sydvästra delen* (1961)
I,4, *Ödeby kyrka: Glanshammars härad* (1969)

Öland

I,1, *Kyrkor pa Öland Inledning* (1966)
I,2, *Böda och St. Olof: Akerbo härad* (1968)
I,3, *Högby kyrkor: Akerbo härad* (1968)
I,4, *Källa kyrkor: Akerbo härad* (1969)
I,5, *Persnäs kyrkor: Akerbo härad* (1970)

Östergötland

I,1,2, *Kyrkor i bankekings härad, norra delen* (1921)
I,3, *Bankekings härad, mellersta delen* (1963)
II, *Vreta Klosters kyrka* (1935)

Skäne

I,1, *Kävlinge kyrkor i Harjagers härad* (1932)
II,1, *Luggude härad, sydvästra delen* (1963)

Småland

I, *Jönköpings och Huskvarna kyrkor* (1940)
II,1, *Kyrkorna i Sjösås uppvidinge härad* (1967)
II,2, *Drews och Hornaryds kyrkor* (1968)
II,3, *Dädesjö och Eke kyrkor: Uppvidinge härad* (1969)
III,1, *Kalmar Slotts kyrkor* (1968)
IV,1, *Växjö Domkyrka* (1970)
V,1, *Bergunda och Öja kyrkor. Kinnevalds härad* (1970)

Södermanland

I,1,2, *Strängnäs Domkyrka* (1968-69)

Stockholms kyrkor

I,1,2,3, *St. Nikolai eller Storkyrkan* (1925-27)
II,1,2, *Riddarholmskyrkan* (1928-37)
III,1, *Ulrika Eleonara elle Kungsholm kyrka med St. Görans kapell* (1915)
III,2, *Hedvig Eleonara kyrka* (1920)
IV,1,2, *S. Jakobs kyrka* (1928-30)
IV,3, *S. Johnnes kyrka och S. Stefans kapell* (1934)
V,1, *Adolf Fredriks kyrka och S. Olovs kapell* (1924)
V,2, *Gustav Vasa kyrka* (1943)
V,3, *Matteus kyrka* (1946)
VI,1,2, *S. Klara kyrka* (1927)
VII,1, *S. Maria Magdalena kyrka* (1934)
VII,2, *Katarina kyrka* (1944)
VII,3, *Sofia kyrka* (1961)
VII,4, *Högalids kyrka* (1966)
VIII,1, *Bromma kyrka och Västerledskyrkan* (1940)
VIII,2, *Spanga och Hässelby kyrkor* (1959)

VIII,3, *Brännkyrka, S. Sigfrids och Enskede kyrkor* (1964)
IX,1, *Skeppsholmskyrkan elle Johans kyrka* (1942)

Uppland
I,1,2, *Kyrkor i Danderyds skepplag* (1918-28)
I,3, *Kyrkor i Värmdo skeppslag* (1949)
I,4, *Kyrkor i Akers skeppslag* (1950)
II,1, *Kyrkor i Väddö och Haverö skeppslag* (1918)
II,2, *Kyrkor i Bro och Vätö skeppslag* (1940)
II, Halvband 2, *Kyrkor i Frösakers härad* (2v.; 1955-56)
II,3, *Kyrkor i Frötuna och Länna skeppslag* (1945)
III,1,2, *Kyrkor i Langshundra härad* (1921-52)
III,3, *Kyrkor i Närdinghundra härad, västra delen* (1953)
IV,1, *Kyrkor i Erlinghundra härad* (1912)
IV,2, *Kyrkor i Seminghundra härad* (1919)
V,3, *Kyrkor i Sjuhundra härad* (1956)
V,5, *Kyrkor i Lyhundra härad* (1961)
V,6, *Estuna och Söderby-Karls kyrkor i Uppland* (1966)
V,7, *Karls Kyrkoruin* (1967)
VI,4, *Kyrkor i Sollentuna härad, Södra delen* (1958)
VI,1-3, *Kyrkor i Färentuna härad* (1954-57)
VI,5, *Kyrkor i Sollentuna härad, norra delen* (1958)
VII,1, *Kyrkor i Bro härad* (1956)
VII,2, *Kyrkor i Håbo härad, södra delen* (1962)
VII,3, *Kyrkor i Håbo härad, mellersta delen* (1963)
IX,1, *Härkeberga kyrka: Trögds härad* (1968)
IX,2, *Iitslena kyrka* (1969)
XI,1, *Svinnegarns, Enköpings-Näs och Teda kyrkor* (1966)
XI,2, *Tillinge kyrka: Asunda härad* (1968)
XI,3, *Sparrsätra och Breds kyrkor: Asunda härad* (1969)
XII,2, *Fittja kyrka: Lagunda härad* (1970)

Värmland
I,1,2, *Kyrkor i Grums härad* (1924)

Västergotland
I, *Kyrkor i Kallands härad* (1913-1922)
II, *Habo kyrka, Vartofta härad* (1970)

Histories

913 Cornell, Henrik. **Den svenska Konstens Historia.** 2nd ed. Stockholm, Aldus/Bonnier, 1966. 2v. illus. index. LC 67-101872.
History of art and architecture in Sweden from the Viking period to about 1800. Supplementary chapter covers the graphic arts from 1600 to 1700. Bibliography (pp. 421-32) arranged by chapters. Excellent collection of plates, plans, and

diagrams. A standard history of Swedish art, particularly good for the Middle Ages. For the advanced student.

914   Grate, Pontus, ed. **Treasures of Swedish Art, from Pre-Historic Age to the 19th Century**. Malmö, Allhem, 1965. 166p. illus. LC 66-51407.
Pictorial survey of art and architecture in Sweden from prehistoric times to the nineteenth century. The brief introductory essay, which sketches the development of Swedish art, is followed by a collection of plates with informative notes. For the general reader.

915   Lindblom, Andreas A. F. **Svensk Konst; från Stenåldern till Rymdåldern**. Stockholm, Norstedt, 1960. 410p. illus. index. LC 60-32013.
Concise history of art and architecture in Sweden from prehistoric times to the present. No bibliography. A well-illustrated recent survey history for the general reader and the beginning student.

916   Lindblom, Andreas. **Sveriges Konsthistoria från Forntid till Nutid**. Stockholm, Nordisk Rotogravyr, 1944-1946. 3v. illus. index.
Comprehensive history of art and architecture in Sweden from prehistoric times to the mid-twentieth century. Well illustrated, but no bibliography. A standard history for the general reader and the beginning student.

917   Roosval, Johnny A. E. **Swedish Art**. Princeton, Princeton University Press, 1932. 77p. illus. (Princeton Monographs in Art and Archaeology, XVIII).
A collection of lectures given at Princeton in 1929 covering most aspects of the history of Swedish art and architecture (with the exception of the eighteenth century). Bibliography in the footnotes. An old but still useful survey of Swedish art and architecture for the general reader.

SPAIN AND PORTUGAL

Topographic Handbooks

918   Gudiol y Ricart, José, and Santiago Alcolea. **Hispania guìa general del arte español**. Barcelona, Argos, 1962. 2v. illus. index.
Handbook of art and architecture of Spain, arranged by provinces. Includes the Canary Islands. No bibliography. For the general reader and the beginning student.

919   Milicua, D. José. **Guide artistique de l'Espagne**. Paris, Tisne, 1967. 559p. illus. index.
Handbook of art and architecture in Spain arranged by place. Provides small illustrations and short descriptions, but no bibliography. For the general reader and the tourist.

920   **Catálogo monumental de España**. Madrid, Ministerio de Instrucción
       Pública y Bellas Artes, 1924– . illus. index.
Official inventory of art and architecture in Spain. Volumes are arranged by
province and city; to date the following have appeared:
    Provincia de Badajoz (3v.; 1925-26)
    La Ciudad de Barcelona (1947)
    Provincia de Cáceres (3v.; 1924)
    Provincia de Cadiz (2v.; 1934)
    Provincia de Laon (2v.; 1925)
    Provincia de Palencia (4v.; 1946-51)
    Provincia de Salamanca (2v.; 1967)
    Zaragoza (2v.; 1957)
    Provincia de Zamora (2v.; 1927).
Within the volumes material is arranged by chronological period. Reference to
specialized literature is made in the footnotes. This is the standard topographical
handbook of art and architecture *in situ* in Spain. It is not yet complete, however,
and several regions have been inventorized by local groups; see (921-925).

921   **Catálogo arqueológico y artístico de la Provincia de Sevilla**. v. 1– .
       Seville, Servicio de Defensa del Patrimonio Artístico Nacional, 1939– .
       illus. index.
Topographical inventory of the art and architecture in the province of Seville,
Spain. Arranged by place, it treats the major architectural monuments, archaeological sites, and the art contents and decorations of the major buildings in the province.
Reference to specialized literature is found in the footnotes. Fills a gap, although
incompletely, in the official inventory of Spanish art and architecture (920). A
reference tool for the advanced student and the scholar.

922   **Catálogo monumental de la Provincia de Toledo**. Toledo, Spain, Publica-
       tiones de la Excelentisma Diputación Provincial de Toledo, 1959. 413p.
       illus. index.
Topographical inventory of the art and architecture of the province of Toledo.
Emphasis is on the architectural monuments, but the art contents and decoration
of the major buildings are also covered. Reference to specialized literature is found
in the footnotes. Fills a gap in the official inventory of Spanish art and architecture
(920). A reference tool for the advanced student and the scholar.

923   **Catálogo monumental de la Provincia de Valladolid**. Valladolid, Spain,
       Editado por la Excelentisma Diputación Provincial de Valladolid, 1960-
       64. 4v. illus. index.
Topographical inventory of the art and architecture in the province of Valladolid,
Spain. Arranged by place, it emphasizes the architectural monuments, but the art
contents and decoration of the major buildings are also covered. Reference to
specialized literature is in the footnotes. Fills a gap in the official inventory of
Spanish art and architecture (920). A reference tool for the advanced student and
the scholar.

924   **Catálogo monumental Diócesis de Vitoria.** Vitoria, Spain, 1967-68. 2v.
        illus. index.
Topographical inventory of the art and architecture in the Diocese of Vitoria.
Arranged by place, it emphasizes the buildings, but the art contents and decoration
of the major structures are also covered. Well illustrated, with thorough reference to
specialized literature in the footnotes. Fills a gap in the official inventory of Spanish
art and architecture (920). A reference tool for the advanced student and the
scholar.

925   **Catálogo de monumentos de Vizcaya.** Bilbao, Spain, 1958. 2v. illus. index.
Inventory of the art and architecture in the province of Vizcaya. Although the
emphasis is on buildings, archaeological sites and the artistic contents of the
buildings are also covered. Reference to specialized literature is in the footnotes.
Arranged by place. Fills a gap in the official inventory of Spanish art and architecture (920). A reference tool for the advanced student and the scholar.

926   **Inventário artístico de Portugal.** Lisbon, Academia Nacional de Bellas
        Artes, 1943– . 8v. to date. illus. index.
Official inventory of art and architecture in Portugal. The first seven volumes
are as follows:
        I, *Distrito de Portalegre* (1943)
        II, *Cidade de Coimbra* (1947)
        III, *Distrito de Santarém* (1949)
        IV, *Distrito de Coimbra* (1952)
        V, *Distrito de Leira* (1955)
        VI, *Distrito de Aveiro* (1959)
        VII, *Concelho de Évora* (2v.; 1966).
Each volume is organized by place. A summary of the political and artistic history
of the locality is followed by a detailed description of the major buildings and
their contents. Specialized literature is referred to in the footnotes. Additional
volumes are planned. A standard reference tool for advanced students and scholars
of Portuguese art and architecture.

Histories

927   **Art Treasures in Spain: Monuments, Masterpieces, Commissions, and
        Collections.** General eds., Bernard S. Myers and Trewin Copplestone. New
        York and Toronto, McGraw-Hill, 1969. 175p. illus. index. LC 70-76758.
Pictorial survey of the architecture, painting, sculpture, and the decorative arts in
Spain from prehistory to the present. Sections were written by a variety of specialists. Contains maps and a glossary-index of museums and monuments, but no
bibliography. For the general reader.

928   Cirici-Pellicer, Alejandro. **Treasures of Spain from Charles V to Goya.**
        Geneva, Skira; Cleveland, World, 1965. 236p. illus. index. LC 65-24418.

Introduction by F. J. Sánchez Cantón. Pictorial survey of art and architecture in Spain from the sixteenth through the early nineteenth centuries. No bibliography. Excellent color plates. For the general reader.

929   Gaya Nuño, Juan A. **Historia del arte español**. Madrid, Editorial Plus-Ultra, 1946. 478p. illus. index.

Concise history of art and architecture in Spain from prehistoric times to the present. Provides a chronological table and a bibliography (pp. 448-50) that lists major books, chiefly in Spanish. For the general reader and the beginning student.

930   Gudiol, Josep. **The Arts of Spain**. Garden City, N.Y., Doubleday, 1964. 318p. illus. index. LC 64-13731.

Survey history of art and architecture in Spain from prehistoric times to the present. Well illustrated and provided with a bibliography (pp. 305-307) of basic books in all languages. A good survey for the general reader and the beginning student.

931   Gudiol y Ricart, José, ed. **Ars Hispaniae: Historia universale del arte hispánico**. Madrid, Plus-Ultra, 1947-1973. 21v. illus. index.

Comprehensive history of art and architecture in Spain. Written by specialists, it covers the period from prehistoric art through the twentieth century. Volume XXI is a history of art and architecture in Latin America (exclusive of Brazil) and the Philippine Islands. Each volume has an excellent classified bibliography of books and periodical articles in all languages. Well illustrated. The standard history of Spanish art and architecture. For the advanced student.

932   Hagen, Oskar. **Patterns and Principles of Spanish Art**. Madison, University of Wisconsin Press, 1943. 2nd ed. 279p. illus. index.

Concise history of Spanish art and architecture from prehistoric times to the present. Bibliographical references in footnotes. This is still a competent survey history for the general reader and the beginning student.

933   Jiménez-Placer, Fernando, and Alejandro Cirici-Pellicer. **Historia del arte español**. Barcelona, Labor, 1955. 2v. illus. index.

History of art and architecture in Spain from paleolithic times through the twentieth century. Well illustrated. No bibliography. General history for the beginning student.

934   Kubler, George, and Martin Soria. **Art and Architecture in Spain and Portugal and Their American Dominions: 1500 to 1800**. Harmondsworth, Penguin, 1959. 445p. illus. index. (Pelican History of Art, Z17). LC 60-666.

Comprehensive and scholarly history of art and architecture in Spain, Portugal, and Latin America from 1500 to 1800. Excellent selection of plates, plans, and diagrams. Good classified bibliography of books and periodical articles (pp. 403-416), with further reference to more specialized literature in the extensive footnotes. A standard history of Spanish, Portuguese, and early Latin American art and architecture for the advanced student and scholar.

935   Lozoya, Juan C. **Historia del arte hispánico**. Barcelona, Salvat, 1931-1949. 5v. illus. index.
Comprehensive history of art and architecture in Spain from prehistoric times through the twentieth century. Well illustrated with plates, plans, and diagrams. Good bibliographies at the end of each chapter, plus a supplementary bibliography for the entire work in Volume 5 (pp. 671-83). A standard history for the advanced student.

936   Pita-Andrade, José M. **Treasures of Spain from Altamira to the Catholic Kings**. Geneva, Skira; Cleveland, World, 1967. 248p. illus. index. LC 67-25118.
Pictorial survey of art and architecture in Spain from prehistoric cave paintings through the fifteenth century. Introduction is by F. J. Sánchez Cantón. Excellent color plates. Popular text for the general reader; the plates are useful to beginning as well as advanced students.

937   Smith, Bradley. **Spain: A History in Art**. New York, Simon & Schuster, 1966. 296p. illus. LC 66-19432.
General survey of art in Spain, from prehistory to 1931, set in a cultural and historical context. Emphasis is on painting, with some sculpture and almost no architecture. Generously illustrated, all in color. General bibliography (pp. 294-96). For the general reader.

938   Lacerda, Aarao de, *et al.* **Historia da arte en Portugal**. Oporto, Portugal, 1943-53. 3v.
Comprehensive history of art and architecture in Portugal from prehistoric times through the nineteenth century. Volume 1 covers the period from prehistory through the fourteenth century; Volume 2 treats the fifteenth and sixteenth centuries; Volume 3 covers the seventeenth through nineteenth centuries. Only the first volume has a bibliography (pp. 555-60), which is a good classified list of books and periodical articles. A standard history of Portuguese art and architecture.

939   Santos, Reynoldo dos. **Historia del arte portugues**. Barcelona, Labor, 1960. 383p. illus. index.
Concise history of art and architecture in Portugal from the pre-romanesque period through the twentieth century. No bibliography. A modern survey for beginning and advanced students.

940   Smith, Robert Chester. **The Art of Portugal, 1500-1800**. New York, Meredith, 1968. 320p. illus. index. LC 68-31684.
Concise history of art and architecture in Portugal from 1500 to 1800. Well illustrated. Bibliography is provided in the notes to the text (pp. 313-16). A good general history of Portuguese art and architecture in English for the general reader and the beginning student.

II. EASTERN EUROPE

GENERAL WORKS

941   Rhodes, Anthony. **Art Treasures of Eastern Europe.** New York, Putnam, 1972. 280p. illus. index. LC 75-186798.
Pictorial survey of the art and architecture of Yugoslavia, Czechoslovakia, Poland, Hungary, Rumania, and Bulgaria from prehistoric times to 1800. Provides a list of major museums in Eastern Europe, brief biographical notes on artists, and a bibliography of general books (p. 273). An attractive pictorial survey for the general reader.

BULGARIA

942   Bozhkov, Atanas. **Bulgarian Art.** Sofia, Foreign Language Press, 1964. 125p. illus. index. LC 64-56569.
Concise history of art and architecture in Bulgaria from the seventh through the twentieth century. No bibliography. For the general reader and the beginning student.

943   Filov, Bogdan D. **Geschichte der altbulgarischen Kunst bis zur Eroberung des bulgarischen Reiches durch die Türken** . . . Berlin, de Gruyter, 1932. 100p. illus. index. (Grundriss der slavischen Philologie und Kultur-geschichte, 10).
History of Bulgarian art and architecture from 679 to 1393. Bibliographies are given at the end of the chapters. This work, along with (944), is a standard history of Bulgarian art and architecture. For the advanced student.

944   Filov, Bogdan D. **Geschichte der bulgarischen Kunst unter der türkischen Herrschaft und in der neueren Zeit** . . . Berlin, de Gruyter, 1935. 94p. illus. index. (Grundriss der slavischen Philologie und Kulturgeschichte, 10).
History of Bulgarian art and architecture from 1393 to 1930. Bibliographies are given at the end of each chapter. Sequel to (943); together they form a standard history of Bulgarian art and architecture.

HUNGARY

945   Hootz, Reinhardt, ed. **Kunstdenkmäler in Ungarn: Ein Bildhandbuch.** Munich, Deutscher Kunstverlag, 1974. 480p. illus.

Illustrated, topographical handbook of the art and architecture of Hungary from prehistoric times to the present. The good collection of plates, arranged by place, contains informative notes as well as plans. A useful chronological list of the works illustrated concludes the volume. No bibliography. A most useful topographical handbook to art and architecture *in situ* in Hungary, especially considering the lack of an official inventory of art and architecture in that country. For the advanced student and the serious art tourist.

946   Kampis, Antal. **The History of Art in Hungary**. London, Wellingborough, 1967. 400p. illus. index. LC 67-78512.
Concise history of art and architecture in Hungary from the ninth century through the first decade of the twentieth century. No bibliography. For the general reader and the beginning student.

947   Nemeth, Lajos. **Modern Art in Hungary**. Budapest, Corvina, 1969. 187p. illus. LC 72-9780.
Survey history of twentieth century art and architecture in Hungary. Bibliography (pp. 171-72) lists books and periodical articles in all languages. For the general reader and the beginning student.

POLAND

948   Piotrowska, Irena. **The Art of Poland**. New York, Philosophical Library, 1947. 238p. illus. index. LC 47-3695.
Concise history of art and architecture in Poland from the early Middle Ages through the early twentieth century. Bibliography (pp. 227-28) lists major works in all languages. For the general reader and the beginning student.

949   Topass, Jean. **L'art et les artistes en Pologne**. Paris, Félix, 1923-28. 3v. illus.
History of art and architecture in Poland from the beginning of the Middle Ages to circa 1920. Volume 1, *Au moyen âge*; Volume 2, *De la prime-renaissance au préromantisme*; Volume 3, *Du romantisme à nos jours*. Bibliographies given at the end of each volume list books in Polish, French, and German. Still one of the few histories of Polish art in a Western language. For the beginning student.

RUSSIA

950   Alpatov, Mikhail V. **Art Treasures of Russia**. New York, Abrams, 1967. 178p. illus. index. LC 67-12683.
Lavishly illustrated general survey of Russian painting, sculpture, architecture, and liturgical arts from the Middle Ages through the nineteenth century. No bibliography. For the general reader.

951   Alpatov, Mikhail V., and Nikolai I. Brunov. **Geschichte der altrussischen Kunst**. Augsburg, Filser, 1932. 2v. illus. index. Repr.: New York, Johnson Reprint, 1969. 423p. illus. index. LC 69-19944.
Comprehensive history of art and architecture in Russia from the tenth century through the seventeenth century. Subjects are treated by type; Alpatov writes on architecture and Brunov on the figurative arts. The reprint has a new preface in English by the authors. The bibliography for the architecture section is on pages 235 and 236; other bibliographies are at the end of the chapters. An old but classic history of old Russian art and architecture; still valuable to the advanced student.

952   **Art Treasures in Russia: Monuments, Masterpieces, Commissions, and Collections**. General eds., Bernard S. Myers and Trewin Copplestone. New York and Toronto, McGraw-Hill, 1970. 175p. illus. index. LC 71-101167.
Pictorial survey of painting, sculpture, architecture, and the decorative and minor arts in Russia from 2500 B.C. to the present. The various epochs are treated by different specialists. Includes maps and a glossary-index of museums and monuments, but no bibliography. For the general reader.

953   Blunt, Cyril G. E. **A History of Russian Art**. London, Studio, 1946. 272p. illus. index.
Survey history of art and architecture from the pre-Christian period through World War II. Brief and inadequate bibliography (p. 268). For the general reader.

954   **Geschichte der russischen Kunst**. Dresden, Verlag der Kunst, 1957-1965. 4v. illus. index.
Collection of essays on various aspects of the art and architecture of Russia, written by Russian specialists and translated into German (Russian title: *Istoriia russkogo iskusstva*). Covers prehistory through the seventeenth century. Good bibliography, with German translations of Russian titles. A standard history of Russian art for the advanced student.

955   Hamilton, George H. **Art and Architecture of Russia**. London, Penguin, 1954. 320p. illus. index. (Pelican History of Art, Z6).
Comprehensive history of the art and architecture of Russia from the tenth through the twentieth century. Good selection of plates, plans, and diagrams. Bibliography (pp. 295-99) lists books chiefly in Western languages. Reference to further, more specialized literature is in the extensive footnotes. A standard history of Russian art and architecture for the advanced student and the scholar.

956   Hare, Richard. **The Art and Artists of Russia**. Greenwich, Conn., New York Graphic Society, 1966. 294p. illus. index. LC 66-16279.
Survey of the history of painting and the minor arts in Russia from the fifteenth to the early twentieth century. Selected bibliography (pp. 282-86). Popular survey for the general reader and the collector.

957   Kornilovich, Kira V. **Arts of Russia**. Cleveland, World, 1967-1968. 2v. illus. LC 67-24469 rev.

Pictorial survey of the art and architecture in Russia from the ancient Scythians through the eighteenth century. Popular text with good color plates. No bibliography. For the general reader.

958   Réau, Louis. **L'art russe**. Verviers, Gerard, 1968. 2v. illus. index. LC 75-408686.

Reissue of the 1921-22 edition (Paris, Laurens). Survey of the art and architecture in Russia from the Greco-Scythian period through the rococo. No bibliography, but there is occasional reference to further literature in the footnotes. An old standard history of Russian art and architecture, still useful to the beginning student.

959   Rice, Tamara T. **A Concise History of Russian Art**. New York, Praeger, 1963. 288p. illus. index. LC 63-16653.

Concise history of art and architecture in Russia from the tenth through the twentieth centuries. Provides a brief, unclassified bibliography (pp. 272-73). A good survey history of Russian art and architecture for the general reader and beginning student.

960   Wulff, Oskar K. **Die neurussische Kunst im Rahmen der Kultur-Entwicklung Russlands von Peter dem Grossen bis zur Revolution**. Augsburg, Filser, 1932. 2v. illus. index.

Comprehensive history of art and architecture in Russia from the eighteenth through the early twentieth century. Volume one, text; Volume two, plates. Brief bibliography (p. 350). For the advanced student.

CHAPTER TEN

ORIENTAL ART

I. GENERAL WORKS

961   La Plante, John D. **Asian Art**. Dubuque, Iowa, W. C. Brown, 1968. 185p.
illus. index. LC 68-14575.
Survey of the art and architecture of India, China, and Japan from circa 2500
B.C. to the beginning of the twentieth century. Provides useful maps and a modest
selection of illustrations in black and white. Bibliography (p. 177) lists major books
in English. Designed as an inexpensive text for the beginning student.

962   Lee, Sherman E. **A History of Far Eastern Art**. Englewood Cliffs, N.J.,
Prentice-Hall, 1964. 527p. illus. index. LC 64-11575.
Concise history of art and architecture in India, China, Korea, Japan, Central Asia,
Southeast Asia, and Indonesia. Excellent selection of plates, plans, and diagrams
from the Stone Age through the eighteenth century. The good bibliography
(pp. 499-511) of books and periodicals in all languages singles out those of special
interest. The standard history of Far Eastern art and architecture. For the
beginning and advanced student.

963   Theile, Albert. **Aussereuropäische Kunst von den Anfangen bis Heute:
ein Überblick**. Cologne, Seemann, 1956. 3v. illus. index. LC A57-4278.
Concise history of non-Western art and architecture from prehistoric times to the
present. Band I, *Die Kunst der Naturvölker: Die altere Kunst Amerikas*; Band 2,
*Die neuere Kunst Amerikas; Kunst Australias; Indische Kunst; Die Kunst des
Islam*; Band 3, *Die Kunst des Fernen Ostens: China, Korea, Japan*. General bibliography (Vol. 3, pp. 274-78) lists major books in all languages. A standard German
history of non-Western art and architecture. For the advanced student.

II. ISLAMIC WORLD

GENERAL WORKS

964   Diez, Ernst. **Kunst der islamischen Völker.** Berlin, Athenaion, 1915. 218p. illus. index.
Concise but scholarly history of Islamic art and architecture from the beginnings through the eighteenth century. Bibliography given at the end of the chapters. A volume in the series "Handbuch der Kunstwissenschaft." An old but classic history, still of interest to the advanced student.

965   Grube, Ernst J. **The World of Islam.** New York and Toronto, McGraw-Hill, 1967. 176p. illus. index. LC 66-19271.
General pictorial survey of the architecture, sculpture, architectural decoration, metalwork, and minor and decorative arts throughout Islamic realms. Includes the arts of the Umayyads, Fatimids, Seljuk Turks in Anatolia and Iran, Atabeks, Ayyubids, Mongol period, Mamluk, Nasrid, Timurid, Ottoman Turks, Safavid Iran, and Islamic art in India. Includes maps, plans, and a brief bibliography (p. 171). For the general reader.

966   Grousset, René, *et al.* **Arts musulmans, Extrême-Orient.** Paris, Colin, 1937. 496p. illus. index.
Concise history of the art and architecture of India, Indochina, Indonesia, China, Japan, Central Asia, and the Islamic world. Well illustrated. Bibliographies at the end of each section. An older but still valuable survey of Oriental art and architecture for beginning and advanced students.

967   Kühnel, Ernst. **Islamic Art and Architecture.** Ithaca, Cornell University Press, 1966. 200p. illus. index. LC 66-19223.
Concise history of art and architecture in the Muslim world from earliest times (Umayyad style) to the twentieth century. Well illustrated with plates, plans, and diagrams. Provides a brief but good bibliography (pp. 185-89). Translation of *Die Kunst des Islam* (Stuttgart, 1963). A good survey history for the beginning student and the general reader.

968   Marcais, Georges. **L'art musulman.** Paris, Presses Universitaires de France, 1962. 186p. illus. index. LC 65-30614.
Concise history of Islamic art and architecture from the eighth century through the eighteenth century. First published in 1946 as *L'art de l'Islam.* Bibliography (pp. 184-86) lists books in all languages. For the beginning student.

969   Otto-Dorn, Katharina. **L'art de l'Islam.** Paris, Michel, 1967. 278p. illus. index. LC 67-107712.
Concise history of Islamic art and architecture from its beginnings through the eighteenth century. Provides glossary of terms, chronological table, and

bibliography (pp. 270-75), which lists books in all languages. French edition of the series "Art of the World." A good survey of Islamic art and architecture for the beginning student.

970   Rice, David T. **Islamic Art**. New York, Praeger, 1965. 286p. illus. index. LC 65-10179.
Concise history of art and architecture in the Muslim world from the seventh through the seventeenth century. Good selection of plates; bibliography (pp. 261-63) lists chief books in English, French, and German. For the general reader and the beginning student.

971   Ry van Beest Holle, Carel J. du. **Art of Islam**. New York, Abrams, 1971. 263p. illus. index. LC 72-92914.
Survey history of the art and architecture of the Islamic world from the time of the Umayyad dynasty through the Safavid dynasty. Includes a chapter of Islamic art of India (Moghul India). The illustrations are well chosen, and the balanced bibliography (pp. 256-58) lists books in all languages. A good survey for the general reader and the beginning student.

972   Sourdel-Thomine, Janine, and Bertold Spuler. **Die Kunst des Islam**. Berlin, Propyläen, 1973. 426p. (text); 416p. (illus.). index. (Propyläen Kunstgeschichte, Band 4).
Comprehensive, illustrated handbook of the art and architecture of the Islamic world from its beginnings through the eighteenth century. Also covers the art and architecture of Persia from the sixth century B.C. to the rise of Islam. The introductory essay characterizing and sketching the history of Islamic art and architecture is followed by a corpus of excellent plates. Separate essays by a group of international specialists discuss in greater detail the development of the various arts and national styles. Notes to the plates provide basic information and reference to specialized literature. The volume concludes with a very good classified bibliography (pp. 401-417) that lists books and periodical articles in all languages. A chronological table coordinates political, religious, cultural, and artistic events in the various regions. A standard handbook for the advanced student and scholar.

IRAN AND AFGHANISTAN

973   Auboyer, Jeannine. **L'Afghanistan et son art**. Paris, Cercle d'Art, 1968. 172p. illus. index.
Concise survey of the art and architecture of Afghanistan from prehistoric times to the fifteenth century. A brief introductory essay traces the development; this is followed by a good collection of plates, with informative notes. Bibliography (pp. 167-72) lists major books in all languages. For the general reader and the beginning student.

974   Belloni, Gian Guido, and Liliana Fedi Dall'Asèn. **Iranian Art.** New York,
       Praeger, 1969. 29p. (text); 101p. (illus.). LC 70-81992.
Pictorial guide to the art and architecture of Iran from prehistoric times to the
seventeenth century. Brief introduction traces the history of art and architecture
in Iran with the help of maps and a chronological table; this is followed by a good
selection of plates with informative captions. Bibliography (p. 29) lists major books
in all languages. A good survey for the general reader.

975   Godard, André. **The Art of Iran.** New York, Praeger, 1965. 358p. illus.
       index. LC 65-11169.
Comprehensive history of art and architecture in Iran from 2,400 B.C. through the
first half of the nineteenth century. Well illustrated with plates, plans, diagrams,
and useful maps; good classified bibliography (pp. 339-45) lists books and periodical articles in all languages. Scholarly but readable text. Standard history of Iranian
art and architecture for the beginning and advanced student.

976   Pope, Arthur U. **An Introduction to Persian Art Since the Seventh Century
       A.D.** New York, Scribner's, 1931. 256p. illus.
Concise history of art and architecture in Persia from the seventh through the
twentieth century. Provides a list of the principal monuments and a brief bibliography (pp. 252-56). An old, general survey history of Persian art and architecture by a leading expert; still useful reading for the general reader and the
beginning student.

977   Pope, Arthur U., and Phyllis Ackerman, eds. **Survey of Persian Art from
       Prehistoric Times to the Present.** London, Oxford University Press, 1965.
       14v. illus. index.
Collection of essays by specialists covering all aspects of Persian art from prehistory
to the present. Volume 14 contains "New Studies 1938-1960: The Proceedings
of the International Congress of Iranian Art and Archaeology, 1960, Part A."
Bibliography is in the footnotes. These authoritative, scholarly essays form a
standard history of Persian art and architecture for the advanced student and the
scholar.

TURKEY

978   Akurgal, Ekrem, *et al.* **Treasures of Turkey.** Geneva, Skira, 1967. 253p. illus.
       index. LC 66-22488.
Pictorial survey of art and architecture in Turkey from the earliest civilizations of
Anatolia through the Islamic period. Excellent color plates. No bibliography.
Popular text for the general reader.

979   Aslanapa, Oktay. **Turkish Art and Architecture.** New York, Praeger,
       1971. 422p. illus. index. LC 72-144222.

Concise history of art and architecture in Turkey from pre-Islamic times through the Ottoman period. Well illustrated. Bibliography (pp. 355-99) is an excellent classified list of books and periodical articles in all languages. A standard history of Turkish art and architecture for beginning and advanced students.

III. INDIA AND CEYLON

980   Abbate, Francesco, ed. **Indian Art and the Art of Ceylon, Central and South-East Asia.** London and New York, Octopus, 1972. 158p. illus. LC 73-151958.
Brief, pictorial survey of the art and architecture of India, Ceylon, Afghanistan, Nepal, Tibet, Siam, Burma, Cambodia, Vietnam, and Indonesia. Popular text. Brief bibliography (p. 154) and chronological table. For the general reader.

981   Ahmed, Jalal U. **Art in Pakistan.** 2nd ed. Karachi, Pakistan Publications, 1962. 151p. illus. index. LC SA 64-1479.
Brief history of art and architecture in Pakistan from the beginning of the Islamic period to the present. No bibliography. For the general reader.

982   Bussagli, Mario, and C. Sivaramamurti. **5,000 Years of the Art of India.** New York, Abrams, 1971. 355p. illus. index.
Illustrated handbook of art and architecture in India from prehistoric times to the present. Excellent plates. For the general reader and beginning student. The corpus of illustrations is useful for the advanced student.

983   Coomaraswamy, Ananda K. **History of Indian and Indonesian Art.** New York, Dover, 1965. 295p. illus. index. Reprint of 1927 edition.
Concise history of art and architecture in India, Nepal, Tibet, Turkestan, Ceylon, and Indonesia from pre-Mauryan times through the Indian medieval. Bibliography (pp. 214-29) provides a good listing of older books and periodical articles. An older, standard history. Still useful to the beginning student.

984   Diez, Ernst. **Die Kunst Indiens.** Berlin, Athenaion, 1925. 194p. illus. index.
History of art and architecture in ancient and medieval India and Indian colonial art of the same time in Ceylon, Java, Burma, Cambodia, Thailand, and Laos. Bibliographies at the end of the chapters. A volume in the "Handbuch der Kunstwissenschaft" series. An old but classic scholarly history of Indian art for the advanced student.

985   Goetz, Hermann. **The Art of India: Five Thousand Years of Indian Art.** New York, Crown, 1962. 280p. illus. index. LC 59-13434.
Concise history of art and architecture in India from prehistoric times to the

present. Provides a glossary of terms, a chronological table, a map, and a good, select bibliography (pp. 263-69) of books and periodical articles in English. A good survey history for the beginning student and the general reader.

986   Härtel, Herbert, and Jeannine Auboyer. **Indien und Südostasien.** Berlin, Propyläen, 1971. 408p. (text); 369p. (illus). index. (Propyläen Kunstgeschichte, Band 16). LC 71-889568.
Comprehensive, illustrated handbook of the art and architecture of India and Southeast Asia from 3000 B.C. to 1700 A.D. Covers also Afghanistan, East Turkestan, and Central Asia. Introductory essay is followed by a corpus of excellent plates, notes to the plates that provide basic information and specialized bibliography, and separate essays on the development of the various media and national styles by a group of specialists. Provides an excellent, comprehensive bibliography (pp. 330-45) that lists books and periodical articles in all languages and a useful chronological table that coordinates the artistic, political, religious, and general cultural events in the various countries. A basic handbook for the advanced student and scholar.

987   Iyer, K. Bharatha. **Indian Art: A Short Introduction.** Bombay, Asia Publishing House, 1958. 87p. illus. index. LC 60-2779.
Brief history of art and architecture in India from earliest times through the eighteenth century. Brief bibliography (pp. 79-80). For the general reader.

988   Kramrisch, Stella. **The Art of India.** 3rd ed. New York, Phaidon, 1965. 230p. illus.
Survey of the art and architecture of ancient and medieval India. Well illustrated, the text concentrates on concepts and characteristics of Indian art. Bibliography (pp. 230-31) lists major works, catalogs of exhibitions, and journals. A good introduction for the general reader and the beginning student.

989   Rawson, Philip. **Indian Art.** New York, Dutton, 1972. 159p. illus. index.
Survey history of art and architecture in India from prehistoric times through the twentieth century. Well illustrated; provides a brief bibliography (p. 157) of popular works in English. For the general reader.

990   Rowland, Benjamin, Jr. **The Art and Architecture of India: Buddhist, Hindu, Jain.** 3rd ed. rev. London, Penguin, 1967. 314p. illus. index. (Pelican History of Art, Z2). LC 67-4077.
Comprehensive history of art and architecture in India from prehistoric times through the period of the Hindu dynasties (nineteenth century). Also covers the Romano-Indian art and architecture in Afghanistan, Turkestan, and Kashmir, and the Indian art and architecture in Ceylon, Siam, Burma, and Java. Provides a good selection of plates, useful maps, plans, diagrams, a glossary of terms, and a good, classified bibliography (pp. 486-92), which lists books and periodicals in all languages. Reference to specialized literature is in the extensive footnotes. A standard history of Indian art and architecture for the advanced student and scholar.

991   Smith, Vincent A. **A History of Art in India and Ceylon.** 2nd ed., rev. by
       K. de B. Codrington. 3rd rev. and enl. ed. by Karl Khandalavala. Bombay,
       D. B. Taraporevala, 1962. 219p. illus. index. LC SA 62-809.
Concise history of art and architecture in India and Ceylon from the Mauryan
period to modern times. Covers Indian-inspired art in Central Asia, Tibet, Nepal,
and Java. Bibliography (pp. 209-210) lists books in English. Reissue of an older
general history for the general reader and the beginning student.

992   Winstedt, Richard, ed. **Indian Art.** London, Faber and Faber, 1947.
       200p. illus. index.
Survey of the art and architecture of India during the ancient and medieval periods.
Introductory essay giving the historical background by H. G. Rowlinson. Popular
text. No bibliography. For the general reader.

993   Zimmer, Heinrich R. **The Art of Indian Asia: Its Mythology and Trans-
       formation.** 2nd ed. Princeton, Princeton University Press, 1955. 2v.
       illus. index.
A comprehensive conceptual and historical study of the art and architecture of
India and Indian Asia from prehistoric times to 1850. Volume one, text; Volume
two, plates. Provided with maps and a chronological table. Thorough reference to
specialized literature is in the notes. A standard work on Indian art and architecture, especially for its chapters on symbolism. For the advanced student.

IV. CENTRAL ASIA

994   Gordon, Antoinette K. **Tibetan Religious Art.** 2nd ed. New York,
       Paragon, 1963. 104p. illus. index. LC 63-22167.
Concise history of Tibetan painting, sculpture, and the minor arts. Provides
bibliography (pp. 99-100) of books and periodical articles in English. For the
general reader and the beginning student.

995   Hummel, Siegbert. **Geschichte der tibetischen Kunst.** Leipzig, Harrasso-
       witz, 1953. 123p. (text); 124p. (illus.).
History of art and architecture in Tibet from prehistory to the present. Provides
maps, a good selection of plates, and a bibliography (pp. 113-17) that lists books
and periodical articles in all languages. A standard history of Tibetan art and architecture for the advanced student.

996   Rice, Tamara T. **Ancient Arts of Central Asia.** New York, Praeger, 1965.
       288p. illus. index. LC 65-19586.
Concise survey of the art and architecture of Central Asia, including the greater
Caucasian area, Russian Central Asia, Afghanistan, and parts of Northern India.

Provides a chronological table and a brief bibliography arranged by chapters (pp. 263-64). For the general reader and the beginning student.

997   Singh, Madanjeet. **Himalayan Art** . . . New York, Macmillan, 1971. 287p.
       illus. LC 68-28652.
Survey history of painting and sculpture in the Himalayas including Nepal, Bhutan, Sikkim, and the Siwalik Ranges. Bibliography (pp. 281-82) lists general books in English. For the general reader.

998   Waldschmidt, Ernst, and Rose Leonore Waldschmidt. **Nepal: Art**
       Treasures from the Himalayas. New York, Universe, 1970. 160p. illus.
       index. LC 72-96964.
Pictorial survey of the art and architecture of Nepal from circa 400 A.D. through the eighteenth century. Brief introduction characterizes the geography, people, and religion of Nepal and provides a short sketch of the art history. Excellent collection of plates with informative captions and a brief but useful note (p. 159) referring to the chief sources for bibliography on Nepal. For the general reader and the beginning student.

V. SOUTHEAST ASIA

GENERAL WORKS

999   Griswold, Alexander B., and Peter H. Pott. **The Art of Burma, Korea,**
       Tibet. New York, Crown, 1964. 277p. illus. index. LC 63-20855.
Concise history of the art and architecture of Burma, Korea, and Tibet from 200 B.C. to the nineteenth century. Provides maps, a chronological table, and a good bibliography of books in all languages (pp. 255-63). For beginning and advanced students.

1000   Groslier, Bernard Philippe. **The Art of Indochina, including Thailand,**
        Vietnam, Laos and Cambodia. New York, Crown, 1962. 261p. illus.
        index. LC 62-11805.
Concise history of art and architecture in Southeast Asia from prehistory to circa 1900. Emphasis is on the architecture and sculpture of the great temples. Provides a useful glossary, a guide to the pronunciation of names, a list of the names of kings, and a bibliography (pp. 240-45) of major books and periodical articles in all languages. For the general reader and the beginning student.

1001   Rawson, Philip S. **The Art of Southeast Asia: Cambodia, Vietnam,**
        Thailand, Laos, Burma, Java, Bali. New York, Praeger, 1967. illus. index.
        LC 67-29399.

Survey history of the art and architecture of Cambodia, Vietnam, Laos, Thailand, Burma, Java, and Bali from earliest times to the modern age. Provides a glossary of terms and a select bibliography of books in all languages (pp. 278-83). For the general reader and the beginning student.

INDOCHINA

1002   Bezacier, Louis. **L'art vietnamien**. Paris, Union Française, 1955. 233p. illus. index.
History of art and architecture in Vietnam from prehistoric times to the nineteenth century. Poor illustrations. Bibliography (pp. 211-13) lists books and periodicals chiefly in French. For the advanced student.

INDONESIA

1003   Bernet Kempers, August J. **Ancient Indonesian Art**. Cambridge, Harvard University Press, 1959. 124p. (text); 353p. (illus.).
Comprehensive study of art and architecture in Indonesia from mesolithic times through the early Islamic period (circa 1650). Brief introduction tracing the development is followed by an excellent corpus of illustrations, with detailed and informative notes. Provides an excellent but unclassified bibliography (pp. 109-114) of books and periodical articles in all languages. A standard history of Indonesian art and architecture for the advanced student.

1004   Bodrogi, Tibor. **Art of Indonesia**. Greenwich, Conn., New York Graphic Society, 1972. 140p. (text); 157p. (illus.). LC 76-154331.
Illustrated survey of the art and architecture of Indonesia from paleolithic times to the present. Well illustrated. Provides a good bibliography (pp. 109-115) listing books and periodical articles in all languages. A good survey history of Indonesian art for the general reader and the beginning student.

1005   Holt, Claire. **Art in Indonesia: Continuities and Change**. Ithaca, New York, Cornell University Press, 1967. 355p. illus. index. LC 66-19222.
Concise history of art and architecture in Indonesia from prehistoric times to the modern age. Discussion of the legends and literature expressed in the fine arts of Indonesia are discussed in the appendices. Bibliography (pp. 331-38) is an unclassified list of books chiefly in English. For the general reader and the beginning student.

1006   Wagner, Frits A. **Indonesia: The Art of an Island Group**. New York, McGraw-Hill, 1959. 256p. illus. index. LC 59-13943.
History of art and architecture in Indonesia from the neolithic age through the twentieth century. Excellent chapters on the impact of Indian and Islamic culture

on the culture of Indonesia precede the discussion of the major epochs of Indonesian art and architecture. Provides a useful glossary, a chronological table, and a bibliography (pp. 243-45) of books and periodical articles in all languages. An excellent history of Indonesian art and architecture for beginning and advanced students.

THAILAND

1007   Le May, Reginald S. **A Concise History of Buddhist Art in Siam.** 2nd ed.
        Rutland, Vt., Tuttle, 1963. 169p. illus. LC 62-18359.
Originally published in 1938, this is a survey history of art and architecture in Thailand from the Dvāravatī period through the schools of Lopburi and Ayudhya. Bibliography (pp. 155-57) lists major books and periodical articles in all languages. A good survey of ancient art and architecture in Thailand for beginning and advanced students.

VI. FAR EAST

GENERAL WORKS

1008   Fontein, Jan, and Rose Hempel. **China, Korea, Japan.** Berlin, Propyläen,
        1968. 362p. (text); 256p. (illus.). index. (Propyläen Kunstgeschichte,
        Band 17). LC 70-426900.
Comprehensive, illustrated handbook of art and architecture of China, Japan, and Korea from 2000 B.C. to the middle of the nineteenth century. Introductory essays on the development of the various arts in the three countries are followed by an excellent corpus of plates. The very informative notes also supply bibliographical references to specialized literature. The volume concludes with an excellent comprehensive bibliography (pp. 318-37) of books and periodical articles in all languages and a thorough chronological table that coordinates artistic events in the three countries with philosophical, political, religious, and general cultural happenings. The standard illustrated handbook of Far Eastern art for the advanced student and scholar.

1009   Kümmel, Otto. **Die Kunst Chinas, Japans und Koreas.** Wildpark-Potsdam,
        Athenaion, 1929. 198p. illus. index.
Concise history of art and architecture in China, Japan, and Korea from prehistoric times to the Ching and Tokugawa periods. Bibliography is given at the end of the chapters. An old but scholarly history, still of interest to the advanced student. Part of the series "Handbuch der Kunstwissenschaft."

1010   Munsterberg, Hugo. **Art of the Far East**. New York, Abrams, 1971. 264p.
        illus. index. LC 68-26866.
Survey history of art and architecture in China, Korea, and Japan from prehistoric
times to the present. Well-chosen illustrations but no plans for the architectural
examples. Bibliography (pp. 260-62) lists books in all languages. For the general
reader and the beginning student.

1011   Shoten, Kadokawa, ed. **A Pictorial Encyclopedia of the Oriental Arts**.
        New York, Crown, 1969. 7v. illus. LC 70-93408.
Illustrated handbook of Far Eastern art and architecture, divided by country; two
volumes are devoted to China, four to Japan, and one to Korea. Provides broad
essays on periods of art and architecture, followed by an extensive collection of
plates. No bibliographies. A useful collection of illustrations for beginning and
advanced students.

CHINA

1012   Abbate, Francesco, ed. **Chinese Art**. London and New York, Octopus,
        1972. 158p. illus. LC 72-171380.
Pictorial survey of art and architecture in China from prehistoric times to the end
of the Ching dynasty. All plates are in color, but some are poorly reproduced.
Inadequate one-page bibliography. For the general reader.

1013   Ashton, Leigh, and Basil Gray. **Chinese Art**. London, Faber, 1935. 375p.
        illus. index.
Concise history of art, exclusive of architecture, in China from the pre-Han period
(3000 B.C.) to the end of the Ching dynasty. Emphasis is on the minor arts.
Bibliography (pp. 360-62) lists major books in English. An old but valuable survey
by leading English scholars. For the beginning student and the collector.

1014   Bachhofer, Ludwig. **A Short History of Chinese Art**. New York, Pantheon,
        1946. 139p. illus. index.
Concise history of art and architecture in China from the neolithic period through
the eighteenth century. Bibliography is provided in the form of notes to the text
(pp. 129-31). This is the best brief survey history of Chinese art and architecture
for the general reader and the beginning student.

1015   Buhot, Jean. **Chinese and Japanese Art, with Sections on Korea and Viet-
        nam**. New York, Praeger, 1967. 428p. illus. index. LC 67-9244.
Concise history of Chinese and Japanese art and architecture with briefer sections
on Korea and Vietnam from prehistoric times through the eighteenth century.
Classified bibliography (pp. 335-43), mostly of works in French. For the general
reader and the beginning student.

1016   Fenollosa, Ernest F. **Epochs of Chinese and Japanese Art: An Outline History of East Asiatic Design.** New and rev. ed. with copious notes by Professor Petrucci. New York, Dover, 1963. 2v. illus. LC 63-5655.
Reprint of the 1921 edition, first published in 1912. Concise history of art and architecture in China and Japan from prehistoric times through the nineteenth century. Provides a glossary of proper names and some bibliographical references in the footnotes. Early pioneering history of Far Eastern art.

1017   Grousset, René. **Chinese Art and Culture.** New York, Orion Press, 1959. 331p. illus. index. LC 59-13323.
Translation of *La Chine et son art* (Paris, Plon, 1951). Concise history of art and architecture in China from prehistoric times through the Ching dynasty. Sets the arts within the development of Chinese culture. Bibliographical footnotes. A good introduction to Chinese art and its cultural context for the general reader and the beginning student.

1018   Jenyns, R. Soame, ed. **Chinese Art.** New York, Universe, 1960-1965. 4v. illus. LC 60-12415.
Illustrated handbook of Chinese art exclusive of architecture covering the period from neolithic times to the end of the Ching dynasty. The volumes consist of a brief introductory essay followed by a good collection of plates. Bibliographies are given at the end of Volumes 1, 3, and 4. Contents:
>   Vol. 1, Lion, Daisy, and Jean Claude Moreau-Gebard. *Bronze, Jade, Sculpture, Ceramics* (1960)
>   Vol. 2, Watson, William, and R. Soame Jenyns. *Gold, Silver, Bronze, Cloisonné, Cantonese Enamel, Lacquer, Furniture, Wood* (1962)
>   Vol. 3, Speiser, Werner, Roger Goeppe, and Jean Fribourg. *Painting, Calligraphy, Stone Rubbing, Wood Engraving* (1964)
>   Vol. 4, Jenyns, R. Soame. *Textiles, Glass and Painting on Glass, Carvings in Ivory and Rhinoceros Horn, Carvings in Hardstones, Snuff Bottles, Inkcakes and Inkstones* (1965).
Good collection of plates for the collector and advanced student.

1019   Medley, Margaret. **A Handbook of Chinese Art for Collectors and Students.** London, G. Bell, 1964. 140p. illus. index. LC 64-54900. Repr.: New York and Evanston, Harper & Row, n.d. LC 74-6765.
Dictionary handbook of Chinese art, exclusive of architecture. Sections cover bronzes, ceramics, decoration, jade and hardstones, and painting; each section has a brief introduction and a dictionary of terms. Brief bibliographies at the end of each section list books in English. General bibliography (pp. 131-32) lists books in English. Appendix lists societies devoted to the study of Chinese art and culture and chief collections of Chinese art. Useful handbook for the beginning student and the collector.

1020   Munsterberg, Hugo. **The Arts of China.** Rutland, Vt., Tuttle, 1972. 234p. illus. index. LC 70-188012.

Concise history of art and architecture in China from prehistory through the Ching period. Bibliography (pp. 221-23) lists major books in English. For the general reader and the beginning student.

1021   Munsterberg, Hugo. **A Short History of Chinese Art**. New York, Greenwood, 1969. 225p. illus. index. LC 70-88990.
Reprint of 1949 edition. General history of Chinese art and architecture from prehistoric times through the Ching dynasty. Bibliography (pp. 213-17) lists major works in English. For the general reader and the beginning student.

1022   Prodan, Mario. **Chinese Art: An Introduction**. New York, Pantheon, 1958. 220p. illus. index. LC 58-11711.
Concise history of Chinese art, exclusive of architecture, from prehistoric times through the Ching dynasty. Chapters on bronzes, ceramics, sculpture, painting, ivories, jade, lacquer, textiles, and jewelry. Bibliography (pp. 209-213) is a classified list of books in all languages. A sensitively written survey for the general reader and the collector.

1023   Sickman, Laurence C. S., and Alexander Soper. **The Art and Architecture of China**. 3rd ed. Harmondsworth, Penguin, 1968. 350p. illus. index. LC 75-422837. (Pelican History of Art, Z10).
Comprehensive history of art and architecture (treated in separate sections) of China from prehistoric times to the early twentieth century. Excellent selection of plates, maps, plans, and diagrams. Two-part bibliography (pp. 327-34) lists major works in all languages, with an additional note on works that have appeared since the first edition. Further reference to specialized literature is found in the extensive footnotes. Useful glossary of terms. The standard history of Chinese art and architecture. For the advanced student and scholar.

1024   Silcock, Arnold. **Introduction to Chinese Art and History**. New York, Oxford University Press, 1948. 256p. illus. index.
Concise survey of Chinese art and architecture cast within the general historical development of the country. Provides maps, chronological table of events in China and the West, guide to the pronunciation of Chinese names, and a brief bibliography listing major books and periodicals in English (pp. 244-46). Still a useful survey for the general reader and the beginning student.

1025   Speiser, Werner. **The Art of China: Spirit and Society**. New York, Crown, 1961. 258p. illus. index. LC 61-10700.
Survey history of art and architecture in China from the Shang dynasty to the twentieth century. Provides glossary of terms, chronological table, and bibliography (pp. 247-48) of books in all languages (those works that have bibliographies are singled out). For the general reader and the beginning student.

1026   Sullivan, Michael. **The Arts of China**. New enl. ed. Berkeley and Los Angeles, University of California Press, 1973. 256p. illus. index. LC 73-78421.

New edition of the author's *A Short History of Chinese Art* (1967). Concise history of the art and architecture of China from prehistory through the twentieth century. Good selection of plates, useful chronological table, and bibliography (pp. 247-48) of major works in English. An excellent survey history for the general reader and the beginning student.

1027   Sullivan, Michael. **Chinese and Japanese Art.** New York, Franklin Watts, 1965. 302p. illus. index. LC 65-10271.
A concise history of Chinese and Japanese painting, sculpture, and architecture. Includes an interesting section on influences. Illustrated with color plates and black and white illustrations. A good introduction for beginning students and general readers.

1028   Swann, Peter C. **Art of China, Korea and Japan.** New York, Praeger, 1963. 285p. illus. index. LC 63-18836.
Concise survey of the art and architecture of the Far East from circa 1550 B.C. to the present. Bibliography (pp. 274-81) lists books in English. For the general reader.

1029   Willetts, William. **Chinese Art.** London, Penguin, 1958. 2v. illus. index.
History of art and architecture in China from prehistoric times to the present. After an introduction that covers the geography of China and that provides a short history of the country, there are chapters on prehistoric civilization. The rest of the work is divided into sections on the major media. Bibliographical references are in the footnotes. A good history of Chinese art and architecture, in part superseded by the author's later work (1030). For the advanced student.

1030   Willetts, William. **Foundations of Chinese Art from Neolithic Pottery to Modern Architecture.** New York, McGraw-Hill, 1965. 456p. illus. index. LC 64-66127.
Illustrated history of art and architecture in China from the neolithic to the present. The text is a revised, abridged, and extensively rewritten version of the author's *Chinese Art* (London, Penguin, 1958. 2v.). Provides a very good selection of plates, plans, and diagrams and a good classified bibliography (pp. 437-41). A good survey history of Chinese art and architecture for beginning and advanced students.

JAPAN

1031   Abbate, Francesco, ed. **Japanese and Korean Art.** London and New York, Octopus, 1972. 158p. illus. LC 72-171382.
Pictorial survey of the art and architecture of Japan and Korea from the seventh century A.D. to the beginning of the twentieth century. All illustrations are in color, but some are poorly reproduced. Inadequate one-page bibliography. For the general reader.

1032   Boger, H. Batterson. **The Traditional Arts of Japan: A Complete Illustrated Guide**. Garden City, N.Y., Bonanza, 1964. 351p. illus. index. LC 64-11726.
Comprehensive survey of the many arts of Japan, including painting, sculpture, architecture, landscape design, floral arrangement, tea ceremony and ceremonial objects, pottery, porcelain, lacquerware, and others. Generously illustrated with black and white illustrations plus a color plate section. Includes maps, chronological outline, and a bibliography (pp. 339-40). A good, sensitive survey for beginning and advanced students.

1033   Buhot, Jean. **Histoire des arts du Japon. I. Des origines à 1350**. Paris, Vanoest, 1949. 270p. illus. index. (Annales du Musée Guimet, Nouv. série, V).
Comprehensive and scholarly history of the art and architecture of Japan from prehistoric times to 1350. Provides good selection of plates, diagrams, and maps, with thorough reference to specialized literature in the extensive footnotes. A standard history of early Japanese art and architecture. For the advanced student and the scholar.

1034   Newman, Alexander R., and Egerton Ryerson. **Japanese Art: A Collector's Guide**. London, Bell, 1964. 271p. illus. index. LC 65-83470.
Handbook of Japanese art containing chapters on various media (books, ceramics, clocks, etc.) and a section on Japanese dating and periods of art history. Good bibliographies are provided at the end of chapters and sections. A good guide to Japanese art, especially the minor arts of interest to collectors.

1035   Noma, Seiroku. **The Arts of Japan**. Tokyo, Kodansha International, 1966-67. 2v. illus. LC 65-19186 rev.
Illustrated history of art and architecture in Japan from prehistory to the present day. Vol. I: *Ancient and Medieval*; Vol. II: *Late Medieval to Modern*. Short essays sketch the development of art and architecture by periods; there are excellent color plates with informative captions. A bibliography of works in English is at the end of each volume. An excellent survey for the general reader and the beginning student.

1036   Paine, Robert T., and Alexander C. Soper. **Art and Architecture of Japan**. London, Penguin, 1955. 294p. illus. index. (Pelican History of Art, Z8).
Comprehensive and scholarly history of art and architecture in Japan from the archaic period to the mid-nineteenth century. Excellent selection of plates, glossary, maps, diagrams, and plans. Bibliography (pp. 291-94) is divided into sections on architecture and art; the first part lists only books in English, while the second part has sections for books in Western languages and those in Japanese. Thorough reference to more specialized literature in the extensive footnotes. The standard history of Japanese art and architecture in English. For the advanced student and the scholar.

1037   Swann, Peter C. **An Introduction to the Art of Japan.** Oxford, Cassirer, 1958. 220p. illus. index.
Concise history of the art, exclusive of the architecture, of Japan from prehistoric times to the Edo period. Bibliography (p. 216) lists books in English. For the general reader and beginning student.

1038   Swann, Peter C. **The Art of Japan: From Joman to the Tokugawa Period.** New York, Crown, 1966. 238p. illus. index. LC 66-22128.
Concise history of art and architecture in Japan from neolithic times to the mid-nineteenth century. Good selection of color plates, modest supplement of black and white plates; liberally provided with plans and diagrams. Provides useful maps, a chronological table, and a bibliography (pp. 226-28) that lists major works in all languages. For the beginning student.

1039   Tsuda, Noritake. **Handbook of Japanese Art.** Tokyo, Sanseido, 1935. 525p. illus. index.
History and handbook of Japanese art and architecture covering the period from prehistoric times to the twentieth century. Text is arranged by periods. Part II provides a useful topographical guide to temples and museums in Japan. Bibliography (pp. 505-508) lists only books in English. An older history, still useful to the advanced student.

1040   Warner, Langdon. **The Enduring Art of Japan.** Cambridge, Mass., Harvard University Press, 1952. 125p. illus. index.
Concise history of Japanese art and architecture from 794 to circa 1750. Consists of chapters on the major periods of Japanese art and architecture. Bibliography (pp. 111-13) provides a list of major books in English. A useful introduction to the broad outlines of Japanese art history. For the beginning student.

1041   Yashiro, Yukio, ed. **Art Treasures of Japan.** Tokyo, Kokusai Bunka Shinkokai, 1969. 2v. illus.
Illustrated handbook of Japanese art, exclusive of architecture, from prehistoric times to the present. Consists of essays on the various periods by Japanese specialists, followed by an excellent corpus of illustrations with descriptive notes. Provides a useful chronological chart of the periods of Oriental art history. A standard handbook of Japanese art for the advanced student.

1042   Yashiro, Yukio. **2000 Years of Japanese Art.** New York, Abrams, 1958. 268p. illus. index.
Illustrated survey of the art of Japan from prehistoric times to the present, exclusive of architecture. The introductory essay, which characterizes the chief epochs of Japanese art, is followed by a collection of excellent plates with informative captions. No bibliography. A good survey for the general reader and the beginning student.

KOREA

1043   Eckardt, Andreas. **A History of Korean Art**. London, Goldston, 1929. 225p. illus. index.
Concise history of art and architecture in Korea from earliest times to the twentieth century. A bibliography is given at the beginning of each section. An older survey history of Korean art and architecture. For the beginning student.

1044   Kim, Chae-won. **Treasures of Korean Art: 2000 Years of Ceramics, Sculpture and Jeweled Arts**. New York, Abrams, 1966. 283p. illus. index. LC 66-23402.
Illustrated history of sculpture and the minor arts in Korea from prehistoric times to the middle of the nineteenth century. Bibliography (pp. 261-63) is an unclassified list of major works; further literature is mentioned in the notes to the text. Excellent illustrations, and good (if brief) text. A good survey of the arts of Korea for the beginning student and the collector.

1045   McCune, Evelyn. **The Arts of Korea: An Illustrated History**. Tokyo and Rutland, Vt., Tuttle, 1961. 452p. illus. index. LC 61-11122.
Concise history of the art and architecture of Korea from prehistoric times through the nineteenth century. Good selection of illustrations, chronological table, and brief but well-selected bibliography (pp. 439-42). A standard history of Korean art and architecture. For beginning and advanced students.

CHAPTER ELEVEN

NEW WORLD ART

I. PRE-COLUMBIAN AMERICA

GENERAL WORKS

1046   Abbate, Francesco, ed. **Precolumbian Art of North America and Mexico.**
        London and New York, Octopus, 1972. 159p. illus.
Pictorial survey of the art and architecture of pre-Columbian North America and
Mexico. Includes Eskimo art. All illustrations are in color. Brief and inadequate
bibliography. For the general reader.

1047   Anton, Ferdinand, and Frederick J. Dockstader. **Pre-Columbian Art and
        Later Indian Tribal Arts.** New York, Abrams, 1968. 264p. illus. index.
        LC 68-11509.
Survey of the art and architecture of pre-Columbian Mexico, Central and South
America, and the later tribal arts of the North American Indian. Good choice of
illustrations. Bibliography (pp. 258-61) lists books in all languages. A good survey
for the general reader and the beginning student.

1048   Bushnell, G. H. S. **Ancient Arts of the Americas.** New York, Praeger,
        1965. 287p. illus. index. LC 65-20077.
Concise history of the arts of pre-Columbian civilizations of North and South
America. Emphasis is on the ancient civilizations of Mexico, Central America,
and northern South America, with only brief mention of North American Indian
art. Good selection of plates, with maps, a chronological table, and a bibliography
(pp. 267-68) of works in English. Good survey for the general reader and the
beginning student.

1049   Disselhoff, Hans-Dietrich, and Sigvald Linné. **The Art of Ancient America:
        Civilizations of Central and South America.** New York, Crown, 1966.
        illus. index. LC 61-16973.

Concise history of pre-Columbian art and architecture covering Mexico, Central America, the Andean lands, greater Peru, Colombia, and San Agustín from prehistory to the Spanish Conquest. Provides useful chronological tables, glossary of terms, good selection of color plates, and modest supplement of black and white plates. Bibliography (pp. 263-66) lists books and periodical articles in all languages. A good survey of pre-Columbian art and architecture for the beginning student.

1050   Emmerich, André. **Art before Columbus.** New York, Simon and Schuster, 1963. 256p. illus. index. LC 63-16027.
Pictorial survey of the art and architecture in Latin America from the second millennium B.C. to the Spanish Conquest. The brief text is accompanied by a good selection of color and black and white plates. Provides a useful glossary of terms and a good bibliography (pp. 245-47) of books in all languages. A good survey for the general reader and the beginning student.

1051   Kelemen, Pál. **Art of the Americas, Ancient and Hispanic, with a Comparative Chapter on the Philippines.** New York, Crowell, 1969. 402p. illus. index. LC 72-87163.
Concise history of art and architecture in Central and South America from prehistoric times through the Colonial period. Contains a chapter on art and architecture in the Colonial Philippines. Provides maps, a good selection of plates, and a bibliography (pp. 359-61) that lists books and periodical articles in English. A good survey history for the general reader and the beginning student.

1052   Kelemen, Pál. **Medieval American Art.** New York, Macmillan, 1943; repr. New York, Dover, 1969. 2v. illus. index.
Comprehensive history of the art and architecture of Mexico, Central America, and the Andean region of South America from circa 100 A.D. to the Spanish Conquest. Good selection of plates, plus maps, plans, diagrams, and a chronological table. Bibliography (pp. 385-405) is an unclassified list of books and periodical articles. A dated but classic treatment of pre-Columbian art and architecture. For beginning and advanced students.

1053   Kubler, George. **Art and Architecture of Ancient America.** London, Penguin, 1961. 396p. illus. index. (Pelican History of Art, Z21).
Comprehensive history of art and architecture in pre-Columbian South and Central America. Covers the civilizations of the Mexican, Mayan, and Andean regions from 1500 B.C. to the Spanish Conquest. Provides good selection of plates, maps, plans, diagrams, and an excellent bibliography (pp. 365-78) that lists the major books and periodical articles in all languages. A standard, scholarly history of ancient American art and architecture for the advanced student and the scholar.

1054   Lothrop, S. K. **Treasures of Ancient America: The Arts of the Pre-Columbian Civilizations from Mexico to Peru.** Geneva, Skira, 1964. 230p. illus. index.
Pictorial survey of the art (exclusive of the architecture) of the ancient civilizations of Mexico, Central America, and the Andean region of South American from

pre-Classical times to the Spanish Conquest. The brief text is accompanied by excellent color plates and commentaries. No bibliography. For the general reader.

MESOAMERICA AND MEXICO

1055   Anton, Ferdinand. **Ancient Mexican Art**. New York, Putnam, 1969. 309p. illus. index. LC 77-75212.
Illustrated history of art and architecture in Mexico from circa 1500 B.C. to the Spanish Conquest. Brief introductory essay is followed by a good selection of plates and commentaries. Provides a useful chronological table, a map, and a bibliography (pp. 299-301) that lists books and periodical articles in all languages. Good survey history for the general reader and beginning student. Plates form a valuable handbook for the advanced student.

1056   Covarrubias, Miguel. **Indian Art of Mexico and Central America**. New York, Knopf, 1957. 360p. illus. index.
History of the art and architecture of the pre-Columbian civilizations of Mexico and Central America, from the Olmec empire through the Aztec empire. Bibliography (pp. 335-60) lists books and periodical articles. Somewhat out of date, but still useful for the advanced student.

1057   Dockstader, Frederick J. **Indian Art in Middle America**. Greenwich, Conn., New York Graphic Society, 1964. 221p. illus. LC 64-21815.
Illustrated handbook of the arts of Central America from earliest times to the present. Covers the ancient cultures of the Aztecs and Mayas as well as the arts of present-day Indians in Central America. Brief introduction sketches the history of art, followed by more detailed comments on the excellent plates. There are maps, a chronological table, and a bibliography (pp. 217-21). Text is directed to the general reader and the beginning student. Plates, especially when combined with the other works by Dockstader (1064, 1068), form a valuable illustrated handbook of Indian art for the advanced student.

1058   Feuchtwanger, Franz. **Art of Ancient Mexico**. London and New York, Thames and Hudson, 1954. 125p. illus. index.
Pictorial survey of the art and architecture of ancient Mexico from 1521 B.C. to 1500 A.D. Brief text with good plates, a map, and a chronological table. No bibliography. A good survey of ancient Mexican art for the general reader.

1059   Medioni, Gilbert. **Art Maya du Mexique et du Guatémala**. Paris, Éditions de la Cyme, 1950. 113p. illus.
Scholarly history of art and architecture of the ancient Mayas. Excellent maps, detailed chronological tables, and a bibliography (pp. 109-112). For the advanced student.

1060   Spinden, Herbert J. **Maya Art and Civilization**. Indian Hills, Colo.,
        Falcon's Wing Press, 1957. 432p. illus. index. LC 56-5124.
This comprehensive study of art and architecture of the ancient Mayas sets the
history of the fine arts within the general cultural context. Bibliography (pp. 399-
412) is an unclassified list of books and periodical articles. Originally published in
1913, it is a classic study of Mayan art and architecture. For the advanced student.

1061   Toscano, Salvador. **Arte Pre-Columbino de México y de la América Central**.
        2nd ed. Mexico City, Inst. de Invest. Estéticas, 1952. 2v. illus. index.
Comprehensive history of art and architecture of pre-Columbian Mexico and
Central America from circa 1500 B.C. to the Spanish Conquest. Good bibliographies
are given at the end of the chapters. An older but standard history of ancient Maya
and Aztec art and architecture. For the advanced student.

1062   Winning, Hasso von. **Pre-Columbian Art of Mexico and Central America**.
        New York, Abrams, 1968. 388p. illus. LC 65-13065.
Illustrated history of art and architecture in Mexico and Central America from
circa 1500 B.C. to the Spanish Conquest. Brief text sketching the history of art
and architecture is accompanied by excellent plates, commentaries on the plates,
chronological tables, maps, and a bibliography (pp. 386-88), which lists books and
periodical articles in all languages. A well-illustrated and concise survey for the
general reader and the beginning student.

SOUTH AMERICA

1063   Anton, Ferdinand. **Alt Peru und seine Kunst**. Leipzig, Seemann, 1962.
        127p. illus.
Pictorial survey of the art and architecture of ancient Peru from 3000 B.C. to
1500 A.D. Excellent plates, maps, brief unclassified bibliography (pp. 99-100) of
books and periodical articles in all languages. Further literature is mentioned in
the footnotes. For beginning and advanced students.

1064   Dockstader, Frederick J. **Indian Art in South America: Pre-Columbian
        and Contemporary Arts and Crafts**. Greenwich, Conn., New York
        Graphic Society, 1967. 222p. illus.
Illustrated handbook of the arts and crafts of the Indian societies of South America
from earliest times to the present. Includes ancient Inca civilizations. Brief introduction, commentaries on the excellent plates, maps, chronological table, and
bibliography (pp. 219-22). Text is directed to the general reader and the beginning
student. Especially when combined with the other works by Dockstader (1057,
1068) the plates form a valuable illustrated handbook of Indian art for the
advanced student.

1065   Lehmann, Walter, and Heinrich Ubbelohde-Doering. **The Art of Old Peru**.
        2nd ed. London, Benn, 1957. 68p. (text); 128p. (illus.).

Illustrated survey of pre-Columbian art and architecture with a brief introduction and notes to the good plates. Bibliography (pp. 66-68) lists major works in all languages. First published in 1924. Once a standard work, it is now out of date in several respects; nevertheless, it is still a valuable collection of plates.

1066   Ubbelohde-Doering, Heinrich. **The Art of Ancient Peru**. New York, Praeger, 1952. 240p. illus. LC 52-7489.
Illustrated survey of the arts of ancient Peru. A brief introductory essay sketching the history of ancient Peruvian art is followed by a good selection of plates and a bibliography (pp. 53-55) that lists books and articles in all languages. Still useful for its plates. For the beginning student and the general reader.

II. NORTH AMERICAN INDIAN

1067   Covarrubias, Miguel. **The Eagle, the Jaguar, and the Serpent: Indian Art of the Americas**. New York, Knopf, 1954. 314p. illus. index. LC 52-6415.
History-study of the arts of the North American Indians covering Alaska, Canada, and the United States. Chapters sketch the history of North American Indian art, discuss its techniques and aesthetics, and describe the various Indian societies. Bibliography (pp. 298-314) is an unclassified list of books and periodical articles in English. An older, classic study of Indian art, still useful to the advanced student.

1068   Dockstader, Frederick J. **Indian Art in America**. 3rd ed. Greenwich, Conn., New York Graphic Society, 1966. 224p. illus.
Survey of the arts of the North American Indian. Well illustrated, it also has a good bibliography (pp. 222-24), which lists books in all languages. A good pictorial survey for the general reader and the beginning student.

1069   Feder, Norman. **American Indian Art**. New York, Abrams, 1971. 446p. illus. LC 69-12484.
Illustrated survey of the arts of the North American Indian. Part I deals with the origins, materials, and techniques of the Indian artists; Part II discusses the arts by culture areas. Covers Indians of the plains, the Southwest, California, the Northwest, the Eastern woodlands, and the Arctic coasts. Excellent plates and a good bibliography (pp. 439-46) that lists major books. A standard illustrated handbook for the general reader and the beginning student.

1070   Feder, Norman. **Two Hundred Years of North American Indian Art**. New York, Praeger, 1971. 128p. illus. LC 70-176395.
Pictorial survey of the arts of the North American Indian based on an exhibition held at the Whitney Museum of American Art. Brief introduction discusses the Indian artists, the function of Indian art, and techniques and materials. Well

illustrated. Provides a good but unclassified bibliography (pp. 121-24). For the general reader and the beginning student.

1071   Haberland, Wolfgang. **The Art of North America**. New York, Crown, 1964. 251p. illus. index. LC 68-15660.

Survey of the arts of the Indians of the United States, Canada, Alaska, and Greenland. Initial chapters treat the Paleo-Indian art of North America; the rest of the work is devoted to an examination of the arts of the American Indian by region. Provides a useful group of five chronological tables, maps, and a good classified bibliography (pp. 212-20), which lists books and periodical articles in all languages. A good survey of North American Indian art for the general reader and the beginning student.

1072   Vaillant, George C. **Indian Arts in North America** . . . New York and London, Harper, 1939. 63p. illus.

Survey of North American Indian art. Selected bibliography (pp. 55-63) is arranged by chapters and lists major books and periodical articles. An old but solid introduction to American Indian art. For the general reader and the beginning student.

III. NATIONAL HISTORIES AND HANDBOOKS

LATIN AMERICA

General Works

1073   Angulo Iñiguez, Diego, Enrique M. Dorta, and Mario J. Buschiazzo. **Historia del arte Hispano-Americano**. Barcelona, Salvat, 1945-56. 3v. illus. index.

Comprehensive history of art and architecture in Latin America from the time of the Spanish conquests to the present. Bibliographies are at the end of each volume. Well illustrated. Standard history of Latin American art and architecture. For the advanced student.

1074   Castedo, Leopoldo. **A History of Latin American Art and Architecture from Pre-Columbian Times to the Present**. New York, Praeger, 1969. 320p. illus. index. LC 69-13421.

Survey history of art and architecture in Latin America from the ancient Toltecs to the present. Fine selection of plates and maps, and a good selected bibliography (pp. 297-99). A good survey of Latin American art and architecture for the general reader and the beginning student.

1075   Kelemen, Pál. **Baroque and Rococo in Latin America**. New York, Macmillan, 1951. 302p. illus. index.
History of art and architecture in Latin America during the Colonial period (seventeenth and eighteenth centuries). Good selection of plates, although they are poorly reproduced; the excellent bibliography (pp. 286-94) lists books and periodical articles in all languages. A somewhat out-of-date but classic history of Colonial Latin American art and architecture.

1076   Solá, Miguel. **Historia del arte hispano-americano**. Barcelona, Labor, 1935. 341p. (text); 51p. (illus.). index.
Concise history of art and architecture in Colonial Latin America (sixteenth through eighteenth centuries). Good selection of poorly reproduced plates. Bibliography (pp. 331-34) lists chiefly Spanish books. This old, general history of Colonial Latin American art and architecture is still a useful source of information. For the beginning student.

Argentina

1077   Pagano, José León. **Historia del arte Argentino**. Buenos Aires, L'Amateur, 1944. 507p. illus. index.
Concise history of art and architecture in Argentina from the pre-Hispanic aborigines to the present. Bibliography is found in the footnotes. A good general history of art and architecture in Argentina. For the general reader and the beginning student.

Colombia

1078   Barney, Cabrera Eugenio. **Temas para la historia del arte en Colombia**. Bogotá, Universidad Nacional de Colombia, 1970. 210p. illus. LC 72-317694.
Concise history of art and architecture in Colombia from 1500 to the present. Poor illustrations. Bibliography (pp. 142-43). For the general reader.

Cuba

1079   Castro, Martha de. **El arte en Cuba**. Miami, Ediciones Universal, 1970. 151p. illus. index. LC 72-19190.
Survey of art and architecture in Cuba from early Colonial times to the present. Bibliographies are at the end of chapters. For the general reader and the beginning student.

Ecuador

1080   Vargas, José Maria. **El arte ecuatoriano.** Puebla and Mexico City, Cajica, 1959. 581p. illus. index.
History of art and architecture in Ecuador from the sixteenth century through the nineteenth century. No bibliography. A standard history of Ecuadorian art and architecture. For the general reader and the beginning student.

Guatemala

1081   Chinchilla, Aguilar E. **Historia del arte en Guatemala 1524-1962: arquitectura, pintura y escultura.** 2nd ed. Guatemala City, Ministerio de Educacion Publica, 1965. 261p. illus. index.
Concise history of art and architecture in Guatemala from 1524 to 1962. Provides an unclassified bibliography (pp. 183-87). For the general reader and the beginning student.

Mexico

1082   Fernandez, Justino. **A Guide to Mexican Art, from its Beginning to the Present.** Chicago, University of Chicago Press, 1969. 398p. illus. index. LC 69-16773.
Concise history of Mexican art and architecture from the time of the ancient Toltecs to the present. There are good bibliographies at the ends of the chapters. A good survey for the general reader and the beginning student.

1083   Rojas, Pedro. **The Art and Architecture of Mexico.** London, Hamlyn, 1968. 71p. (text); 146p. (illus.).
Pictorial survey of the art and architecture of Mexico from 10,000 B.C. to the present. Provides a chronological table, a map, and notes to the plates. No bibliography. For the general reader.

1084   Rojas, Pedro, ed. **Historia general del arte mexicano.** Mexico, Editorial Hermes, 1962-64. 3v. illus. index. LC 64-54702.
Comprehensive history of art and architecture in Mexico from pre-Columbian times to the present. Vol. I: *Época Prehispánica*, by R. Guerrero; Vol. 2: *Época Colonial,* by P. Rojas; Vol. 3: *Época Moderna Y Contemporánea*, by R. Tibol. There are extensive bibliographies at the end of each volume. Well illustrated. The standard history of Mexican art and architecture for beginning and advanced students.

1085   Smith, Bradley. **Mexico: A History in Art.** New York, Harper & Row, 1968. 296p. illus. index.
Pictorial history of the art of Mexico, exclusive of architecture, from prehistoric times (1700 B.C.) to 1940. Well illustrated. Provides a bibliography (pp. 294-95) that lists major books. For the general reader.

Venezuela

1086   Calzadilla, Juan, ed. **El arte en Venezuela**. Caracas, Circulo Musical, 1967.
        239p. illus. LC 67-98176.
Concise history of art and architecture in Venezuela from pre-Spanish aboriginal
art to the present. Provides an appendix with biographies of artists and architects
(pp. 196-239). No bibliography. The standard history of art and architecture for
Venezuela. For the general reader and the beginning student.

UNITED STATES

1087   Abbate, Francesco, ed. **American Art**. London and New York, Octopus,
        1972. 158p. illus.
Pictorial survey of the art and architecture of the United States from the early
nineteenth century to the present. All illustrations are in color. Inadequate one-
page bibliography. For the general reader.

1088   Cahill, Holger, and Alfred Barr, eds. **Art in America: A Complete
        Survey** . . . New York, Halcyon, 1939. 162p. illus.
Brief survey of art and architecture in America from Colonial times to the early
twentieth century. Consists of essays written by various specialists. Bibliography
(pp. 153-62) lists major books and periodical articles. Still a useful survey for the
general reader.

1089   Chase, Judith W. **Afro-American Art and Craft**. New York, Cincinnati,
        and Toronto, Van Nostrand, 1972. 271p. illus. index.
Survey of Afro-American painting, sculpture, and minor arts. Introductory chapter
discusses the African background and early history of Afro-American art. Bibliography (pp. 138-39) provides a classified list of major books. For the general reader
and the beginning student.

1090   Goodrich, Lloyd. **Three Centuries of American Art**. New York, Praeger,
        1967. 145p. illus. index.
Pictorial survey of art and architecture in America from Colonial times to the
present. Brief introductory text accompanies a good selection of plates. No bibliography. For the general reader.

1091   Green, Samuel M. **American Art: A Historical Survey**. New York, Ronald
        Press, 1966. 706p. illus. index. LC 66-16844.
Comprehensive history of art and architecture in America from Colonial times to
circa 1960. Fairly well illustrated; has a good glossary of terms, informative notes
to the text, and a good classified bibliography (pp. 663-68). Balanced, unbiased
text. An excellent survey history of American art and architecture.

1092   LaFollette, Suzanne. **Art in America**. New York, Harper & Row, 1968.
        361p. illus. index. LC 72-2187.
Reprint of 1929 edition. Survey history of art and architecture in America from
Colonial times to the early twentieth century. No bibliography. For the general
reader.

1093   Larkin, Oliver W. **Art and Life in America**. Rev. and enl. ed. New York,
        Holt, Rinehart and Winston, 1960. 559p. illus. index. LC 60-6491.
General history of art and architecture in America from circa 1600 to the present.
Emphasis is on the cultural context of the fine arts. Thorough and useful bibliog-
raphical notes (pp. 491-525). For the general reader and the beginning student.

1094   McLanathan, Richard. **The American Tradition in the Arts**. New York,
        Harcourt, Brace, & World, 1968. 492p. illus. index. LC 65-21032.
History of art and architecture in America from Colonial times to the mid-
twentieth century. Well illustrated. A classified list of major books is provided in
the bibliography (pp. 471-78). For the general reader and the beginning student.

1095.   McLanathan, Richard. **Art in America: A Brief History**. New York,
        Harcourt Brace Jovanovich, 1973. 216p. illus. index. LC 72-92358.
Concise history of art and architecture in America from Colonial times to the
present. Good selection of plates. Good, partially annotated bibliography of
books and periodical articles (pp. 211-12). A good survey for the general reader.

1096   Mendelowitz, Daniel M. **A History of American Art**. 2nd ed. New York,
        Holt, Rinehart and Winston, 1970. 521p. illus. index. LC 71-111303.
History of art and architecture in America beginning with American Indian art and
concluding with American art of the present. Well illustrated. Bibliography (pp. 510-
12) lists basic books. A standard history of American art and architecture for the
general reader and the beginning student.

1097   Myron, Robert, and Abner Sundell. **Art in America: From Colonial Days
        through the Nineteenth Century**. New York, Crowell-Collier, 1969. 186p.
        illus. index. LC 69-10347.
Survey history of art and architecture in America from Colonial times to the end
of the nineteenth century. Brief bibliography (p. 183). For the general reader and
the beginning student.

1098   Pierson, William H., Jr., and Martha Davidson, eds. **Arts of the United
        States: A Pictorial Survey**. New York, McGraw-Hill, 1960. 452p. illus.
        LC 60-9855.
Brief survey of art and architecture in America from Colonial times to the present.
The 18 brief essays on various arts at different periods are by a number of specialists. Conceived as an accompaniment to a slide collection at the University of
Georgia, the illustrations are postage-stamp-size reproductions of the slides. No
bibliography. With the slides, this is a valuable teaching tool directed to the general
reader and the beginning student.

1099   Richardson, Edgar P. **The Way of Western Art, 1776-1914.** Cambridge,
        Mass., Harvard University Press, 1939; repr. New York, Cooper Square,
        1969. 204p. illus. index. LC 73-79604.
Survey history of art and architecture in America and Western Europe in the
period 1776 to 1914, with emphasis on the interrelationships between European
and American art and architecture. No bibliography. Still a valuable study for
beginning and advanced students.

CANADA

1100   Colgate, William G. **Canadian Art, Its Origin and Development.** Toronto,
        Ryerson, 1943. 278p. illus. index.
Concise survey of the history of art in Canada, exclusive of architecture, from 1820
to 1940. Bibliography (pp. 267-70) provides a useful list of primary sources as
well as major books and articles. A good survey history of Canadian national art.
For the general reader and beginning student. The bibliography will be of use to
the advanced student.

1101   Hubbard, Robert H. **An Anthology of Canadian Art.** Toronto, Oxford
        University Press, 1960. 187p. illus. LC 60-52060 rev.
Concise history of art and architecture in Canada from the founding of New France
to the present. Well illustrated. Brief introduction traces the history of art and
architecture in Canada, followed by more detailed notes to the plates, a section of
artists' biographies, and useful bibliographical notes (pp. 167-69) which evaluate
the state of art historical scholarship in Canadian art. A good survey history of
Canadian art and architecture for the general reader and beginning student.

1102   Hubbard, R. H. **The Development of Canadian Art.** Ottawa, National
        Gallery of Canada, 1967. 137p. illus. index.
Survey history of Canadian art and architecture from the foundation of New France
to the present. Compiled from a series of lectures delivered at the National Gallery
in Ottawa. Well illustrated. No bibliography. A good survey of Canadian art and
architecture by a leading specialist. For the general reader and the beginning student.

1103.   McInnes, Graham C. **Canadian Art.** Toronto, Macmillan, 1950. 140p.
        illus. index. LC 52-6306 rev.
Survey of the history of art in Canada, exclusive of architecture, beginning with
Indian art and ending in 1933. Appendices give lists of principal events in Canadian
history, art institutes and museums, and Canadian artists. No bibliography. A
balanced if cursory history of Canadian art for the general reader.

CHAPTER TWELVE

ART OF AFRICA AND OCEANIA
(WITH AUSTRALIA)

I. GENERAL WORKS

1104   Abbate, Francesco, ed. **African Art and Oceanic Art.** London and New
York, Octopus, 1972. 158p. illus. LC 72-172111.
Very brief pictorial survey of both sub-Saharan African and Oceanian art, most of
which is sculpture. All color illustrations. Weak one-page bibliography. For the
general reader.

1105   Trowell, Kathleen M., and Hans Nevermann. **African and Oceanic Art.**
New York, Abrams, 1968. 263p. illus. index. LC 68-16798.
Pictorial survey of the arts of sub-Saharan Africa and primitive Oceania, in the
latter case consisting of New Guinea, Melanesia, Micronesia, and Polynesia. The
section on Africa is treated according to modes or types of art, with a chapter on
the sculpture of some ancient African kingdoms. The art of Oceania is treated by
region. Provided with maps and good photographs showing African artists at work.
Bibliography (pp. 259-60) lists books and some periodical articles in all languages.
For the general reader and the beginning student.

II. AFRICA

1106   Bascom, William. **African Art in Cultural Perspective: An Introduction.**
New York, Norton, 1973. 196p. illus. index. LC 73-4680.
Survey of the traditional art of Africa with emphasis on the general anthropologi-
cal context. There is a brief chapter on Egypt and North Africa, though the bulk
of the work is devoted to sub-Saharan Africa. Useful maps, rather poorly reproduced; well-chosen illustrations. Bibliography (pp. 189-91) lists books in all
languages. A good introduction for the beginning student.

1107   Bodrogi, Tibor. **Art in Africa.** New York, McGraw-Hill, 1968. 131p. illus.
        LC 68-12065.
Introduction to the traditional arts of sub-Saharan Africa. The brief text is followed
by a selection of plates and a bibliography (pp. 97-101). For the general reader.

1108   Berman, Esmé. **Art and Artists of South Africa: An Illustrated Biographi-
        cal Dictionary and Historical Survey of Painters and Graphic Artists since
        1875.** Cape Town, A. A. Balkema, 1970. 368p. illus. index. LC 75-54902.
Two-part handbook of painters and graphic artists in South Africa since 1875.
The entries in the first part, the biographical dictionary, give basic biographical
information, list of major exhibitions, collections that own the artist's work, and
(for the major artists) reference to further literature. The second part is an historical
survey of painting and graphic art in South Africa since circa 1850. Basic reference
tool to art of South Africa.

1109   Laude, Jean. **The Arts of Black Africa.** Berkeley, University of California
        Press, 1971. 289p. illus. index. LC 71-125165.
Concise history of the arts of sub-Saharan Africa treating both historical and contemporary traditional arts. Provides a useful comparative chronological table of
artistic and cultural events in Africa and Western Europe. Bibliography (pp. 279-
84) lists books in all languages. For the beginning student.

1110   Leiris, Michel, and Jacqueline Delange. **African Art.** London, Thames and
        Hudson, 1968. 460p. illus. index. (The Arts of Mankind, 11). LC 73-
        353276.
Comprehensive handbook of the traditional arts of sub-Saharan Africa. Well illustrated with plates, plans, and diagrams. Provided with maps, glossary, and bibliography (pp. 385-408), which lists books and periodical articles in all languages.
Although the bibliography is unclassified, it is extensive and the most important
works are marked with an asterisk. For beginning and advanced students.

1111   Leuzinger, Elsy. **The Art of Black Africa.** Greenwich, Conn., New York
        Graphic Society, 1972. 378p. illus. index. LC 72-172085.
Pictorial handbook of the arts of sub-Saharan Africa. Introduction discusses the
geography, function, materials, and techniques of art in Africa. This is followed by
an excellent collection of plates arranged according to stylistic regions; there is a
map and a succinct summary introduction for each region. The select bibliography
(pp. 363-69) is an excellent classified list of books and periodical articles in all
languages. A good introduction for the general reader and the beginning student.
The excellent plates make it of value to the advanced student as well.

1112   Leuzinger, Elsy. **Africa: The Art of the Negro Peoples.** 2nd ed. New York,
        Crown, 1967. 247p. illus. index. LC 60-13819.
Concise study of the traditional arts of sub-Saharan Africa. Part one gives a general
introduction; part two discusses the regional styles of African art. Includes useful
maps, a table of cultures, a glossary of terms, and a good selected bibliography

(pp. 228-32) of books and periodical articles. A good survey for the general reader and the beginning student.

1113   Rachewiltz, Boris de. **Introduction to African Art**. New York, New American Library, 1966. 200p. illus. index. LC 66-18260.
Concise survey and history of sub-Saharan African art from prehistoric times to the present. Provides a good, classified bibliography (pp. 161-92). For the general reader and the beginning student.

1114   Wassing, René S. **African Art, Its Background and Traditions**. New York, Abrams, 1968. 285p. illus. index. LC 68-28387.
The traditional arts of sub-Saharan Africa are covered, with emphasis on their relationship to social life, economics, religion, and technology. Introductory chapter: "The African and His Environment." Well illustrated. Bibliography (pp. 274-75) is a brief alphabetical listing of major books. For the general reader and the beginning student.

1115   Willett, Frank. **African Art: An Introduction**. New York, Praeger, 1971. 288p. illus. index. LC 76-117394.
Concise history of the art and architecture of sub-Saharan Africa from the earliest times to the present. Provides a good selection of plates, many useful maps, diagrams, and a few plans. Bibliography (pp. 275-79) is an unclassified list of major books and periodical articles in all languages. The footnotes provide further reference to specialized literature. A good general survey for the beginning student and the general reader.

III. OCEANIA

1116   Ambesi, Alberto C. **Oceanic Art**. Feltham, England, Hamlyn, 1970. 159p. illus. index. LC 78-563041.
Pictorial survey of the arts of Melanesia, Micronesia, Polynesia, New Zealand, and Hawaii. No bibliography. For the general reader.

1117   Bodrogi, Tibor. **Oceanian Art**. Budapest, Corvina, 1959. 43p. (text); 170p. (illus.).
Pictorial survey of the arts of Melanesia, Micronesia, Polynesia, and Indonesia. Illustrations of works in the Ethnographical Museum in Budapest. Provides a list of principal collectors and collections of Oceanic art, and a brief bibliography (pp. 39-40) of major works in all languages. For the general reader.

1118   Bühler, Alfred, Terry Barrow, and Charles P. Mountford. **The Art of the South Sea Islands, including Australia and New Zealand**. New York, Crown, 1962. 249p. illus. index. LC 62-11806.

Survey of the arts of Melanesia, Micronesia, Polynesia, as well as the aboriginal arts of Australia and the Maori art of New Zealand. Introductory chapters discuss the geographical setting and the religious, social, and technological factors. These chapters are followed by excellent characterizations of the major regional styles. Bibliography (pp. 235-40) provides a thorough list of major books and periodical articles in all languages. A good survey for beginning and advanced students.

1119   Guiart, Jean. **The Arts of the South Pacific.** New York, Golden Press, 1963. 461p. illus. index. (The Arts of Mankind, 4). LC 63-7331.
Well illustrated study of the native arts of Australia, Torres Straits, New Guinea, Melanesia, Micronesia, Polynesia, and Hawaii. Provided are a glossary-index, maps, and a bibliography (pp. 419-38), which is an alphabetical list of major books and periodical articles in all languages. A good illustrated handbook for beginning and advanced students.

1120   Schmitz, Carl A. **Oceanic Art: Myth, Man and Image in the South Seas.** New York, Abrams, 1971. 405p. illus. index. LC 69-12797.
Comprehensive study of the native arts of New Guinea, Melanesia, Polynesia, and Micronesia. The general introduction sketches the history of art in Oceania from prehistoric time to the present. Sumptuously illustrated. Bibliography (pp. 402-405) lists books and periodical articles. For the general reader and the beginning student.

1121   Smith, Bernard W. **Place, Taste, and Tradition: A Study of Australian Art since 1788.** Sydney, Smith, 1945. 287p. illus. index. LC 46-1408 rev.
Concise history of art and architecture in Australia in the nineteenth and twentieth centuries. Emphasis is on the general cultural climate. Bibliography (pp. 272-75) lists books and periodical articles. For the general reader and the beginning student.

1122   Tischner, Herbert. **Oceanic Art.** New York, Pantheon, 1954. 32p. (text); 96p. (illus.).
Pictorial survey of the arts of Melanesia, Micronesia, Polynesia, and New Zealand. Brief text, with notes to the plates. Bibliography (pp. 17-20) lists books and periodical articles. For the general reader and the beginning student.

1123   Wingert, Paul S. **Art of the South Pacific Islands.** New York, Beechhurst, 1953. 64p. illus.
Brief survey of the arts of Melanesia, Micronesia, Polynesia, New Zealand, and Hawaii. Short bibliography (p. 46) of major books. For the beginning student.

1124   Wingert, Paul S. **An Outline of the Art of the South Pacific.** New York, Columbia University Press, 1946. 61p. illus.
Brief guide to the art of Melanesia, Micronesia, Polynesia, Australia, and New Zealand. Text is in outline form. Appendix gives lists of American museums that have collections of Oceanic art. Good classified bibliography of books and articles (pp. 45-57). An older but useful introduction for the beginning student.

IV. AUSTRALIA

1125   Berndt, Ronald M., ed. **Australian Aboriginal Art.** New York, Macmillan, 1964. 117p. illus. index. LC 64-12214.
This survey of the art of the Australian aborigines deals with pre-Colonial rock paintings as well as with the more recent traditional aboriginal arts. Consists of a collection of essays by specialists. Well-chosen illustrations and a good bibliography (pp. 108-112), which lists books and periodical articles in all languages. A good introduction for the general reader and the beginning student.

1126   Hughes, Robert. **The Art of Australia.** Rev. ed. Harmondsworth, Penguin, 1970. 331p. illus. index. LC 72-18946.
History of art and architecture in Australia from prehistoric times to the present. Well illustrated. Bibliography (pp. 317-20) is a good list of books and periodical articles. A standard history of Australian art and architecture for the general reader and the beginning student.

1127   Moore, William. **The Story of Australian Art, from the Earliest Known Art of the Continent to the Art of Today.** Sydney, Angus & Robertson, 1934. 2v. illus. index.
Survey of art and architecture in Australia from prehistoric times to the early twentieth century. Provides a dictionary of Australian artists (pp. 155-234). For the general reader and the beginning student.

APPENDIX

SELECTED LIST OF FINE ARTS BOOKS
FOR SMALL LIBRARIES

Julia M. Ehresmann

The titles selected here have been chosen for libraries serving readerships with general and, for the most part, non-scholarly interests. These include small to moderate-sized public libraries, well-developed high school libraries, and the libraries of community colleges whose offerings in the fine arts are restricted to art appreciation or basic survey courses.

In areas for which good books exist on two levels—both the quite general and the serious but sub-scholarly—at least one example of each type is included. After the question of suitability according to level, other criteria for inclusion are quality of scholarship, effectiveness of presentation, and, where appropriate, sufficiency of illustration. Availability has been a significant but not decisive consideration. It is assumed that the annotations in the body of the text will be consulted in selecting titles for acquisition.

If this list falls short of representing a balanced "Opening Day" collection, it is because the broad subject of the fine arts itself is not yet evenly covered by books for the non-specialist.

PART I—REFERENCE WORKS

BIBLIOGRAPHIES

Item Number	Author and Title
2	Chamberlin. *Guide to Art Reference Books.*
7	Lucas. *Art Books.*
62	*Art Bibliographies Modern.*
102	Rowland. *The Harvard Outline and Reading List.*
132	Garrett and Garrett. *The Arts in Early American History.*
135	Roos. *Bibliography of Early American Architecture.*

INDEXES

DIRECTORIES

DICTIONARIES AND ENCYCLOPEDIAS

PART II—HISTORIES AND HANDBOOKS OF WORLD ART HISTORY

PREHISTORIC AND PRIMITIVE ART

Prehistoric

Primitive

PERIODS OF WESTERN ART HISTORY

Ancient

Egyptian

Ancient Near Eastern

Mesopotamia

Item Number	Author and Title
421	Moortgart. *Art of Ancient Mesopotamia.*

Iran

427	Porada. *Art of Ancient Iran.*

Scythia

433	Jettmarr. *Art of the Steppes.*
434	Rice. *Scythians.*

Aegean

437	Boardman. *Pre-Classical.*
438	Demargne. *Birth of Greek Art.*
441	Marinatos. *Crete and Mycenae.*
442	Matz. *Art of Crete and Early Greece.*

Classical Greek and Roman

443	Becatti. *Art of Ancient Greece and Rome.*
447	Ruskin. *Greek and Roman Art.*

Greek

454	Boardman, *et al. Art and Architecture of Ancient Greece.*
455	Brilliant. *Arts of the Ancient Greeks.*
466	Richter. *Handbook of Greek Art.*
470	Schuchhardt. *Greek Art.*

Etruscan

475	Mansuelli. *Art of Etruria and Early Rome.*
479	Richardson. *Etruscans.*

Roman

Medieval and Byzantine

Early Christian

Byzantine

Early Medieval

Romanesque

Baroque and Rococo

19th and 20th Centuries

19th Century

20th Century

20th Century (cont'd)

Item Number	Author and Title
759	Selz. *Art Nouveau.*
762	Muller. *Fauvism.*
769	Rosenblum. *Cubism and Twentieth Century Art.*
770	Schwartz. *Cubism.*
772	Dube. *Expressionism.*
778	Rickey. *Constructivism.*
779	Vallier. *Abstract Art.*
783	Taylor. *Futurism.*
788	Gaunt. *Surrealists.*
790	Richter. *Dada.*
795	Hunter, *et al. New Art Around the World.*
796	Lucie-Smith. *Late Modern.*

EUROPEAN NATIONAL HISTORIES AND HANDBOOKS

799	Olivier-Michel, *et al. Guide to the Art Treasures of France.*
803	Laclotte. *French Art from 1350 to 1850.*
812	Grimschitz. *Ars Austriae.*
851	Lindemann. *History of German Art.*
853	Vey and de Salas. *German and Spanish Art to 1900.*
863	Arnold. *Concise History of Irish Art.*
867	Garlick. *British and North American Art to 1900.*
877	Chastel. *Italian Art.*
880	Monteverdi. *Italian Art to 1850.*
883	Hammacher and Vandenbrande. *Flemish and Dutch Art.*
897	Rooses. *Art in Flanders.*
901	*Guide to Dutch Art.*
903	Timmers. *History of Dutch Life and Art.*
906	Nørlund. *Danish Art through the Ages.*
914	Grate. *Treasures of Swedish Art.*
930	Gudiol. *Arts of Spain.*
937	Smith. *Spain: A History in Art.*
940	Smith. *Art of Portugal.*
941	Rhodes. *Art Treasures of Eastern Europe.*
946	Kampis. *History of Art in Hungary.*
950	Alpatov. *Art Treasures of Russia.*
956	Hare. *Art and Artists of Russia.*
959	Rice. *Concise History of Russian Art.*

ORIENTAL ART

Item Number	Author and Title
961	La Plante. *Asian Art.*
962	Lee. *History of Far Eastern Art.*
965	Grube. *World of Islam.*
967	Kühnel. *Islamic Art and Architecture.*
971	Ry van Beest Holle. *Art of Islam.*
975	Godard. *Art of Iran.*
979	Aslanapa. *Turkish Art and Architecture.*
982	Bussagli and Sivaramamurti. *5,000 Years of the Art of India.*
985	Goetz. *Art of India.*
988	Kramrisch. *Art of India.*
996	Rice. *Ancient Arts of Central Asia.*
998	Waldschmidt and Waldschmidt. *Nepal.*
999	Griswold and Pott. *Art of Burma, Korea, Tibet.*
1000	Groslier. *Art of Indochina.*
1001	Rawson. *Art of Southeast Asia.*
1005	Holt. *Art in Indonesia.*
1006	Wagner. *Indonesia.*
1007	Le May. *Concise History of Buddhist Art in Siam.*
1010	Munsterberg. *Art of the Far East.*
1011	Shoten. *Pictorial Encyclopedia of the Oriental Arts.*
1019	Medley. *Handbook of Chinese Art.*
1020	Munsterberg. *Arts of China.*
1025	Speiser. *Art of China.*
1026	Sullivan. *Arts of China.*
1028	Swann. *Art of China, Korea and Japan.*
1030	Willetts. *Foundations of Chinese Art.*
1032	Boger. *Traditional Arts of Japan.*
1035	Noma. *Arts of Japan.*
1042	Yashiro. *2000 Years of Japanese Art.*
1044	Kim. *Treasures of Korean Art.*
1045	McCune. *Arts of Korea.*

NEW WORLD ART

1047	Anton and Dockstader. *Pre-Columbian Art and Later Indian Tribal Arts.*
1049	Disselhoff and Linné. *Art of Ancient America.*
1051	Kelemen. *Art of the Americas.*
1055	Anton. *Ancient Mexican Art.*
1062	Winning. *Pre-Columbian Art of Mexico and Central America.*
1064	Dockstader. *Indian Art in South America.*
1068	Dockstader. *Indian Art in America.*

NEW WORLD ART (cont'd)

Item Number   Author and Title

1069   Feder. *American Indian Art.*
1071   Haberland. *Art of North America.*
1074   Castedo. *History of Latin American Art and Architecture.*
1082.   Fernandez. *Guide to Mexican Art.*
1085   Smith. *Mexico: A History in Art.*
1089   Chase. *Afro-American Art and Craft.*
1091   Green. *American Art.*
1093.   Larkin. *Art and Life in America.*
1095   McLanathan. *Art in America.*
1096   Mendelowitz. *History of American Art.*
1102   Hubbard. *Development of Canadian Art.*

AFRICA AND OCEANIA

Africa

1105   Trowell and Nevermann. *African and Oceanic Art.*
1106   Bascom. *African Art in Cultural Perspective.*
1111   Leuzinger. *Art of Black Africa.*
1115   Willett. *African Art.*

Oceania

1118   Bühler, *et al. Art of the South Sea Islands.*
1119   Guiart. *Arts of the South Pacific.*
1126   Hughes. *Art of Australia.*

AUTHOR AND TITLE INDEX

In this index, authors and editors are listed by their last names and initials only. References are to item number, not to page number. Title entries are made for main entries only.

SUBJECT INDEX

References are to item numbers, not to page numbers.